Contents

Foreword

School reform is as American as apple pie. As John Tharp's book clearly shows, Americans have been engaging in school reform since the implementation of the Quincy Graded School in 1848. Ever since then, a plethora of educational reform plans has been advanced to reform schooling, up to James Comer's school development plan.

Beginning with Seymour Sarason's groundbreaking book *The Predictable Failure of Educational Reform*, released in 1990, reformers, policy wonks, and thoughtful legislators have had to pay more attention to studying why past reforms came a cropper and ultimately failed. But until John Tharp's 3-year archival study, which is presented in this book, no one had ever taken the Sarason criteria and systematically applied them to past reforms to tease from the historical record the traces, patterns, and trend lines that brought the real record of disappointment clearly into focus. And no one had then engaged in a prediction about an actual educational reform plan still underway in America—the Comer plan based on that analysis.

I suppose that John Tharp's book will bring forth the usual amount of hand-wringing and whining from do-gooders, consultants, and reformers. His recommendations will certainly be controversial and hotly debated because he doubts that the schools can actually be fundamentally reformed, at least not along the criteria advanced by Sarason. Of course, schools have changed, and there will be more changes in them in the future. But reform signals a fundamental and deep kind of change. Whereas deep changes in schooling have been attempted, few have ever lasted long on the American landscape, with the exception of the creation of the graded school.

I recommend to the thoughtful reader who wants to come to a clear understanding of educational reforms in America this archival analysis of educational reform by John Tharp, a public school teacher and high school principal still at work trying to provide a sound education to the students under his stewardship. No one ever said that change is easy, but John Tharp's book lays out how difficult, steep, and daunting the challenges have been and will continue to be to those who try. The record is definitely not for the faint of heart.

I think what John has done is to finally clear away the reform rubble and let us take a look at the real ground zero. For that, we owe him a debt of gratitude. Now, at last, we can see clearly the challenges that are present and must be surmounted.

Fenwick W. English
R. Wendell Eaves Senior Distinguished
Professor of Educational Leadership
School of Education
The University of North Carolina at Chapel Hill

1

A Chronology of Past School Reforms

> Schooling is fundamentally a moral, not a technical, enterprise. Schools, as social institutions, express our values more than achieve goals. . . . Schools are less about instructing facts and more about constructing morality.
>
> —Noblit and Dempsey (1996, p. 3)

In 2007 public school reform was a prescription for schools to improve standardized test scores in hopes of meeting the federal government's No Child Left Behind (NCLB) mandates. Unfortunately, for public school students, even the most well-intentioned reforms could not supersede reality.

Under NCLB, falling short of a single adequate yearly progress goal meant that an entire school failed for the school year. As professor Thomas Sobol writes in the September 20, 2006, edition of *Education Week*, "the test results associated with the NCLB law show that, despite scattered gains, school achievement continues to be closely tied to family background" (p. 44). Viewed in that context, NCLB, like other school reform ideas in the United States, amounted to nothing more than politicians' tinkering with the educational system while significant educational change remained elusive.

It is not surprising to learn then, as renowned school reform expert Seymour Sarason (2004) points out, that "knowing a child's test score tells us absolutely nothing about the context of learning and the role of the different factors which are endogenous to the learning process and experience" (p. 7). Thus, factors such as learning and the learning process, factors hard to quantify, became secondary in the adequate yearly progress bottom-line numbers analysis. The bottom-line analysis had more in common with economic theory than education. Although research indicated that schooling needed to change, the American people accepted schools the way they were. People were hesitant and fearful of schooling that looked different from what they had experienced as students.

Although the topic of school reform remained fascinating yet perplexing, the utility of educational policymaking via school reform ideas such as NCLB remained questionable. I crafted this study to uncover those basic concepts and methods that school reform plans must understand and employ to successfully transform schooling.

SIGNIFICANCE OF THE STUDY

This study was a comparative analysis of select reform plans to determine if the success or failure of Yale University professor Dr. James Comer's school development plan (SDP) could be predicted. Five reform plans were chosen and compared to the SDP.

I studied the historical roots of school reform and the case history of school desegregation efforts to gain insight into the sociopolitical, economic, and philosophical roots that spawned Dr. Comer's vision of comprehensive educational restructuring. First, the topic of school reform was traced to antiquity. Second, the SDP developed in the midst of the civil rights movement, a grassroots movement whose members believed that desegregation of public facilities—namely, schools—would lead to societal equality. Third, Comer unfolded his plan as a way to help disadvantaged poor and minority students in that slow-moving desegregation era.

I created a rubric by identifying 26 variables—the indicators of observable characteristics—from Sarason's works. According to Sarason, a reform plan must address these variables in a significant way to successfully reform schooling. These indicators were compiled and organized into four main categories: change theory, teaching theory, the teaching profession, and school power and politics. If a reform plan significantly addressed and improved each element on the rubric, I reasoned, the reform plan had the potential to change schooling.

I created the "failure of school reform" rubric based on Sarason's writings (1990, 1993, 2002, 2004) on school reform. I organized Sarason's ideas, or indicators of observable characteristics on the rubric, under four elements—change theory, teaching theory, the teaching profession, school power and politics. It was to this framework that I comparatively assessed the SDP.

To make comparisons between the SDP and the Lancastrian plan, the age-graded plan, the Gary plan, the Trump plan, and the coalition of essential schools (CES) plan, I began with a brief study of the history of public education in America. I then explored the roots of democracy and the creation of democratic education. This was followed by a study of school reform, the significance of school desegregation for the SDP, and the recycling of school reform. I wrote historiographies for each reform plan and followed them with a brief study of the significance of child development theory—the philosophical basis for the SDP.

The Comer SDP sought change by improving the public school climate. The SDP ostensibly contained core principles that made education suitable and successful for all children. Comer believed that the utilization of the three guiding principles of consensus, collaboration, and no-fault was the prescription for improving school climate and education for all children (Comer, Haynes, Joyner, & Ben-Avie, 1996). The premise of the SDP was that it allowed adults to work together for the benefit of all children, including poor and minority children, and it gave stakeholders the necessary power for collaborative decision making.

I conducted a cursory historiography for each reform plan. I presented the goals of the reform plan, the fundamental beliefs underlying each reform, and the larger societal issues of the period. More detailed research gathered from the archives served as the data set for this study. I organized the archival data for each reform plan by plugging the data into the rubric. This information is cataloged in Appendixes A–F.

A study of the history of schooling made it clear that the problems in schooling from different eras remained the same in 21st-century schools. For example, the high percentages of students struggling to pass tests in 2007 were similar to the struggles that students had in passing tests and advancing in grade level over 100 years ago (Ayers, 1909). The same struggle to get all students to pass and gain promotion to the next grade has not been overcome in the past 100 years.

By studying the history of school reform and specific reform plans the research gained insight into the successes and failures of the selected plans throughout history. I sifted through the archives to find out the foundational philosophical beliefs that public education was rooted in, and this information provided guidance for understanding the current era of school reform.

I based the comparative study on archival information available for the Lancastrian plan, the age-graded plan, the Gary plan, the Trump plan, and the CES plan. All of these reform plans wanted to improve the process of education for the masses. I was able to find archival data to study and complete a rubric for each plan. I selected reform plans from different eras throughout the 19th and 20th centuries. The chosen reforms spanned 200 years of history, and each was distinctive in its own time.

All selected reform plans were methods designed to improve the mass education system for all students. The analysis of history provided me with an understanding of how the public education system became what it was in 2007. I found that although many novelties existed in modern times—the Internet, cell phones, nuclear proliferation—the concept of raising youth and developing the human mind remained constant. Studying similar reform plans from different eras provided me with answers about the elusive quest to transform schooling to best educate youth. The following is a comprehensive list of other possible school reform plans:

21st Century Community Learning Centers
90/90/90 Schools
Accelerated Schools Plan
Advancement via Individual Determination
Allen Plan
America's Choice
Batavia System
Cambridge Plan
Community for Learning Program
Comprehensive High School
Comprehensive School Reform
Co-Nect Plan
Core Knowledge
Dalton Laboratory Plan

Direct Instruction Model
Edison Project
Exito Para Todos
Herbartian Method
High Schools That Work
Joplin Plan
Kindergarten Idea
Middle Start
Modern Red Schoolhouse
Monitorial Method
Montessori Method
New Math Plan
Newton Plan
Open Court
Oswego Plan
Outcome Based Education
Pestalozzian Method
Project Zero Plan
Pueblo Plan
Small Learning Communities
Small Schools Movement
Success for All / Roots & Wings
Torrance Plan
Total Quality Management
Turning Points
Urban Learning Centers
Urban School Development
Winnetka Plan
Year-Round Education

Each of the five reform plans chosen matched the SDP in terms of a determination to improve mass education for all students at a particular moment in time, and each had an abundance of archival information. Each reform plan occurred at a unique period in American history, and each enjoyed widespread popularity in its day. Table 1.1 provides a brief comparison of each plan.

Table 1.1.   Reform Plans in Historical Time

Reform Plan	Date	Founder	Historical Moment	Original Location	Premise
Lancastrian	1806	Joseph Lancaster	Early republic	New York City	1,000:1 (student:teacher ratio)
Age-graded	1848	Horace Mann	Industrialism	Quincy, MA	Graded schooling classification
Gary	1906	William Wirt	Progressivism	Gary, IN	Work, study, play
Trump	1959	J. Lloyd Trump	Sputnik/Cold War	Champaign, IL	Large, small, independent study
SDP	1968	James Comer	Civil rights movement	New Haven, CT	"Emergency room" mentality
CES	1984	Theodore Sizer	Postindustrialism	Providence, RI	80:1 (student:teacher ratio)

Note. SDP = School Development Plan; CES = Coalition of Essential Schools.

The Lancastrian plan began in 1806 in the early infancy of the United States; the age-graded plan occurred during a time of mass immigration and a perceived need for large-scale cultural diffusion; the Gary plan was a turn-of-the-century plan that had firm roots in the industrial revolution and the ideals of efficiency and mass production; the Trump plan of 1959 rose 2 years after the Soviets launched *Sputnik*, the first satellite sent into space, with the perceived notion that schools needed to become better or else the United States would lose the Cold War; the CES plan arose at the time that the federal government's *A Nation at Risk* study (National Commission on Excellence in Education, 1983) reported that our schools were hopelessly mediocre and that the Japanese business ethic would soon lead to their dominance in America if our schools did not change and begin producing more intelligent workers.

DEMOCRACY AND THE CREATION
OF DEMOCRATIC EDUCATION

I found that the seeds for democratic education were planted in England and then transplanted to the American colonies. The seeds sprang forth after the American Revolution as the American public education system developed. The *Oxford English Dictionary* informed all that the earliest usage of the word *democracy* came from Sir Thomas Elyot of England in 1531, who used it in his book *The Boke Named the Governour* to describe the necessity of education for proprietors of government. The dictionary reads,

1. Government by the people; that form of government in which the sovereign power resides in the people as a whole, and is exercised either directly by them (as in the small republics of antiquity) or by officers elected by them. In mod. use often more vaguely denoting a social state in which all have equal rights, without hereditary or arbitrary differences of rank or privilege.

The earliest reference attributed to Elyot states,

1531 ELYOT *Gov.* I. Ii, An other publique weale was amonge the Atheniensis, where equalitie was of astate amonge the people. . . . This maner of

gouernaunce was called in greke *Democratia*, in latine, *Popularis potential*,
in englisshe the rule of the comminaltie.

In 1531, *English democracy* meant that the governors held power in service
to the monarchy, and Elyot wrote that an educational system needed to teach
governors how to rule effectively. In 2007, *American democracy* meant that
the people held the power in service to the common good and that an educational system needed to teach the people how to rule effectively.

Eggleston (1901) wrote a history of the origins of education in the
United States and established the development of schooling in the Americas as a natural progression of educational events that occurred in England in the seventeenth century. Education in England had its beginnings
in religious monasteries in the fifth century. Much later, Henry VIII dis-
rupted educational efforts during his reign in the early 16th century, but he
did not silence all instruction, and soon, free Latin and grammar schools
came into existence: "The tide wave of zeal for founding new Latin
schools reached its flood about the time that emigration to America began,
and the impulse was felt in all the early colonies" (p. 211).

Grammar schools taught Latin to beginning students, but this tradition
would eventually end in the Americas, and English replaced Latin (Eggleston, 1901). The early schools were used to train men for service in the
church, and the priests performed services in Latin: "Valued at first as a
means of producing clergyman, we find the grammar school in the fif-
teenth century esteemed in Scotland as a training place for public officials
'for the king's use'" (p. 219). Education expanded in the Americas, and in
1647, Massachusetts passed a state law requiring all towns to create and
support a school. Eggleston wrote, "The outcome of this law adopted, in
what was the most religious as it was the most intolerant period of New
England history, has been the development of a national system of secu-
lar education for many millions" (p. 231).

Not all colonists pursued the advancement of education. One-time governor of Virginia Sir William Berkeley stated in 1671 that Virginia did not
have any free schools, because "learning has brought disobedience and
heresy and sects into the world" (quoted in Eggleston, 1901, p. 262). The
ideal of public education was ingrained in the minds of most of the founding fathers, however, and many helped further mass schooling for com-
moners.

James Madison, the father of the U.S. Constitution, studied ancient Greece and Rome for a model of government and brought the ancients' democratic ideas with him to Philadelphia in the summer of 1787. That summer, 55 delegates debated, compromised, and issued a document that provided a federal democratic system of government for the United States of America. The former U.S. Constitution, known as the Articles of Confederation, did not successfully mold the 13 states into a union to allow democracy to flourish. The states had a great deal of independent power, and the national government was weak and ineffective.

The new U.S. Constitution included rights for state governments but installed a much stronger central government. Although Madison ensured that the new U.S. Constitution protected the individual rights of the people, anti-Federalists voiced opposition, fearing that state and local power would be reduced to virtual representation and that a tyrannical government was in the making, thus lessening the democratic power of the people.

The American experiment in democracy began with this compromised less-than-equal plan that the founding fathers hoped would lay a foundation that could be improved on by future generations. John Adams envisioned a democratic future that included women and racial minorities as equal citizens (McCullough, 2001). James Madison worried about the impact of the undemocratic institution of slavery and did not think the future of the country could include freed persons of color (Rakove, 1990). George Washington feared that ideological differences over the function of government would tear the infant democracy apart (Wills, 1994). These extraordinary men and this monumental yet contradictory founding set the stage for a democratic system of acquiring knowledge in public schools.

SCHOOL REFORM: SEARCHING FOR EQUITY, FRATERNITY, AND NATURAL RIGHTS

I discovered that mid-19th-century leaders promoted a government-sponsored system of education to help unite a diverse citizenry of immigrants. Led by a Massachusetts lawyer named Horace Mann, these leaders heralded public schooling as the method for uniting all people under a common American ethos. The concept of universal public education found its roots in the writings of Montesquieu in *The Spirit of Laws* (1748) in which the French thinker espoused a democracy ensuring "the greatest virtue" for the people," but the people "must be imbued with a selflessness, benevolence of attitude to others, and a devotion to country" (quoted in Alexander & Alexander, 1998, p. 21).

Founding leaders such as Thomas Jefferson, Adams, and Madison wrote of the virtues of public schooling for all children. Through universal public education, people learned to function as a community, participate in the duties of government, and positively contribute to the economy and society with their labor.

With these ideas unfolding in the young republic, public schools steadily grew in size and inclusiveness. By 1840 Mann led others who believed that knowledge and education were the natural rights of all people (Alexander & Alexander, 1998). In terms of equality, however, Mann did not include every ethnicity, nor was he motivated by democracy but rather a fear of rising crime rates, increased immigration, and a lack of methods for social control (M. B. Katz, 1971): "Children of poor and lower-class families received no education at all or were attached as apprentices to learn a trade and develop manual skills" (quoted in Alexander & Alexander, 1998, p. 22). African American children were almost totally excluded from education because laws barring the education of slaves were passed in Southern states and African Americans were provided little or unequally segregated educational opportunities in Northern states (Lightfoot, 1978). Mann's (1844) common school movement constituted an attempt to unite citizens with recent European immigrants under one American ethos. The common school movement proposed to help prevent conflict and train immigrant workers to help business flourish (Fowler, 2000).

Horace Mann's common school movement came in an era when values shifted from liberty and individualism to fraternity, order, and economic growth (Fowler, 2000): "Fraternity, defined as a sense of national unity, was the foremost value for Horace Mann and many of his fellow reformers" (p. 334). Mann reasoned that schools could bring all people together and unite them as Americans. This developed a sense of community and nationalism: "Tocqueville saw the strong individualism of Americans as troublesome and potentially dangerous" (Noblit & Dempsey, 1996, p. 201). Rights were important, this ideology posited, but people's rights were better guaranteed when all shared a sense of belonging and purpose in community.

The romanticized image of public schools as places where people could "pull themselves up by their bootstraps" obscured the picture of what schools were. The history of public education began in many ways with Mann and the common school. Mann's school concept was more about socialization and control (M. B. Katz, 1971) than it was about cultivating the minds of all children in the liberal arts. The bureaucratic structure of public education placed power in the hands of the government, and it operated schools to serve the needs of the economy. This had not changed and still held true in 2007.

A CASE HISTORY OF SCHOOL DESEGREGATION

Comer began the SDP in two all-Black elementary schools in New Haven, Connecticut, in 1968. Even though the *Brown v. Board of Education* Supreme Court ruling of 1954 made segregated schools illegal, many schools and school systems still found themselves segregated. This case history informed the research about the legal history of this era and the enduring school segregation that motivated Comer to take action.

In crafting this study, I discovered that the roots of the Comer SDP spawned from the civil rights movement in the United States. Comer created a child-centered process to help schools and school people educate poor and minority students in the slow-moving desegregation era. It did not matter to Comer if African American children sat next to White children in school. He theorized that children needed to be properly cared for and educated in a school building—especially, children from disadvantaged backgrounds.

The civil rights movement shaped the history of school desegregation in the United States. In 1896, the U.S. Supreme Court ruled that "separate but equal" facilities—including schools—were constitutional. African Americans were beyond servitude for only 31 years when the Court handed down this decision. During slavery, it was illegal for the enslaved to learn to read. From 1865 through Reconstruction, the struggle began to make literate the masses of African Americans. Beginning in 1896, the fight was against the system that wanted to recommit African Americans to illiteracy.

Dr. Comer was born into an era when African Americans relentlessly pressed the federal and state governments to change the discriminatory segregation laws. Beginning in the 1960s, Comer wanted to help African American children gain what the *Brown* decision promised. It was the legal fights for enforcement of *Brown* that gave birth to the SDP.

Alexander and Alexander (1998) report that the *Brown* decision marked the beginning of school desegregation and equal educational opportunities for African American children—at least in the textbooks of American history. The case aimed to stamp out de jure segregation in schools, mainly existent in the Southern states. With the subsequent *Brown II* decision of 1955, school systems were ordered to racially integrate "with all deliberate speed." It was 1970 before most school systems in the South ended de jure racial school segregation.

Many Northern cities maintained de jure segregation laws well into the 1950s and 1960s to control the influx of African Americans who had been flooding into cities in search of factory jobs and a better way of life since the 1920s. Most major Northern urban centers created Black codes to keep Blacks separate in housing, school, jobs, and social affairs. Other cities in the North contained few Black citizens and did not maintain any segregationist laws. M. B. Katz (1971) reports that cities such as Boston, however, did not care much for the hopes and aspirations of its poor and minority groups.

> The hostile reaction of school boards like Boston's in the 1960's to the problem of *de facto* segregation, for instance, revealed how the long-standing insensitivity of a school system to its poorer clientele had hardened into a pattern of interacting with community groups. Incident after incident suggested that the school board simply did not care to try to understand the aspirations of some black people: it appeared, very simply, that the wishes of black people did not matter much. (p. 116)

States in the North and the West that maintained separate schools in the 1960s, vestiges of de jure segregationist laws, were spared the job of having to integrate in 1974. The Supreme Court handed down the *Milliken v. Bradley* decision that year, ruling that major metropolitan centers with many separate localized school districts did not have to work together to create a desegregation plan (Alexander & Alexander, 1998).

As school desegregation languished, many schools remained segregated. Schools in New Haven, for example, remained racially polarized. Comer and his team went into two all-Black elementary schools in New Haven and began implementing the SDP. These two schools scored at the bottom of the school district in all measurable outcomes. The federal government would not equalize the schools in New Haven, and the SDP became the answer to help improve schooling in these two high-poverty schools.

WAS EDUCATION REFORM RECYCLED?

Noblit and Dempsey (1996) provides a compelling lens to view school reform—as periodic reform shifts back and forth from calls for excellence, to equity, and so forth. These researchers found that school reform dates back to antiquity. They categorized the current "excellence versus equity" debate as "modern manifestations of more deep-seated ideas, 'oratorical' and 'philosophical' about education in our culture" (Cuban, 1988, p. 1).

Excellence was the current manifestation of the *oratorical* ideology, whereas *equity* represented *philosophical* belief. Should students have been required to read the "great books," or was it better for students to self-select authors and titles? School reforms of the 20th century that came from the oratorical concept of excellence include the Committee of Ten of 1893, the reforms of the late 1950s, and the reforms of the 1980s.

Philosophical notions of "equity" were found in the cardinal principles of 1918, the progressivism of the 1920s–1940s, and the new curricula and programs of the 1960s and 1970s. Leaders in the drive for excellence, such as E. D. Hirsch, Allan Bloom, and Mortimer Adler, believed that "our nation was greater, according to the modern orators, when we had less diversity and more agreement about what was to be valued" (Noblit & Dempsey, 1996, p. 47). They believed that the great ideas had already been thought, the essential truths already discovered.

Teachers appeared to be telling the truth when they left staff development meetings declaring that they had already seen in the past the latest educational trend or development. Noblit and Dempsey (1996) state that education reform was recycled. School reform in the 20th century shifted back and forth from an oratorical concept of excellence to the philosophical concept of equity. The oratorical excellence ideology of the National Education Association's Committee of Ten report in 1893 suggested that high school should prepare students for college and for life, with increased graduation requirements.

Reforms of the late 1950s concluded that more emphasis needed to be placed on science, math, and foreign language, given that the Soviets launched *Sputnik* in 1957 (Noblit & Dempsey, 1996). Again, in the 1980s, excellence was sought when state governors came together in an unprecedented move to advocate and implement school reform. Led by Republican governor Lamar Alexander of Tennessee and Democratic governor Bill Clinton of Arkansas, they pushed for reforms that included increased high school graduation requirements, standardized testing, career ladders, and school choice. State governments became more active in mandating and monitoring their school districts (Fowler, 2000).

As school reform shifted back and forth from ideas that promoted excellence for all to equity-related services, various reform proposals sprang forth. The Lancastrian plan of the early 19th century proposed an equitable way to educate the masses, followed by the age-graded plan, which promised efficiency and mass education. Later, the Gary plan modeled a way to save on costs and provide whole-child development for all students, a combination of excellence and equity. The Trump plan sought to improve education with added rigor (excellence), whereas the SDP worked to improve the educational system for the poor (equity). Finally, the CES plan called for a higher level of cognitive significance in secondary education, with exhibitions to prove student mastery of big ideas for all students, an attempt at both excellence and equity.

THE LANCASTRIAN PLAN

A brief historiography of the Lancastrian Plan provided an interpretation of the importance of this reform in the early years of the American republic. The Lancastrian plan came forth at the dawning of the mass education movement and was instrumental in the development of this movement. Although the Lancastrian plan was significant in ushering in the mass education program, it fizzled as an accepted school reform idea by the mid-19th century.

In 1801 Jefferson assumed the presidency of the United States and harkened in a new era in national politics as the first Democratic–Republican Party member elected to the nation's highest office. As president, Jefferson doubled the size of the country with the Louisiana Purchase, kept U.S. trade open with the Middle East by going to war against the Barbary pirates, and substantially decreased the national debt. Jefferson also strongly believed in education for the common man. He viewed education as the way to improve the human condition.

Spring (2001) writes that Thomas Jefferson believed that "individuals were born with reason and a moral sense, and education can improve the workings of these faculties and contribute to the increase of human knowledge" (p. 64). In 1916 professor John Reigart observed that Jefferson supported the Lancastrian model (also spelled *Lancasterian* by some authors) for educating children (Reigart, 1916). This plan of school organization promised mass education for children at an unbelievably low cost.

Joseph Lancaster (1973) opened the first Lancastrian school in the Southwark area of London, England, in 1798. Six years earlier, at the age of 14, he had traveled to Jamaica "to teach the blacks" (Reigart, 1916, p. 9). He was a Quaker who "was nearly overwhelmed by his success in attracting pupils" to his school (p. 9). In London, he taught children in a room in his father's house. He wanted to include children whose parents could not afford to pay tuition, so he admitted many nonpaying pupils from low-income families that otherwise did not see any utility in paying tuition for their children to learn to read and write (Cubberley, 1934).

Lancaster realized that his operational costs must be minimal given that tuition payments would not come from all students. Out of this reality grew the Lancastrian system of schooling. In it, he used older students, known as *monitors*, to teach the rest of the students. In the 1973 reprinting of Lancaster's 1805 book *Improvements in Education*, editor Francesco Cordasco states in the introduction:

Although the techniques were very old (extending back to the efforts of John Brinsley [c. 1570–c. 1630], with evidences of the use of monitors in Elizabethan grammar schools), it was Lancaster who established in the monitorial system a practical and inexpensive method of instruction for poor children on a large scale. The term 'monitorial' derives from the practice of employing the older or more intelligent children to teach small groups of the other children. (p. 9)

The Lancastrian model, also known as the monitorial plan, educated up to 1,000 students in one room, with one teacher. It had a machine-like efficiency to it, and "machinery had a positive symbolic connotation" (Kaestle, 1973b, pp. 164–165). Lancaster soon imported his plan to the young United States. It gained acclaim quickly, and hundreds of schools adopted the plan.

Lancaster gained success in England with his plan because it offered a way to educate the increasing population of poor in London at a time when additional funds were not available (Kaestle, 1973a). "His success came to the attention of some English noblemen, and in 1805 he even gained the patronage of George III" (p. 83). "The plan was so cheap, and so effective in teaching reading and the fundamentals of religion, that it soon provided England with a sort of a substitute for a national system of schools" (Cubberley, 1934, p. 129).

At the same time that Lancaster developed his school plan, Dr. Andrew Bell introduced a monitorial system of schooling and gained Church of England support for his plan (Cubberley, 1934). However, "it was the Lancastrian plan which was brought to the United States, Church-of-England ideas not being in much favor after the Revolution" (p. 129).

As the United States entered the 19th century, proponents of democracy pushed for a system of education to teach the electorate, believing that literacy made a country strong. Opponents of mass education disapproved, not willing to endure the burden of taxation to pay for mass schooling. The Lancastrian plan seemed to be an attractive compromise.

> Under the plans previously in use education had been a slow and an expensive process, because it had to be carried on by the individual method of instruction, and in quite small groups. Under this new plan it was now possible for one teacher to instruct 300, 400, 500, or more pupils in a single room, and to do it with much better results in both learning and discipline than the old type of schoolmaster had achieved. (Cubberley, 1934, p. 134)

Although a few wealthy persons already paid tuition for the private education for their children, most did not possess the money to educate them, nor did they possess the ideology that tuition payments benefited their children. "It was not the monitorial system of education which was controversial, or Joseph Lancaster. What was disputed was the *education* of the poor; its desirability, its form and its cost" (Lancaster, 1973, p. 6). With costs at a minimum, more people accepted the common school ideology, and school attendance increased (Reigart, 1916).

In Lancastrian schools, one teacher existed in a large open room, and up to 1,000 pupils were educated in this classroom (English, 1992).

> The pupils were sorted and seated in rows, and to each row was assigned a clever boy who was known as a monitor, and who was the key to the entire system. . . . The teacher first taught these monitors a lesson from a printed card, and then the monitors . . . took their rows to "stations" about the wall and proceeded to teach the other boys what they had just learned. (Cubberley, 1934, pp. 131–32)

The monitors worked with about 10 children each, walking students around the sides of the large open room to posted stations of lessons (Lancaster, 1973). Monitors came early to school and received lessons from the teacher, which they were to teach their pupils for that day (Cubberley, 1934). "It is obvious that a school like this of Mr. Lancaster's, consisting of from 700 to 1,000 boys, would soon fall into decay, without very close attention to order and method" (Reigart, 1916, p. 11).

After completing a lesson, the students returned to their seats in a strict, orderly fashion and began a new lesson.

> When they finished, they would march to the front of the room and stand around the monitor's desks, where they would receive instructions . . . they would march to the rear part of their section and recite or receive further instruction. (Spring, 2001, p. 71)

As the students gained proficiency with the lesson, they were sent on to the next monitor and lesson.

Lancaster began his schooling plan based on the philosophy that poor people's children deserved an education (Lancaster, 1973). In his school, he emphasized the importance of time management and kept students busy so that they did not have idle time to misbehave. Some student misbehavior occurred in Lancastrian schools, "but Lancaster was most kindhearted, and even his use of outlandish forms of punishment was due to his efforts to find substitutes for flogging, towards which he had the greatest aversion" (Reigart, 1916, p. 77). If students misbehaved, they were

publicly shamed and humiliated, with no physical punishment employed
(M. B. Katz, 1971):

> Children who talked frequently or were idle were punished by having a
> wooden log placed around their necks. Extreme offenders were placed in a
> sack or basket suspended from the roof of the school in full view of the rest
> of the pupils. (Spring, 2001, p. 72)

He believed that students gained interest in lessons when an incentive was
involved, such as competition with one another:

> Like traditional pedagogy, the monitorial system emphasized recitation, but
> now, due to the use of student monitors, children could be almost continu-
> ally engaged in active, competitive groups. The constant stimulation of
> monitorial instruction would increase motivation; the highly regimented
> procedures would maintain order in huge schools as well as inculcate disci-
> pline. (Kaestle, 1983, p. 41)

It was the strict, regimented orderliness of the Lancastrian plan that allowed it to gain popularity and emulation. It improved the previous school
models that contained a great deal of wasted time and bored, unruly students (Spring, 2001).

> The Lancaster school wrote the author of the memoir "allowed the pupils to
> advance according to their industry and application to their studies." They
> "were not held back by duller scholars," he said, as is "often the case under
> our present school system." (Kaestle, 1983, p. 43)

New York City implemented the Lancastrian plan first in the United
States, in 1806, with the ideology that the schools helped children whose
parents did not do a good job raising them (Spring, 2001). "It was, in great
measure, due to the 'limited state of funds' that the society introduced in
their first school, in 1806, the monitorial system, at that time in vogue in
England" (Reigart, 1916, p. 5).

The Lancastrian model found widespread popularity in New York City
and then in the state of Pennsylvania. It also was implemented in Georgia,
Maryland, North Carolina, Michigan, and Louisville, Kentucky, and later
in Mexico and in South American countries (Cubberley, 1934). Charles

Andrews (1830), a teacher at the male African Free School in New York City, wrote in 1830 that the introduction of the Lancastrian plan to his school in 1809 greatly improved the school.

> The introduction of this excellent plan produced a very favorable change in the school, and in its affairs generally: the number of pupils soon increased, and their order and general decorum became objects of favorable remark, even among those who had previously been in the habit of placing but little to their credit. (p. 18)

According to Andrews, the Lancastrian plan created a structure that was conducive for effective teaching and learning.

> To supply instruction to the thousands of neglected children there was at hand a ready-made plan, remarkably cheap in operation, and, with all its faults, apparently superior in method and discipline to the schools of the day. (Reigart, 1916, p. 13)

Because of the popularity of his plan abroad, Lancaster eventually moved to the United States. At the height of the plan's popularity, however, he was hit by a horse and buggy and killed in New York City in 1838 while attempting to walk across a street (Spring, 2001). After his death, the Lancastrian plan waned and eventually ended as a viable reform plan.

The Lancastrian plan was replaced by the American plan of education (English, 1992). The American plan required all students to attend primary school to learn the basics in reading, writing, and arithmetic, in age-graded classrooms (English, 1992). Lancaster, Pennsylvania, had thoroughly embraced the Lancastrian plan but decided to end its use by 1838 because many people in the community believed that the use of young and inexperienced students for most of the teaching was not effective (Riddle, 1905). Lancaster, Pennsylvania, instead set up a primary and secondary school system with an age-graded structure and with more teachers and teacher assistants:

> On the score of economy and where the main object is to educate a large number of children at the least possible expense, the committee does not doubt that the Lancasterian system has the advantage over every other. But where thorough and complete instruction is sought for, they are constrained

to think that other and more successful methods may be found. And, believing as they do, that the board will consider quality rather than the cheapness of the schools they are about to establish, the committee do not hesi-
tate to recommend the abandonment of a system which they are constrained
to believe incurably defective and superficial. (p. 82)

Although many found structural fault with the Lancastrian plan, it succeeded in transforming the educational landscape of America by helping
foster the development of mass education. "The Lancastrian schools . . .
made the common school common and much talked of, and awakened
thought and provoked discussion on the question of public education"
(Cubberley, 1934, p. 136).

The Lancastrian plan provided low-cost education for the masses of
children when the idea was first popularized. "As a result, the Lancastrian
system became the most widespread and successful educational reform in
the Western world during the first thirty years of the nineteenth century"
(Kaestle, 1983, p. 41).

THE AGE-GRADED PLAN

The next plan reviewed was the age-graded plan—the only plan studied
that successfully became part of the structure of the public education system. The orderly and seemingly logical classification of pupils in the age-
graded plan contributed to its acceptance by the citizenry, even though no
human development research exists that supports its pupil classification
system.

The Lancastrian plan was heralded because it was inexpensive and effective. It spread throughout the country because it improved school instruction, discipline, and student motivation (Cubberley, 1919). "Lancaster introduced activity, emulation, order, and a kind of military
discipline" (p. 93). Martin (1972) finds strength in the Lancastrian model
and other one-room schoolhouse configurations:

In the one-room school, older children managed younger children as they
did—and still do—in every neighborhood, in large families, and in children's play not controlled by adults. Children in one-room school expected
each other to lead, direct, help, carry, follow, and ask. Their relationships

seemed natural to them, but it was only because the form of the social group—the school—that nudged them into these behaviors. (p. 31)

Many favored this plan because schools needed only one teacher, thereby keeping costs down. Because of its low costs, the plan "hastened the adoption of the free school system in all the northern states by gradually accustoming people to bearing the necessary taxation which free schools entail" (p. 96).

Textbook expansion and the creation of curriculum guides produced the necessary conditions for the development of graded schools in the early 19th century and led to the move away from the Lancastrian plan (Cubberley, 1919). Goodlad and Anderson (1959) write about this phenomenon:

> Textbooks series—first in reading and arithmetic and later in science, social studies, health, and so on—came to be rigorously ordered by grades. The work considered appropriate for a given grade level determined the content of the textbook, and then the content of the textbook came to be regarded as appropriate for the grade. In time, more fundamental procedures for determining the curriculum were scarcely considered. (p. 47)

With the conditions right, the age-graded plan in American public education took off when the father of the common school, Horace Mann, returned with the idea from a visit to Prussia in 1843 (Spring, 2001). Quincy Grammar School headmaster John Philbrick officially instituted it in Quincy, Massachusetts, in 1848 (English, 1992).

The purpose of the age-graded plan was to make education effective and efficient in producing learners (Spring, 2001). Many reasoned that teaching hundreds of children of varying ages and abilities in a single room at a single time was "not only inefficient but also inhumane" (Tyack, 1974, p. 44). According to educational researcher Larry Cuban (1989), however, the age-graded plan indelibly harmed school children, especially those deemed at risk:

> One of the most inflexible of the structures of schooling is the graded school. The graded school categorizes, segregates, and, as a last resort, eliminates those whose performance and behavior deviate too sharply from the norm. The graded school—consisting of one teacher and one class of 30 or so students of roughly the same age who spend about 36 weeks together

before moving on to another grade or class—assumes that students possess
equal mental and physical capacities, have equal amounts of help available
from their families, and will be taught by teachers with equal skills and
knowledge. (p. 782)

Martin (1972) says that the one-room school "forced the teacher to
cater to the differences among children" (p. 29), whereas the age-graded
plan destroyed differentiation. Goodlad and Anderson (1959) state that
children's abilities differed in some areas and grew unevenly. The researchers report that "in the first grade there is a spread of four years in
pupil readiness to learn as suggested by mental age data" (p. 3).

The age-graded plan evolved beginning with the separation of schools
into primary, intermediate, and grammar schools (Cubberley, 1919). Next,
schools divided into separate classes in the same building: "It began by
the employment of assistant teachers, known as 'ushers,' to help the 'master,' and the provision of small recitation rooms, off the main large room,
for their use in hearing recitations" (p. 229). Finally, by the mid-19th century, newly built schools contained many small classrooms. The development of textbooks and standardized course studies led to the idea that it
was unnecessary for several teachers to instruct the same material in a
school:

> The waste in maintaining two duplicate schools in the same building, each
> covering the same two or three years of school work, when by re-sorting the
> pupils the work of each teacher could be made more specialized and the
> pupils better taught, was certain to become obvious as soon as school su-
> pervision by teachers began to supersede school organization by laymen. (p.
> 232)

The age-graded plan aimed to separate students to create more effective
schools. The belief was that students with "similar age and attainments"
(M. B. Katz, 1971, p. 35) accomplished more in the age-graded plan than
in the one-room schoolhouse model. R. H. Anderson (1993) questions the
research-based success of the age-graded plan:

> It is strange that the graded school, with its overloaded, textbook-dominated
> curriculum, and its relatively primitive assumptions about human develop-
> ment and learning, has held its ground this long. To my knowledge there has

never been a respectable body of research or scholarly reflection on the academic and social legitimacy of segregating students by age and providing them with a standard curriculum. (p. 10)

Principal Beggs (1964), the Decatur-Lakeview high school administrator who implemented the move to the Trump plan believed that future schools would be nongraded and that public school quality would be improved:

> The ungraded school of the future will have realistic expectations for learners. . . . Schools will be expected to teach students to think, to discriminate, to judge. . . . The ungraded school is a common-sense approach to providing for differences between and within people. (p. 221)

One notable criticism of the age-graded plan was that many students did not have the capacity to move and stay at grade level and thus suffered permanent left-behind status because the plan's inflexibility did not cater to their needs (Cuban, 1989).

The age-graded plan received unquestioned faithfulness from the American public. Most people seemed to believe that the age-graded plan allowed teachers to maximize instruction with grade-appropriate materials. It was an accepted norm in schooling from infant day care through the 12th grade. English (1992) posits:

> The development of graded schools does not represent a sharp break with past organizational decisions in American schools. Rather, it was the last in a series of reactions to confront industrial-social changes in America, at a time when the population was rapidly becoming urbanized. . . . The graded school . . . restored order to American urban schoolhouses. (p. 122)

The age-graded plan was criticized because many children did not keep up with the course work deemed at grade level and were held back while others surpassed grade level (Cubberley, 1919). To deal with this issue, an idea known as the Batavia plan assigned assistant teachers to "laggards" (p. 373) to help them catch up with the rest of their peers. For the bright students, Harvard University president Eliot created the Cambridge plan, a faster-paced course of study. The brightest students completed 8 years of an average student's school program in 6 years. Cubberley reported that "supplementary class, over-age classes, or ungraded classes" were to help slow students while enabling bright students to accelerate ahead:

> Their purpose is not only to make the graded system more flexible, and thus break up somewhat the so-called "lock-step" of the public school, but also to meet the needs of both the dull and the bright children, by providing special instruction better adapted to their stage of progress than is the regular instruction of the average school grade. (p. 374)

The concept of retention reigned as a major philosophical issue in the age-graded plan. Should schools have passed students along to keep pace with their peers, or should they have strictly maintained grading standards (Buckingham, 1921)? This debate lingered into the 21st century and had not been settled by 2007. Martin (1972) reminds the educational community that individual differences get lost in the age-graded plan's quest for order and uniformity:

> Each child differs from every other child, and some children are more intelligent than others. Furthermore, every child is brighter in some things than he is in others. Hell, he might be in the fourth form for arithmetic, but in the seventh form for reading. (p. 29)

A retention-versus-promotion debate ensued in the early 20th century when New York City Public School superintendent William Henry Maxwell discovered that 40% of his students did not move through school with their age group. Other school districts found similar results:

> The number of elementary-school graduates practically doubled in the ten years intervening between 1908 and 1918, although during the same time the population of the country increased no more than 15 percent. No doubt one of the causes of the large increase in the number of graduates was the effort to reduce over-ageness throughout the country. (Buckingham, 1921, p. 219)

Ayers (1909) writes that in Chicago in 1906, 43,560 first graders were enrolled in school but that only 12,939 eighth graders were, too. Teachers maintained high grade standards, but the expense equaled a large number of student retentions. A retention critic's argument blamed this philosophy for the dwindling numbers (Buckingham, 1921). Student promotion advocates stated that they "are of the opinion that the schools are run for the benefit of the children rather than for the sake of standards" (p. 221).

Tyack (1974) reports that in 1922 New York City superintendent William L. Ettinger found that 83,000 students out of 716,000 — about 12% — were not promoted to the next grade. For Ayers (1909), the tragedy of schooling is in the retention of students who are deemed below grade level (*grade level* was the vocabulary used when this was written, but Ayers and his peers used the term *retarded*). Instead of promoting success, schools promoted failure and a sense of hopelessness for too many children.

> Under our present system there are large numbers of children who are destined to lives of failure . . . . Success is necessary to every human being. To live in an atmosphere of failure is tragedy to many. It is not a matter of intellectual attainment; not an intellectual matter at all but a moral matter. The boys and girls coming out of school clear-headed and with good bodies, who are resolute, who are determined to do and sure that they can do, will do more for themselves and for the world than those who come out with far greater intellectual attainments, but who lack confidence, who have not established the habit of success but within whom the school has established the habit of failure. (p. 220)

With all the criticisms and a seemingly poor theoretical framework to support its ideology, the age-graded plan enjoyed unheralded success:

> Despite these problems, the graded school has succeeded beyond the dreams of the 19th century reformers who invented it. By the early 1900s the graded school was *the* way to organize education, and so it has remained. It is no accident that the education systems in most developed nations are built on the graded school. (Cuban, 1989, p. 782)

Thus, the age-graded plan remained a reform plan that succeeded to become a structural fixture in public education.

THE GARY PLAN

The turn-of-the-century industrial-revolution spirit of mass production inspired educational elites to adopt factory model business principles to make their profession more respectable. This assembly-line approach to teaching and learning ran contrary to John Dewey's "school is life" philosophy. Gary, Indiana, superintendent William Wirt, who studied under Dewey, sought to assuage these competing ideologies with his efficiently operated "work–study–play" community schoolhouses.

In 1906, United States Steel Corporation built the most modern steel plant in the world, southeast of Chicago. This factory led to the creation of a new town on the Indiana sand dunes named Gary. At about the same time, the newly formed three-member Gary school board hired Wirt as school superintendent. They provided him free reign in creating a plan for educating Gary's youth.

Wirt created a work–study–play plan to keep children off the streets and make public schooling economical (Ravitch, 1988). Under this plan students were "platooned" to save space. While one third of the children played outside, another third studied in classrooms, and the remaining third worked in shop classes. All three groupings rotated, and students used hallway lockers to store their books and other belongings (Elwell, 1976).

Wirt received his education from DePauw University, in Greencastle, Indiana, earning a bachelor's (1898) and doctoral (1916) degrees (Starr, 1958). He also studied under John Dewey at the University of Chicago and served as his hometown school superintendent in rural Bluffton, Indiana, before the Gary Board of Education hired him in 1908 (Ravitch, 1988). Wirt's "initial motivation for the Gary school system focused more on a desire to attack the seat-bound academic formalism that often permeated schools and bored children" (Levine, 2002, p. 52).

Over the next 30 years, Wirt invented, tinkered, and led the school system's work–study–play (or platoon) school model, a plan that eventually spread across the nation. "In 1929 a nation-wide survey found 1,068 schools in 202 cities throughout the country using the 'platoon' system" (Starr, 1958, p. 728). "More than 100 cities were represented at the first national conference of the National Association for the Study of the Platoon or Work-Study-Play School Organization held in Washington, D.C. in 1926" (Elwell, 1976, p. 21). In its prime, the Gary plan received acclaim as the standard bearer of progressive child-centered education that modeled scientifically managed efficiency (Callahan, 1962).

Educational researchers characterized the early 20th century as a time when public education received heavy influence from businesses. Leaders created an ideal of schools that efficiently produced educated pupils (Callahan, 1962). Frederick Winslow Taylor's time-and-motion studies led to the assembly-line approach in industry, and many business and community leaders decided that schools could efficiently produce educated students using the same principles that factories used on raw materials.

Callahan (1962) writes that "educators were put under pressure to demonstrate that they were not allowing part of the expensive 'plant' to stand idle" (p. 126). As a result, the rise of the platoon school began as a way to best utilize the school building to maximize usage and minimize waste. Franklin Bobbitt, professor at the University of Chicago, published an article entitled "Elimination of Waste in Education" in 1912, describing the Gary plan as a good example of scientific management put to use in the schools' making maximum use of the school facility (cited in Levine, 2002).

Wirt's Gary plan rotated students from academic courses to industrial work time and finally into physical education and other outdoor classes. Carter V. Good wrote about the Gary plan in a biographical sketch of Wirt in the *Dictionary of American Biography*:

> Division of pupils of a school into two groups or platoons, with a schedule of classes arranged so that one platoon was studying the fundamental or tool subjects in home rooms while the other platoon was engaged in activity subjects in special rooms. (Starr, 1958, p. 528)

All facets of a school building were constantly in use, never sitting empty (Cohen & Mohl, 1979). Wirt theorized that his work–study–play model fit with Dewey's idea of a whole-child developmental school that taught students mathematics and writing along with swimming, music, nature, and industrial education and other courses (Callahan, 1962).

At its prime, schools in Gary stayed open around the clock for the entire year and had intensive adult education programs in the evenings. Gary was a city mostly composed of new European immigrants. The children as well as adults needed English-language classes and Americanization training.

Elwell (1976) describes the many new ideas that Wirt's plan attempted: "In the first decade of this century, few school systems had attempted any of the innovations that characterized the Gary system" (p. 20). These ideas included an 8-hour school day, a single building housing 1st through 12th grades, individual student schedules, single-subject teachers, daily auditorium programs, new administrative roles, summer school, a full-time vocational program, and release time for religious instruction.

The more usage that school buildings received, Wirt theorized, the less expensive the public education enterprise would be (Ravitch, 1988). Wirt envisioned the school as a community center, and this ideology increased support of the school in the community (Cohen & Mohl, 1979). Good's biographical sketch of Wirt described the popularity of his plan: "Books and articles were written about it; visitors came to observe it" (Starr, 1958, p. 728). What's more, the platoon system's appeal was not limited to its economic benefits:

> Its popularity lay not only in its appeal to economy-minded taxpayers pressed by rising school enrollments but also in the way it adapted the progressive idea of a "community school" to an urban industrial center. (p. 728)

John Dewey and his daughter Evelyn called the Gary plan an exemplar of progressive education and profiled it in their collaborative book *Schools of To-Morrow* (Dewey & Dewey, 1915). The Deweys believed that the Gary plan modeled the progressive educational ideals of making education child centered and focusing on the development of the total child.

> But the biggest idea . . . is the social and community idea. . . . The question he tried to answer was this: What did the Gary children need to make them good citizens and happy and prosperous human beings, and how could the money available for educational purposes supply all these needs? (p. 176)

They praised Wirt for a plan that made sense economically while including the greater community. Wirt wanted schools to remain open for community activities throughout the evening hours to further increase their economic utility.

> Gary schools use the community as much as possible as a contributor to the educational facilities, and in so doing they give good return in immediate

results . . . But these schools have done much by showing a good business management, by spending the taxpayer's money in an economical way. (Dewey & Dewey, 1915, pp. 203–204).

The platoon system, according to Wirt and endorsed by the Deweys, maximized usage of school buildings, which made good fiscal sense.

Despite all the notoriety it received, the Gary plan faced criticism because it lacked empirical data to support its apparent success. Elwell (1976) reports on a 1918 Rockefeller Foundation–funded study by the General Education Board: The "report was thorough and scientific [and] found much to criticize and to doubt in the way the schools operated" (p. 20). Gary's dropout rates, attendance rates, and achievement scores were no better than those of other schools in Indiana. The shops lacked proper supervision, and the shop class curriculums and overall student development seemed to be lacking. Older students—serving as teaching assistants for younger children—helped in shops, but the practice did not appear to contain educational merit.

Many classroom observations found teachers using old-fashioned methods and failing to match class work with practical experience, and the Gary school system did not evaluate its teaching methods to determine their merit (Elwell, 1976). Despite it critics, however, the Gary plan garnered much praise.

A decade into the implementation of his plan in Gary, the mayor of New York City, John Mitchel, recruited Wirt to assist his city in developing the platoon school model for the New York public school system (Callahan, 1962). Ravitch (1988) characterizes Mitchel's primary goal for recruiting Wirt "to relieve the city of the burdensome problems of the public schools" (p. 195). At the time, New York City needed many more schools to house and educate current schoolless children and newly arriving immigrants. Ravitch says, "Mitchel was intrigued by the prospect of ending the part-time problem, enlivening the curriculum, and at the same time saving huge sums of money in the school construction program" (p. 203). Before Mitchel's election to office, the previous two New York mayoral administrations spent $5 million and $7 million to build new schools, but with the adoption of the Gary plan, Mitchel cut the amount to $1 million.

Cohen and Mohl (1979) describe Mitchel's leadership as "progressive passion for businesslike efficiency to city government—a commitment to scientific management, however, which often outweighed the social needs of city residents" (p. 36). Mitchel wanted to educate more students, with better quality, and at a cheaper rate than current spending levels. The fact remained, however, that public schools could not turn a profit; therefore, taxes and spending levels had to be increased to educate more students.

Gary schools mirrored society with racial segregation—namely, through separate White and Black schools. When Wirt and his school system were "confronted with Negro migration, the Gary schools were just as segregated as schools without a reformist tradition" (Ravitch, 1988, p. 228).

By the 1920s, school systems adopted the platoon school model "not because of its progressive child-centered tendencies, but because of the money that was saved by doubling pupil enrollment in a single building" (Ravitch, 1988, p. 227). Wirt ran the Gary school system until his death, from a sudden heart attack in 1938, and the Gary plan fell apart soon after (Cohen & Mohl, 1979). Increased cognitive curricular mandates were on the horizon, mandates that the platoon school could not fulfill.

Callahan (1962) attributes the success of the Gary plan to its association with the ideals of scientific management. In the age of Taylorism, anything associated with efficiency gave it what Callahan called a "halo effect." Additionally, the Gary plan provided districts that contained an influx of immigrant children a way to educate them without the enormous cost of building new schools. With students rotating from workshops to classrooms to the gymnasium, schools could double the amount of students that they could accommodate without building new facilities.

THE TRUMP PLAN

In 1956, the National Association of Secondary School Principals created the Commission on the Experimental Study of the Utilization of the Staff in the Secondary School to address problems in education (Trump, 1959). With Dr. J. Lloyd Trump as its director, the commission viewed the teacher shortage as a major obstacle to ensuring high-quality education for all students: "In 1955 . . . 45,000 more teachers than were readily available were needed in high schools" (Trump & Baynham, 1961, p. 1).

This coupled with the fact that the Soviet Union launched *Sputnik* in 1957 — the first human-made orbiting satellite — spurred fears that it might surpass the United States in the Cold War and win. It was left to the public schools to quickly reform to help the United States keep its competitive edge against the Soviet threat (Tyack, 1974). In 1959, Dr. Trump, professor of education at the University of Illinois, proposed a reorganization of schools to make education student centered, and he conceived of the school principal as instructional leader instead of business manager.

Trump created a plan to improve educational quality (Trump, 1959). His proposal called for flexible scheduling, a new plan for student learning, more time for teacher planning coupled with nonprofessional staff for assistance, better relations with the community, and an evaluation system to assess student learning.

The Trump plan radically changed the school day schedule. Traditionally, schools divided the day into class periods. For example, a student would attend six classes each day for 50 minutes each. "Today's school schedules students tightly so that they go from one class or study hall to another, six or more periods a day, with the same periods repeated five days a week" (Trump, 1959, p. 13). The Trump plan divided the day into uneven units of time based on the needs of individual students and their developmental ability.

Trump (1959) devised time for large-group instruction, small-group instruction, and individual study time. His idea was for students to spend 40% of their time in school working independently. Another 40% of the day was used for large-group instruction, and the remaining 20% was used for small-group instruction. "The school of the future will schedule students in class groups an average of only 18 hours a week, instead of the present 30 hours" (p. 14). Trump based his new school schedule on the premise that schools must do a better job "to provide for the individual differences of the students and to determine which learning experiences are the most significant for the success of the individual" (p. 5).

The different class groupings that Trump (1959) proposed corresponded to the varied activities in which he believed students should engage during a typical school day. Large-group instruction allowed a teacher to lecture to hundreds of students at once, without having to repeat the same information five times a day. Small groups of students and a teacher then met for discussion. Students then spent the remaining time in independent study, where they would "read . . . create, memorize, record . . . self-appraise" among other activities in "materials centers, museums, workshops, libraries, and laboratories" (p. 10).

> Tomorrow's schools will put flexibility of school arrangements ahead of the rigidity of the bell. The day will be divided into 15- or 20-minute modules of time, instead of equal periods, with no standard intermissions when the entire school crowds the halls and rest rooms at once. (Trump & Baynham, 1961, p. 41)

Ridgewood High School in suburban Norridge, Illinois, adopted the Trump plan and implemented a schedule that caused confusion; but when aided with technology, the school met the needs of its students. An article in *Education Digest* in January 1965 chronicles the 4 years of the Trump plan at the school. Superintendent Eugene Howard said:

> Instead of having six or seven periods a day to juggle, we had 21. . . . Ridgewood became the first school in the country to operate with a computer-built modular schedule. Costs run about $5 per student, which includes a weekly schedule for every student, every teacher, and a master schedule for the school office. (Ridgewood High School, 1965, p. 14)

The Trump plan proposed to reconfigure how students spent their days in school by providing them with less structure and more time for independent study. It was theorized that this would free up teachers to provide individualized instruction for students: "The secondary school of the future will provide for closer relationships between students and teachers" (Trump, 1959, p. 19). This transformation did not happen overnight, and the needs and maturity levels of students dictated who worked well independently and who needed structured learning. Superintendent Howard addressed this concern:

> Students are not born with the ability for independent study. Some students don't even have it when they enter graduate school. So we're asking a great deal when we ask students to participate in planning their own learning and then to put the plan in effect. There's a lot to be learned about teaching youngsters to work by themselves; I know we haven't learned it all by any means. (Ridgewood High School, 1965, p. 15)

The Trump plan proposed to improve the quality of teaching in a time when a great teaching shortage existed. "Attracting and retaining highly qualified teachers is a formidable problem" (Trump, 1959, p. 5). Also, the nature of the job had changed, and the differences were perceived negatively by the teachers. "Teachers gradually have inherited so many clerical and routine tasks that little evidence of the unique nature of teaching remains" (Trump & Baynham, 1961, p. 52).

> Staff specialists, community consultants, general aides, clerks, and instruction assistants, along with professional teachers, will comprise the staff . . . more adults to work with students but fewer adults will need to be professional teachers. (p. 33)

Trump used the additional staff to free up teachers to deal solely with the issues of teaching.

Trump's innovative plan of the early 1960s also recommended team teaching and independent study time for students as a better way to educate students, as opposed to "the lock-step rigidity of the self-contained classroom" (Beggs, 1964, p. 4). "Schools must be organized so that individual teacher competencies are better utilized and personal satisfactions more fully realized" (Trump & Baynham, 1961, p. 9). The plan took advantage of teachers who possessed subject expertise; namely, it allowed teachers to teach in teams, teaching to their strengths but also assisting when others possessed greater knowledge in a subject.

Teachers spent more time developing quality lesson plans and evaluating their students and less time on clerical and nonprofessional duties (Trump & Baynham, 1961). This was possible because the Trump plan increased the number of clerical staff and other support staff and so allowed teachers more time and freedom to perform the tasks that they were trained to do. Evanston (Illinois) High School adopted a "schools within a school" plan and utilized the philosophies of Dr. Trump's reform to improve teaching and learning. Some Evanston teachers exulted: "There is a different spirit in team teaching and team classes. It's more demanding for students and more stimulating for teachers" (Trump & Baynham, 1961, p. 85).

Teacher training became a collaborative and deliberative process, with school districts working in close collaboration with university schools of education. Trump described the difference between the self-contained classroom and the school of tomorrow that he envisioned:

> The self-contained classroom locks them in and denies their differences. It makes a farce out of the concept of equality of educational opportunities for all students because it refuses them access to the wide range of varied talents possessed by different teachers. Tomorrow's schools will recognize the differences among teachers by: team teaching; differentiated assignments and work loads; salary differentials. (Trump & Baynham, 1961, p. 47)

Lakeview High School in Decatur, Illinois, adopted the Trump plan, creating a system of instruction that included "team teaching, large and small group instruction with independent study, multimedia teaching aids and flexible scheduling" (Beggs, 1964, p. xii). Former Lakeview principal David W. Beggs III wrote in 1964 that teachers worked in isolation too much and that many of the daily lessons in the classrooms did not enhance student understanding.

Dr. Trump believed that teacher-centered instruction was not sound educational practice—that is, when "teachers talked and talked and talked to fill the pitcher" (p. 19). Along with team teaching, a 15-period, 27-minute module master schedule, which permitted time for independent study and large-group lectures, was created to foster better teaching and learning. He explained:

> School programs should reduce the time required for listening to teachers' talk. Conversely, the school should provide more time and better places for pupils to engage in independent study, covering required content as well as materials of special interest. . . . The school program needs to help pupils to find avenues of social action in the community after helping them prepare for constructive efforts. (quoted in Pileggi, 1969, p. 568)

Trump rejected the notion that the brain was like a muscle that needed exercising or that it was like a vessel just waiting to be filled up with information (Beggs, 1964).

Dr. Trump announced his "Images of the Future" plan in 1959 to the National Association of Secondary School Principals Commission on the Experimental Study of the Utilization of Staff in the Secondary School. His plan introduced team teaching, large-group lectures, medium- and small-group seminars, and individual study time to reform school. Ridge-wood High School applied the Trump plan to its entire school in 1961. The *Education Digest* (Ridgewood High School, 1965) article notes:

> The plan at Ridgewood included the following innovations: Instead of classes of 25–30 students, the students met in groups of four to six, 10–15, and 65–130. Instead of standard classrooms, there were many assorted working spaces, from individual carrels to large lecture halls. Instead of classroom teachers, the teachers were grouped in cooperative teams that utilized a variety of teaching spaces. (p. 13)

In addition, in 1982, New York City school superintendent Richard R. Doremus wrote "What Ever Happened to . . . Wayland (Mass.) High School?" Wayland High School introduced the Trump plan in 1963 with great fanfare. It did not last long. High staff turnover and new ideas came in with new leaders—which spelled the end of the Trump plan at Wayland (Doremus, 1982).

CES PLAN

A new sense of urgency calling for drastic reforms in public education emerged in the 1980s led by the federal government's *A Nation at Risk* report (National Commission on Excellence in Education, 1983). This government-produced study prophesized the end of U.S. supremacy in the world because a majority of the country's students came out of public schools wholly unprepared for the increasingly competitive global market:

> By the 1980s, the Soviets were no longer the bogeyman of American education. Fear now centered on stories about high schools turning out illiterates while Japanese students routinely outperformed Americans on standardized tests. (Schaller, 1992, p. 88)

To regain a competitive edge for America, citizens demanded that teachers work harder to increase students' proficiency levels. International test scores in science and mathematics consistently showed U.S. students far below those of competitive nations. By the end of the decade, many state governments had adopted policies to obtain higher academic accountability and standards for teachers and students.

Dr. Theodore Sizer published a critique of the American high school in his 1984 book *Horace's Compromise*. In it, he presented glaring educational deficiencies and proposed fundamental changes for public and private high school education. Sizer's book was a culmination of several years of personal observation that he and several Brown University colleagues had conducted. In an investigation called "A Study of High Schools," the group toured the country, visiting school after school and documenting what they saw in each school. Sizer commenced the journey with the belief that too many good reforms existed but were not used, and he wanted to know why. His book came on the heels of *A Nation at Risk* and coincided with president Ronald Reagan's harsh criticisms of public education.

Sizer (1984) believed that high schools needed to be less about course credit and more about significant cognitive development. The traditional process of taking classes and covering content was more of a rite of passage than an educationally significant practice (Sizer, 1984). Sizer developed the CES as a result of his study. He based his ideas on "the relationships between students and teachers. . . . We favor the pedagogies of 'coaching' and 'questioning' as outlined in Mortimer Adler's *Paideia Proposal*" (p. 11).

Sizer (1992) reasons that by following new principles that were "more sensible and sensitive" (p. 224), schools were better. Furthermore, educators were forced to make compromises that were not necessarily in the best interest of students and learning but occurred because the educational system forced concessions. With that ideology, he created the CES, "which [would] experiment with ways to reduce the compromises school people and students must now make" (p. 225).

> Sizer's approach to school reform did not include criticizing teachers. Instead, he sought to illuminate how the mindlessness of American secondary schooling forced even well-intentioned teachers to compromise their ideals. (Muncey & McQuillan, 1996, pp. 6–7)

Sizer's work (1996) bore the fruit of nine ideas that served as the core of the CES reform model. Sizer did not believe the ideas to be radical or fantastic. Instead, the majority were common sense, even though "they implied substantial changes in the way that most high schools currently functioned" (p. 156). With a thoughtful and deliberative implementation process of all nine coalition principles, Sizer believed that beneficial results and boosted student achievement would result. The common principles were as follows (pp. 154–155):

1. The school should focus on helping adolescents learn to use their minds well. Schools should not be "comprehensive" if such a claim is made at the expense of the school's intellectual purpose.

2. The school's goals should be simple: that each student masters a limited number of essential skills and areas of knowledge. While these skills and areas will, to varying degrees, reflect the traditional academic disciplines, the program's design should be shaped by the intellectual and imaginative powers and competencies that students need rather than necessarily by "subjects" as conventionally defined. The aphorism "less is more" should dominate: curricular decisions should be guided by the aim of thorough student mastery and achievement rather than by an effort merely to cover content.

3. The school's goals should apply to all students, while the means to these goals will vary as those students themselves vary. School practice should be tailor-made to meet the needs of every group or class of adolescents.

4. Teaching and learning should be personalized to the maximum feasible extent. Efforts should be directed toward a goal that no teacher have direct responsibility for more than eighty students. To capitalize on this personalization, decisions about the details of the course of study, the use of students' and teachers' time, and the choice of teaching materials and specific pedagogies must be unreservedly placed in the hands of the principal and staff.

5. The governing practical metaphor of the school should be student-as-worker rather than the more familiar metaphor of teacher-as-deliverer-of-instructional-services. Accordingly, a prominent pedagogy will be coaching, to provoke students to learn how to learn and thus to teach themselves.

6. Students entering secondary school studies are those who can show competence in language and elementary mathematics. Students of traditional high school age but not yet at appropriate levels of competence to enter secondary school studies will be provided intensive remedial work to assist them quickly to meet these standards. The diploma should be awarded

upon a successful final demonstration of mastery for graduation—an "Exhibition." This Exhibition by the student of his or her grasp of the central skills and knowledge of the school's program may be jointly administered by the faculty and by higher authorities. As the diploma is awarded when earned, the school's program proceeds with no strict age grading and with no system of "credits earned" by "time spent" in class. The emphasis is on the students' demonstration that they can do important things.

7. The tone of the school should explicitly and self-consciously stress values of unanxious expectation ("I won't threaten you but I expect much of you"), of trust (until abused), and of decency (the values of fairness, generosity, and tolerance). Incentives appropriate to the school's particular students and teachers should be emphasized, and parents should be treated as essential collaborators.

8. The principal and teachers should perceive themselves as generalists first (teachers and scholars in general education) and specialists second (experts in one particular discipline). Staff should expect multiple obligations (teacher-counselor-manager) and a sense of commitment to the entire school.

9. Ultimate administrative and budget targets should include, in addition to total students loads per teacher of eighty or fewer pupils, substantial time for collective planning by teachers, competitive salaries for staff, and an ultimate per-pupil cost not to exceed that at traditional schools by more than 10 percent. To accomplish this, administrative plans may have to show the phased reduction or elimination of some services now provided students in many traditional comprehensive secondary schools.

The CES reform was less about telling schools how to reform and more about providing a philosophical basis for local schools to change themselves: "The focus of the CES work is less on issues than the life of schools and classroom, and the work is predicated on the idea that the issues and the stimulus for change should come from the practitioners themselves" (McDonald et al., 1999, p. 6).

> As readers will quickly observe in all our work, we have focused on the "triangle" of students, teachers, and the subjects of their study. We know that the game of school learning is won or lost in classrooms, and we felt that America's present system of schooling makes winning often very difficult indeed. Any improvement in American high schools must take into account the stubborn realities of this triangle. Understand the triangle, and the subsequent necessary steps become clear. (Sizer, 1984, p. 5)

In 1997, the CES governing body, known as the CES Congress, met to add the 10th common principle to the CES plan. Although the United States was an exemplar of democracy and freedom, a widening gap between rich Americans and poor Americans concerned CES members, who worked in schools that increasingly segregated students according to socioeconomic status (Cushman, 1998a). "Among schools there was one important difference, which followed from a single variable only: the social class of the student body" (Sizer, 1984, p. 6). The 10th principle stated:

> 10. The school should demonstrate non-discriminatory and inclusive policies, practices, and pedagogies. It should model democratic practices that involve all who are directly affected by the school. The school should honor diversity and build on the strengths of its communities, deliberately and explicitly challenging all forms of inequity and discrimination.

Although society did not implement significant strategies to help economically disadvantaged citizens, the congress decided that schools must work to erase achievement gaps and other disparities that left poor and minority students behind.

The goal of CES was to make learning more significant by not relying on structures set up over 100 years ago. For example, the American high school curriculum was still based on the system that the Committee of Ten set up in 1893. This committee created the academic subjects of English, math, science, social studies, and elective courses. Students moved from one class to the next, all equal in time and all disconnected from the others. The CES plan changed this fundamental structure. Sizer (1984) writes, "I would organize a high school into four areas or large departments: 1. Inquiry and Expression, 2. Mathematics and Science, 3. Literature and the Arts, 4. Philosophy and History" (p. 132).

School life was more like real life because math, philosophy, English, and the other subjects flow naturally from one another. The real world did not separate life into neat, disconnected academic disciplines. Teachers spent more time helping students think, and students spent more time thinking. As philosopher Jerome Bruner said, "we get interested in what we get good at" (quoted in Sizer, 1984, p. 165). Full implementation of the CES plan ended the warehousing of students in schools and promoted learning opportunities based on the natural curiosities of students.

COMER SDP

The Comer SDP was a child-centered and data-driven school reform process (Comer, 1997). Comer created the SDP as a process to help schools with high percentages of struggling students to improve (Comer, 1980). While employed at the Yale Child Study Center in 1968, Comer believed that if schools created and maintained strong bonds between home and school, then students would have the positive backing needed to become successful (Comer et al., 1996).

The Comer SDP relied on child development theory and emphasized whole child development as the key to raising children to survive independently (Comer et al., 1996). As adults, people who had developed their total selves positively contributed to democratic society. Oftentimes, when a child was sent to school, his or her path and development were based on the economic and educational levels of his or her parents. Based on this fact, schools placed students in different groupings according to their perceived ability. Using this theory, the ability of a child was preordained at birth (Scheurich & Imber, 1991). M. B. Katz (1971) says that ability grouping was a "social sorting device. They have utilized the mantle of science to disguise the fact that schools reinforce existing patterns of social structure" (p. 122).

The SDP wanted to especially help students who were pushed into low-level tracks or classes because they did not appear to have strong parental support, did not seem to be interested in their own education, and seemingly frustrated teachers and other students because they were labeled cognitively slow.

The SDP also wanted to help teachers and administrators realize that all children were capable of learning and that lower-class parents wanted their children to perform well in school just as middle-class parents strove to make sure that their children succeeded. M. B. Katz (1971) supports this line of thinking: "My premise that the desire that children become functionally literate and able to understand mathematics is nearly universal; it is as true of poor as of affluent parents" (p. 143).

The SDP asserted that the home was an important factor in contributing to the success or failure of children in school and society in general. Also, the empowered school, society, and social networks to which a child had access all influenced his or her development and shaped his or her overall self (Comer et al., 1996). The SDP wanted to bring parents and teachers into a close relationship that positively influenced a child and contributed to his or her total development along the related pathways: physical, psychological, social, ethical, cognitive, and lingual.

> All children can learn and develop well. Children are social beings who need the support and involvement of caring adults for their five internal developmental pathways to become fully realized and to grow physically. If children's physical needs are met, they have the potential to develop psychosocially. For some children, the home, school, social networks, and society nurture and facilitate development. For other children, however, negative influences in their environment inhibits their total development. (p. 15)

The SDP took on an "emergency room" mentality in dealing with students in schools. If a child struggled with reading, for example, then the child was taught to read. Less focus was placed on assigning blame to whoever did not successfully teach the child in the past (Comer et al., 1996). M. B. Katz (1971) agrees and says, "Once again . . . take the schools out of the business of making attitudes. Have them attend to skills, especially, in the beginning, reading" (p. 143). Move beyond the blame game, Comer (1997) believed—teach children where they were when they came to you.

This was not a quick-fix school reform measure. It could not be implemented overnight and automatically turn a low-performing school into a school with high test scores. This was an ecological system of human development (Malloy, 1997). In the past, school reform had used a one-dimensional approach to solve a multidimensional problem. Comer's plan was a process, and it took years and ongoing dedication to make it work.

The SDP relied on site-based management and posited that the people who were most directly affected by decisions should make the decisions (Comer et al., 1996). These stakeholders included parents, teachers, administrators, other adults in the community, and, to some extent, students. Murphy and Beck (1995) and Sergiovanni (1994) report positive results from site-based management because all adults worked together to help in the positive development of children and teenagers.

The African proverb "It takes a whole village to raise a child" was the premise under which the SDP functioned (Comer et al., 1996). For M. B. Katz (1971) "decentralization should include a shift of power to teachers and students, away from administration, as well as to local communities" (p. 146). All adults had to work together to help children develop properly.

The SDP operated on three guiding principles: consensus, collaboration, and no-fault. Comer believed that voting on issues led to winners and losers; people campaigned for their cause instead of participating in "coalition building" (p. 149). Consensus urged all concerned to work toward an agreed solution that was acceptable to everyone.

Collaboration required parents, teachers, administrators, and others involved in the process to respect others' points of view. A collaborative environment encouraged inclusion and respect among all members of the school community. M. B. Katz (1971) reports that schools and teachers suffered "from the suffocating atmosphere in which teachers have had to work. . . . Teachers do not run schools. . . . They are . . . harassed by the administration, which . . . continually gets in their way" (p. 131). When all adults felt respected and equal, it fostered a willingness to work together in pursuit of common goals.

Coupled with the no-fault principle, the assignment of blame for problems was discouraged. Instead, the examination of problems was required from a viewpoint where all shared equal responsibility for positive change (Noblit, Malloy, & Malloy, 2001). This atmosphere of shared responsibility created a positive environment in which the best interests of the children remained the primary concern of the entire school community (Comer et al., 1996).

> Simply designing and placing a shared decision-making structure in a school setting is unlikely to be effective unless there are supportive components . . . Site-based management designs generally fail to establish structures and processes that help school communities work through cultural change. Shared decision making is difficult when the staff continues to be isolated. The professionalization of teaching grates against the belief that everyone- parents, community members, cafeteria workers- should have a say in what is important. (Squires & Kranyik, 1996, p. 29)

The no-fault principle helped people move past blaming and focused on people's emotions to solve conflicts that hindered collaborative work efforts. When conflicts and arguments developed between adults in a school, a standstill ensued. The no-fault principle operated "on the premise that other people's mistakes result from misunderstandings, misinterpretations, or miscommunications and not a deliberate attempt to offend" (Comer et al., 1996, p. 57).

As long as the adults were not talking and working together, the problem carried over into other aspects of the school, and children suffered. The goal was to talk out the problem, listen to each other, solve the conflict, and move on (Comer et al., 1996).

Comer, Haynes, and Hamilton-Lee (1988) believe that many of the problems that children encounter in school stem from a lack of understanding and communication between the home and the school, as well as from a lack of respect from society. Children—especially, those from poor minority families—were better able to adapt when schools understood their needs. Many schools did not offer teachers, parents, and children a forum where they could express what they were thinking, to an attentive audience that took them seriously. The SDP worked to establish strong relationships among people. It dealt with how students interacted with teachers, how teachers perceived students, and how parents and the community related to a school (Noblit et al., 2001).

The principle of no-fault worked to improve personal relationships by diminishing the act of blaming so that attention was focused solely on the needs of children (Noblit et al., 2001). When people did not feel that they were in a safe environment to express how they felt, they resorted to blaming to express their emotions. A group of researchers from Northwestern University, Prince George's County School District (Maryland), and Yale University, including Dr. Comer, conducted a study of the SDP and its effect on urban education:

> Because of their own negative experiences with schools and government, many poor parents of color do not believe that the school sincerely wants to educate their children or involve them as participant parents . . . From the teacher's vantage point, the children come to school academically and socially unprepared, and their parents show little practical interest in promoting their children's learning and social skill development. (Anson et al., 1991, p. 58)

The no-fault principle began with the premise that a conflict had arisen from a misinterpretation or misunderstanding (Comer et al., 1996). The act committed or words spoken were not intentional acts aimed at causing harm. The parties involved in the conflict were brought together, preferably with a trained SDP facilitator as a mediator, and they ironed out differences.

No-fault also dealt with the ages-old parent–teacher conflict that had each side blaming the other for the failings of the children. Teachers contended that they were not able to educate students, because the parents provided no support at home (Comer et al., 1996); parents had the idea that the school did not care about and would not educate their children. When this conflict occurred, people did not feel safe and comfortable to express how they felt; therefore, they resorted to blaming:

> Individuals need to express their emotions. . . . Blaming occurs when individuals feel unsafe or uncomfortable. . . . By blaming, the team avoids self-reflection and, thus, the ability of the team to work collaboratively is undermined. (p. 57)

The no-fault principle was often misunderstood, and it caused further confusion and dissension. What about a person who was at fault? Shouldn't that person receive blame? Wasn't that person getting away with what he or she had caused (Noblit et al., 2001)? This led to some sensitive situations, especially if the conflict was between a student and a teacher. The misunderstanding led a teacher to seek punishment, and many times through reflection, the teacher saw that the situation could have been handled differently. A student may not have reacted had he or she not been backed into a corner.

The no-fault principle was misconstrued as meaning that (a) it was no one's fault that the student was not able to read or write, (b) it was no one's fault that the child was misbehaving, and therefore (c) discipline and punishment should not have been doled out (Noblit et al., 2001). This was equally harmful—especially to the student who was not taught that his or her negative actions had consequences. Also, the teacher's authority in the classroom was usurped, and he or she therefore had trouble maintaining an atmosphere conducive to learning.

When dealing with personal conflicts, strong feelings and emotions prevented resolutions. It was seen as counterproductive to deal with personal problems when there was work to be done. However, if personal conflicts were not resolved, they interfered with the collaborative process and broke down the system of working together to positively benefit children (Comer et al., 1996).

Teams must be taught to suspend judgment and simply describe the behavior that led to particular emotions. . . . The tendency [exists] to blame others rather than to engage in self-reflection that can result in finding one's own errors or lack of development. . . . No-fault does not mean that we withhold our honest thoughts and feelings. Rather, no-fault is about providing a safe environment in which we can share our thoughts and feelings directly with the individuals and teams that have provoked the feelings. (p. 59)

The principles of consensus and collaboration meant that all persons who were involved agreed to a decision before it was put into action (Comer et al., 1996). Oftentimes, a vote was taken and the majority got its way whereas the minority did not, but because all did not agree with the decision, all did not attempt to follow through with it.

To reach consensus, all personnel had to be given the opportunity to express how they felt on the subject. It was important that the other members heard and then transcended what they believed and gave consideration to other views, even if they did not personally believe them (Comer, 1997). Listening skills were important, and members received training. This approach took time; all sides had to be listened to, and decisions were not carried out until consensus was reached. This created a win-win situation instead of the winner-loser mentality, and a policy had a much greater chance of being internalized and fulfilled when reached through consensus (Comer et al., 1996).

Collaboration required all persons involved to work together for the benefit of the children. Many teachers, accustomed to working in isolation, had a difficult time with collaboration. They worked with a principal whom they respected for exhibiting authority and caring, but they had a difficult time working collaboratively, especially with teachers from other disciplines or grade levels (Haynes, 1998).

Comer believed that all schools benefited from the positive relationships that the SDP established. Schools with high percentages of disadvantaged children could not be effectively educated without its principles. Child development theory concluded that all children were at risk if they did not have the proper nurturing from home or school. Continuing his interview with O'Neil (1997), Comer explains:

If you look at the trends in social problems, the greatest growth is in the white middle class. Teenage pregnancy was once three times as great among blacks as whites. It's now one and a half times higher. Thirty years ago, Daniel Patrick Moynihan made us aware of the disturbing fact that single parents headed 25 percent of black homes. That's now true of the white community. So we're dealing with a systematic problem; it just happened to show up in the most vulnerable group first. (p. 10)

Comer said that the SDP provided a means to create and sustain a positive school climate and that it helped students develop. Teachers, parents, and administrators positively influenced children when they worked together toward their best interests (Comer, 1980).

The SDP was a data-driven school improvement process because it measured the impact of its implementation in schools to help figure out what worked and what needed to be improved in each school (Comer et al., 1996). The SDP received criticism because outstanding gains in standardized test scores were not necessarily shown. Comer and others realized that test scores did not indicate success or failure of the SDP: "Measuring program outcomes, such as improved student performance on standardized tests is meaningless unless there is a commensurate assessment of the level and quality of program implementation" (p. 123).

The SDP conducted studies of its schools. It documented and evaluated its schools for three reasons:

> to provide formative process data to improve and strengthen program implementation; to provide measures of program impact on salient outcome variables, including those identified in Comprehensive School Plan goal statements; to contribute to the theory on how schools change and how students succeed. (Comer et al., 1996, p. 123)

Data gathered from all stakeholders helped in formulating decision making in the best interests of the children. The stakeholders included students, parents, and school staff—including teachers, administrators, janitorial, secretarial, professional, and nonprofessional support staff.

Studies showed improvements in SDP schools. For example, a 1986 analysis of achievement data in the Benton Harbor area schools (Michigan) showed significant gains in reading and mathematics and higher-than-average gains made for the school district as a whole (Comer et al., 1996). In 1987, the research office of Prince George's County public schools showed gains in the California Achievement Test between 1985 and 1987 that were greater for SDP schools than for the district as a whole. Moreover, the analysis of fourth graders in the first two SDP schools in New Haven showed steady gains in mathematics and reading between 1969 and 1984. "The grade equivalent scores for the two schools increased from about 3.0 in reading and mathematics in 1969 to 6.0 in reading and 5.0 in mathematics in 1984" (p. 130).

Additional studies to assess the quality of the SDP implementation were conducted by Comer and the SDP staff at Yale University (Comer et al., 1996). An experimental Comer study on "behavior and school adjustment effects" found that SDP students experienced "greater positive changes in attendance and teacher ratings of classroom behavior, attitude toward authority, and group participation, when compared to non-SDP students" (p. 132).

Another study compared the self-concept of fourth- and sixth-grade students to non-SDP students according to the six self-concept dimensions on the Piers Harris Self-Concept Scale: "On the post-test measures, SDP students scored significantly higher than the control group of non-SDP students on all six self-concept dimensions and significantly higher than the normative group on total self-concept" (Comer et al. 1996, p. 133).

Other studies comparing SDP schools with schools that were geographically and demographically similar showed significantly better climates in the SDP schools: "It is clear from our research that where the program is implemented well, strong positive school-level and student-level outcomes result" (Comer et al., 1996, p. 145).

The SDP was based on child development theory and the premise that all children developed properly when provided the necessary support by the adults in their lives. Taken as a whole, the data appeared to show that the SDP fostered positive change in schools.

SCHOOL REFORM AND CHILD DEVELOPMENT

Comer (1997), Sarason (1971), and M. B. Katz (1971) report that the ecological approach to education served children best. School reform relied on child development theory and emphasized whole-child development as the key principle in guiding adult interactions with students. The neighborhood or circumstances from which a child came would not determine one's life chances.

Oftentimes, when a child was sent to school, his or her path and development were preordained based on the economic and educational levels of his or her parents or guardians (M. B. Katz, 1971). Schools placed students in groups according to their perceived academic abilities, a system known as *tracking*. Proponents of tracking believed that slow children held back the brighter, more motivated students who became bored while a teacher attended to the needs of the former. The academically gifted did not reach their full potential in mixed classes.

> But critics miss the essential point in that they fail to see the connection between the educational processes in the schools and the level of academic skills the caste system requires of blacks, which can force not only 'good schools' but also well-intentioned black or white school personnel to apply the same subtle devices against black children. (Ogbu, 1978, p. 132)

More often than not, ability stemmed from the socioeconomic level of a child's parents. If one was from a disadvantaged background—if one did not speak, dress, or act as though one was from the mainstream culture—and if one's parents did not appear to be interested in educational development, then one was placed in the lowest track at school, and further educational opportunities were limited. The goal was to indoctrinate these students with middle-class values and prepare them for assembly-line work (M. B. Katz, 1971).

Comer (1997) says that students who were not empowered from their home to thrive in an academic environment found school difficult. However, because the home was not properly preparing a child for school did not mean that parents did not care about education. Comer noted that children who were not prepared in the mainstream culture had difficulty in school because their home training was different:

> We realized that the children were bright and able but that the climate wasn't right. We also realized that the teachers wanted to succeed, but they were stuck with a mechanical model of teaching and did not understand what else was necessary. They weren't prepared to respond to students' lack of social and emotional skills, which led to students' acting out or withdrawing from classroom activities. The teachers' responses were to try to control the behavior, to 'get the badness out of the children.' That led to difficulty with the parents, who themselves very often had not done well in

school. Parents ended up withdrawing from the school or attacking it. So children, parents, and teachers all wanted to succeed, but all behaved in ways that kept them from being successful. (quoted in O'Neil, 1997, p. 7)

WHY STUDY THE SDP? THE SIGNIFICANT HISTORICAL ORIGINS OF COMER'S PLAN

Dr. Comer came of age and graduated from college in the 1960s, an intellectually radical time in the United States. At the time, urbanization, suburbanization, and the growth of transportation and communication systems reshaped the landscape. Urban education could not keep up. African American students in the northern and western regions of the country found themselves concentrated in strained urban schools.

In 1968, Comer established the SDP in two African American elementary schools in urban New Haven that were deemed the worst schools in the city. The history before 1968 was studied to gain an understanding of the national political landscape that led to Comer's creation.

Although the Supreme Court decided *Brown v. Board of Education* in 1954, it took until the 1969 *Alexander v. Holmes* "at once" Supreme Court mandate for many Southern schools and school districts to comply with federal school desegregation orders. Meanwhile, in the northern and western parts of the country, the school desegregation era ended in 1974, when the Supreme Court decided in *Milliken v. Bradley* that locally created school districts did not fall under the desegregation mandate. Midwestern urban areas, for example, contain hundreds of separate school districts in a single metropolitan region. Therefore, schools such as those in New Haven remained racially polarized.

In the midst of the political, social, economic, and military struggles of the 1960s, Comer incorporated the child psychology and educational writings and theories of Lewin (1936); Kelly (1966); Reiff (1966); Becker, Wylan, and McCourt (1971); and Hartman (1979) to help create a new reform plan for public education. When Comer and the SDP staff embarked on a journey into the two New Haven schools, they were at the bottom of the district in every measurable category and served the poorest and most underprivileged youths in the city. Comer reported that after the first year, his team should have been kicked out the schools; however, they were not.

Over the course of the next several years, they helped make the schools and the students successful.

PHILOSOPHICAL BELIEFS UNDERLYING THE SDP

After studying the history of public education and school reform, I gained knowledge of the philosophical underpinnings of the SDP by examining the theories that Dr. Comer subscribed to when crafting his reform plan.

The SDP wanted to change basic school structures to create a school that gave more power to people involved at the grassroots level, and it created an ideology that diminished biased ideologies so that all children were served. Comer (1972) believes that student problems in schools stem from greater societal issues and conflicts. "We are a society that has failed to gear itself to enable people to meet their basic needs," Comer said. "The failing public school system is only a by-product of this larger failure" (p. 55).

Comer's plan focused on helping students whom the system pushed into low-level tracks and classes because they did not appear to have strong parental support, did not seem to be interested in their own education, and were deemed so slow that without separation they would continue to frustrate teachers and bother other students. The mission was to help teachers and administrators realize that all children could learn and that lower-class parents wanted their children to perform well in school, just as any middle-class parents did.

Schools with predominately African American student populations struggled when they did not maintain a healthy social contract among the school, community, and parents. According to the SDP philosophy, simply because the home was not properly preparing a child for school did not mean that the parents or guardians did not care about education.

The SDP asserted that the home was an important factor in contributing to the success or failure of children in school and society. Recognizing that school, society, and the social networks to which a child had access all influenced his or her development and shaped the child's overall self, the SDP attempted to bring parents and teachers together to positively influence children along the six pathways to development: physical, psychological, social, ethical, cognitive, and lingual (Comer et al., 1996).

Students who were not empowered from their home to thrive in the academic environment found school difficult. However, this did not mean that they were hopeless. M. B. Katz (1971) believes that because schools were based on racist and class-biased ideologies that had not changed, they contributed to the failure of their students. Additionally, racism created more hurdles which minority students had to surmount to receive equal educational opportunities. During the desegregation era, persistent racist remarks and attacks fueled the fire and grew into tremendous obstacles. Comer (1972) writes that the "black experience" in America could serve as a great lesson for all:

> A close look at the black experience reveals that black problems are simply the most extreme examples of American problems; that blacks have been only the most victimized by a generally inappropriate social policy. It reveals that, while black and white conflict is very real and painful, the root problem is beyond black and white. The black experience can teach us all much about how America must change. (p. 70)

The quality of relationships that existed among students, parents, teachers and school administrators determined school climate. The overall behavior, attitude, and achievement of students reflected a school's climate. When a school wanted to improve its climate, it had to change the way that it interacted with its students (Comer et al., 1996).

The SDP prescribed an increase in the amount of parent–teacher communication and interaction to positively influence and motivate children. If students understood that the adults in their lives—parents, teachers, administrators, cafeteria staff, counselors, custodial workers—were working together and if these adults exhibited positive behavior toward the students, then student behavior and motivation would improve and result in increased levels of achievement (Comer et al., 1996).

In Chiles and Hill's (1993) interview with him, Comer addressed the reasons why predominately Black schools failed whereas White schools tended to succeed. Comer said that it was not simply a matter of race; rather, the outward appearance may have been that Whites were succeeding and African Americans were not. Comer indicated that the problem amounted to the availability of opportunities—namely, that Whites had more opportunities and African Americans had fewer. Therefore, statistics broken down by race showed Whites outstripping African Americans. Comer further explains:

> Blacks have been closed out of the economic and social mainstream of the society. In the Black community, you are more likely to have undereducated parents unable to give their children the kinds of experiences they need to succeed in school, even when the parents want their kids to succeed and try to do all the right things. Often they don't know some of the things you can do from a very early age to help a child succeed in school. But it's not only some Black parents, its White parents as well. When you do an analysis of Blacks and Whites, what you're really measuring is Whites who have greater opportunity and Blacks who have had less opportunity, so Whites overall show up better. But if you compare Whites from Appalachia with Blacks from Prince Georges County, Maryland, or Shaker Heights, Ohio [Black middle-class communities], Blacks will do better. (p. 88)

Comer was empowered in his own life to achieve academic success by his mother and father (Comer, 1997). Time and again, they stressed the importance of education to him. Comer worked his way through college and medical school and succeeded. The fact troubled him that many of his friends who were just as intelligent did not go to college. Many did not even finish high school. Although menial factory labor was available, the drudgery of that work was readily apparent, and other opportunities quickly diminished.

His experience propelled him to spend his career searching for ways to empower all children to become motivated to reach their full potential. His boyhood friends in Indiana were not "lazy" or "obstinate," as many "at risk" children were labeled. Instead, they did not receive the proper preparation needed to succeed in school, and teachers misconstrued this as lack of intelligence and lack of effort.

The same educational problems in existence in the mid-20th century, when Comer was a child, still existed in 2007. However, the problems were magnified in 2007 because the plentiful amounts of low-skill jobs that were available in the past no longer existed in the United States. This meant that the working class that had historically been educated to perform blue-collar, low-skill jobs suddenly needed higher levels of education. Factory jobs moved overseas, and increased technological advances domestically rendered low-skill tasks obsolete. Education in 2007 was more critical than in the past because children needed it to gain admittance to and perform in the high-skill jobs that existed in the United States.

SUMMARY

I began this study with a review of what experts wrote about education. With this examination of the literature, I gained perspective about the history of public education in America, the roots of democracy and the creation of democratic education, school reform, the significance of school desegregation for the SDP, the recycling of school reform, the SDP and the five other reform plans, and the significance of child development theory for the SDP. This study continued with an examination of the selected reform plans as compared to Sarason's description of the failure of school reform.

An analysis of the five mentioned school reform ideas served as comparisons for the SDP. Could its success or failure be predicted? If past school reform plans similar in ideology and implementation to the SDP failed, what did this mean for the future of the SDP? Did it thrive and expand, or did it degenerate (Noddings, 1998)? What necessary conditions existed for the SDP to succeed? What was the explicit purpose of public schools? Did schools develop citizens for a democracy, prepare workers for businesses, or simply socialize children and immigrants? Was the real purpose one of these, a combination of all, or none?

That purpose engendered more discussion than ever before. Comer's purpose for the SDP centered on the ideal that all students—especially, disadvantaged youth—really needed public education to help them become positively contributing citizens during adulthood, more or less an amalgamation of the three stated goals (Comer et al., 1996).

2

Profiling the Failures of School Reforms

> Too few adults really believe that poor kids or minority kids can make
> it. Don't educate them to use their minds, the conventional wisdom
> goes, because they aren't interested, and anyway, we do them a big
> service by preparing them for semiskilled jobs.
>
> —Theodore Sizer, *Horace's Compromise* (1984, p. 220)

Few school reform plans in history transformed schools in the manner that they intended. Features of some reform plans became part of the structure of the American educational system. The perceived efficiency of the age-graded plan, for instance, led to wholesale adoption of age-graded schooling. Other times, only parts of a reform plan survived. Among its many features, the Dalton plan promoted individualized instruction. Although the reform plan itself faded, the method of individualized instruction was incorporated by countless classroom teachers (Cubberley, 1919). On the whole, most reform plans, including the Gary plan, the Trump plan, and the Lancastrian plan, became footnotes in history.

The purpose of this study was to determine if the success or failure of the Comer SDP could be predicted by assessing it according to Sarason's "failure of school reform" descriptors (1990, 1993, 2002, 2004). Past and present school reform plans were examined using qualitative data extracted from each plan's archival record. The reform plans were analyzed against a rubric based on Sarason's descriptors. This rubric served as a qualitative tool for comparative assessment of the reform plans. I sought to better understand the difficulties school reform plans encountered as they butted against a large human social structure, namely, K–12 education. Finally, this study served as a lens through which future educational policymakers can contemplate new school reform proposals.

METHOD OF ANALYSIS

This investigation commenced with a comparative examination of the SDP and five select reform plans. The key ideas of the Lancastrian plan, the age-graded plan, the Gary plan, the Trump plan, and the CES plan were identified to find similarities and differences between them. A narrative summary of the findings was developed.

Sarason believed that no matter how altruistic the goals of any school reform plan were, none would succeed for reasons that I compiled in the rubrics in this study. I determined that a successful school reform plan must address the following four elements: change theory, teaching theory, the teaching profession, and school power and politics. I provided descriptive indicators of observable characteristics under each element that guided analysis. The data were used to measure the selected reform plans. Figures 2.1–2.4 illustrate the features of the rubric that guided the assessment of the reform plans.

I assessed each reform plan with a rating system that measured each element. Each element's measure resulted from the scores of each indicator. A rating of *high, medium, low*, or *not applicable* was the scoring method for each indicator. A rating of *high* meant that the reform plan fully integrated that indicator in the reform (see Table 2.1).

The entire change theory element was rated according to the overall success of each indicator: *very effective, effective, somewhat effective*, or *not effective*. A *somewhat effective* rating meant that the reform plan scored *high* or *medium* on a few of the indicators (see Table 2.2). For example, the CES rated *very effective* for teaching theory because all variables were rated *high*. The Lancastrian plan rated *not effective* for the teaching profession because all the variables were rated *low*. An explanation of the elements and indicators follows.

Table 2.2 explains the rating scale for the elements, while Table 2.1 lists the rating scale for the indicators. A *high* rating on all indicators equated

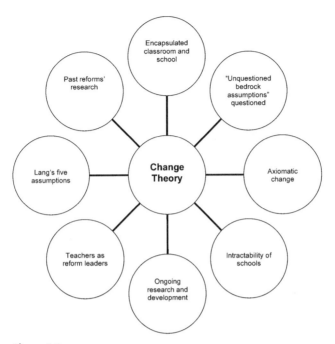

Figure 2.1.

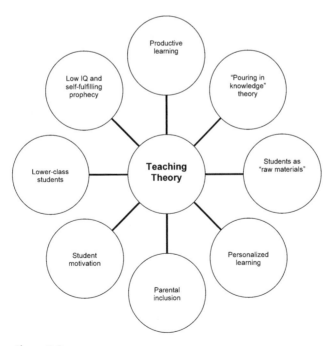

Figure 2.2.

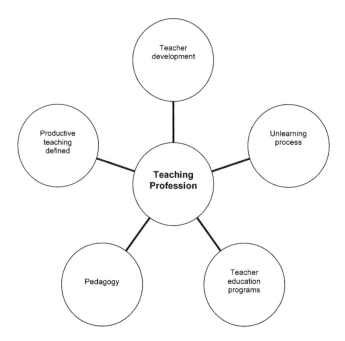

Figure 2.3.

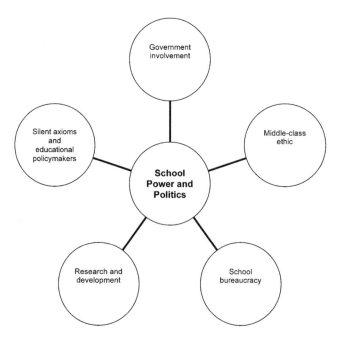

Figure 2.4.

Table 2.1. Criteria for Rating the Indicators of Observable Characteristics

Rating Level	Indicators of Observable Characteristics
High	The archival data provided compelling evidence that this indicator was fully integrated by the reform plan.
Medium	The archival data provided some evidence of integrating the indicator by the reform plan.
Low	The archival data provided evidence that the reform plan did not include this indicator as a component of the plan.
Not applicable	No archival data existed to effectively measure this indicator.

to a *very effective* rating for an element, whereas a *low* rating for each indicator resulted in a *not effective* rating on a particular element.

Under each indicator, I included a brief explanation—often in the form of a brief descriptive quotation from Sarason—and a one-sentence statement from the author that served as a guide in determining how each reform plan rated on the indicator. For example, under the change theory element, the first indicator was "the encapsulated classroom and school." I explained the meaning of the indicator and cited the following passage from Sarason (1990): "the axiom was that education (schooling) best takes place in encapsulated classrooms in encapsulated schools" (p. 111). Sarason did not agree that schooling necessarily had to take place in a classroom, with rows of desks, a chalk board or white board, and one teacher instructing with a prescribed curriculum to all the students born of a particular year, at the same time.

I organized the explanation of the rubric to make the research method understandable. A summary explanation of each indicator is followed by a quotation from Sarason as a point of reference. Next, I included a statement that guided the search through the gathered archival data (see

Table 2.2. Criteria for Rating the Elements

Rating Level	Elements
Very effective	The reform plan provided a comprehensive inclusion of the variables. The plan scored a high rating for each indicator.
Effective	The reform plan included most of the variables. The plan scored a high on most of the indicators and nothing lower than a medium.
Sometimes effective	The reform plan scored at least medium on the majority of the indicators.
Not effective	The reform plan consistently scored a low on the majority of the indicators.

Appendixes A–F) to determine whether the reform plan satisfied the criteria for that particular indicator. For example, under "encapsulated classroom and school," I wrote "the reform plan significantly addressed the problems inherent in the encapsulated classroom and school and included alternative learning situations." This statement reminded me to look for substitutes to the encapsulated classroom in the raw data.

Tables 2.3–2.6 follow, with summary rubics of change theory, teaching theory, the teaching profession, and school power and politics.

Table 2.3.   Summary Rubric for Change Theory

Indicator	Rating
Encapsulated classroom and school	
"Unquestioned bedrock assumptions" questioned	
Axiomatic change	
Intractability of schools	
Ongoing research and development	
Teachers as reform leaders	
Lang's five assumptions	
Past reforms' research	

Table 2.4.   Summary Rubric for Teaching Theory

Indicator	Rating
Productive learning	
"Pouring in knowledge" theory	
Students as "raw materials"	
Personalized learning	
Parental inclusion	
Student motivation	
Lower-class students	
Low IQ and self-fulfilling prophecy	

Table 2.5.   Summary Rubric for the Teaching Profession

Indicator	Rating
Teacher development	
Unlearning process	
Teacher education programs	
Pedagogy	
Productive teaching defined	

Table 2.6. Summary Rubric for School Power and Politics

Indicator	Rating
Government involvement	
Middle-class ethic	
School bureaucracy	
Research and development	
Silent axioms and educational policymakers	

CHANGE THEORY

"I predicted that as it was being conceived and implemented educational reform would go nowhere" (Sarason, 2002, p. 178). Change theory represents the first element that I created based on Sarason's work. Eight indicators of observable characteristics are listed under this element that I found from Sarason (1990, 1993, 2002, 2004) as being necessary for a reform plan to achieve change in schools and school systems.

Encapsulated Classroom and School

The encapsulated classroom and school indicator means that learning does not necessarily best take place with a student sitting in a desk in rows with many other students as one teacher provides whole-class instruction with a prearranged and fragmented curriculum. "The axiom was that education (schooling) best takes place in encapsulated classrooms in encapsulated schools" (Sarason, 1990, p. 111). The reform plan significantly addressed the problems inherent in the encapsulated classroom and school and included alternative learning situations.

"Unquestioned Bedrock Assumptions" Questioned

The "unquestioned bedrock assumptions" questioned indicator requires that basic school structures that had been in place for over 100 years had to be questioned, critiqued, and, in most instances, radically changed. Theory and analytic and evaluative data were vital elements that must have been in place when considering a reform proposal (Sarason, 2004). "Unreflective acceptance of assumptions and axioms that seem obviously right . . . faced with failure after failure. . . . You don't examine your bedrock assumptions" (Sarason, 1990, p. 148). The reform plan challenged fundamental beliefs about schooling, for example, the notion that all students needed math, and reshaped schooling based on researched theory.

Axiomatic Change

The axiomatic change indicator calls for a change in the teaching and learning process, not just everything else around it. In the modal class-room, "the average number of questions asked by students is two. . . . Teachers' rate of question asking varies from about 40 to 150" (Sarason, 1990, p. 87). The reform plan confronted accepted norms and proposed significant out-of-the-box changes in school, such as converting "teacher as all-knowing" and "student as passive recipient" into a more collabora-tive and inquiring teacher–student relationship.

Intractability of School

The intractability of schools indicator states that just because a reform sounds altruistic does not mean that it is a good idea. "Schools have been intractable to change and the attainment of goals set by reformers. A ma-jor failure has been the inability of reformers to confront this intractabil-ity" (Sarason, 1990, p, xiii). School reform needed to provide for the de-velopment of teachers as well as students and make school significant and less boring for students. The reform plan addressed the intractability of schools by going beyond good intentions into research-based reform. The reforms understood that teachers did not go along with the plan just be-cause it appeared to be a good idea.

Ongoing Research and Development

The ongoing research and development indicator demands diagnostic re-search and development as necessary for reform plan development. "Busi-ness executives would never . . . undertake a major reform that they did not sedulously monitor, evaluate, and report. Publicity is not evaluation" (Sarason, 1990, p. 129). Research and development was a significant part of the reform plan and was included with the funding source to provide ongoing measurement of the reform.

Teachers as Reform Leaders

The teachers as reform leaders indicator asserts that if teachers do not lead the reform plan, then the plan will not succeed. Reform plans were developed and implemented without much consultation with teachers. It was assumed that teachers would go along with the reform because the ideologies of the plan were said to be in the best interests of educating students (Sarason, 1990, 2004). A reform plan needed to provide for inclusion of teachers in the decision-making process from the beginning: "The omission of this step comes close to being universal in school systems. That omission in part explains why reform efforts fail as they do, why teachers regard administrators as people who have forgotten what it is like to be teachers" (Sarason, 2004, p. 166). The reform plan, from the beginning, was led by teachers.

Lang's Five Assumptions

Eugene Lang, a businessman, created the "I Have a Dream" Foundation in 1981 to pay for college for elementary school students at PS 121 elementary school in New York City. "Lang formed a foundation for the purpose of stimulating other affluent people to adopt a school and to provide assistance" (Sarason, 1990, p. 126).

Sarason listed five assumptions that he believed Lang made in creating the foundation. The following is an application of the five assumptions of change to the select reform plan (Sarason, 1990, p. 125):

Outside agent: "Change will not or cannot come about from within."

Parents and community: "The change must involve parents and community resources"

Motivate students and families: "Sustaining motivation in students and families' demands that one enter their lives in whatever ways are necessary in and out of school."

Power relationships altered: "The outside force for change inevitably alters existing attitudes and power relationships."

Less discontinuity between school and nonschool: "Students experience less discontinuity (personal, educational, and social) between the school and nonschool worlds."

The reform plan contained all of the essential aspects of the five assumptions.

Past Reforms Researched

The past reforms researched indicator requires that careful attention be paid to the history of school reforms—successes and failures:

> Each new wave of reform learns nothing from earlier efforts and comes up with recommendations that have failed in the past. What is called reform is based on an acceptance of the system as it has been and is. Change will not occur unless there is an alteration of power relationships among those in the system and within the classroom. (Sarason, 1990, p. xiv)

Reform efforts continually lacked regard for any significant research and evaluation of past reforms to use as guides to help prevent future failure. "You apply the conclusions, you deliver the knowledge, you perform the operation as if the object of it is a passive, anesthetized patient" (Sarason, 1990, p. 129). The reform plan researched past reforms to use as a guide in the development of its ideas.

TEACHING THEORY

"But if we did not have to teach the curriculum, *what would we do with them?*" (Sarason, 1993, p. 42). Teaching theory is the second element that I crafted, and it has eight indicators that a reform plan must incorporate to significantly revolutionize teaching and learning in schooling.

Productive Learning

The productive learning indicator requires a clear definition of productive learning versus examples of unproductive learning by the reform. Sarason emphasized productive learning as an imperative to effective classroom contexts. A productive learning context was cognitive, affective, emotional, motivational, and attitudinal (Sarason, 2004).

Sarason (2004) indicates that a sense of openness and mutual respect from teacher to learner increased student performance: "In a context of productive learning, respect is a way of openly acknowledging that the learner needs and wants explanation of your behavior, words, and directions" (p. 58). Definitions of productive learning and unproductive learning needed to be defined by a reform plan. The reform plan provided a definition for the concept of productive learning that included whole-child development theory. The definition was at once cognitive, affective, emotional, motivational, and attitudinal.

"Pouring in Knowledge" Learning Theory

The "pouring in knowledge" learning theory indicator means that the 19th-century learning theory that students are like empty water vessels waiting to be filled up must be scrapped. "'Pouring in' knowledge into the minds of children is to extinguish curiosity and interest" (Sarason, 1993, p. 101). The reform plan found the "pouring in" concept of learning to be unacceptable and subscribed to cognitively significant theory, for example, Vygotsky's social–cognitive interactive theory of learning.

Students as "Raw Materials"

The students as "raw materials" indicator highlights the industrial revolution concept that students are the raw materials in an assembly-line process and that the finished products would be educated children. The factory model approach to schooling characterized students as "raw material: something to be molded and shaped in as cheap and efficient way as possible" (Sarason, 1993, p. 62). The reform plan utilized a philosophical humanist approach to teaching children that included whole-child development at its core and did not rely on rat theory or the business model to educate humans.

Personalized Learning

The personalized learning indicator stresses student-centered instruction beginning with students' interests, skills, and abilities. Sarason (2004) identifies learning as "social-personal-transactional in nature, that takes place in an observable context which has purposes which may give it an observable formal or informal structure or a nonobservable, covert structure" (p. 42).

Student-centered learning permits bidirectional transactions and a "multi-sensory process" (p. 48) that included teachers' learning from students and students' learning from teachers. Sarason believed that knowledge was acquired by action, not passive receptivity, and asked, "Who is learning what and from whom, and what is the conception of learning undergirding what one has observed?" (p. 45). The reform plan emphasized teaching students versus teaching content. It operated on the premise that teachers began learning from the position of each student.

Parental Inclusion

The parental inclusion indicator emphasizes teachers' seeking advisement from parents on how to motivate, discipline, and teach their progeny. Sarason (2004) states that a parent has much more invested in his or her children than a teacher who only worked with select children for 10 months. A parent offered information and advice to teachers regarding his or her child, and this began to help answer the question of "how do we make school learning relevant to students' life experience outside of school?" (p. 62). Sarason further suggested that teachers meet with the parents of all his or her students before the first day of school. The reform plan required a commitment from teachers to work collaboratively with parents in the education process.

Student Motivation

The student motivation indicator requires movement away from rat theory—an unsuitable theory for the study of humans. The theory of learning was important, and Sarason called for student-focused constructivist ideas: "Piaget and Schaefer-Simmern engagement was a constructive process: action on and in turn being acted on, an ongoing transformation between 'in there' and 'out there,' a willing pursuit powered by curiosity, interest, and the desire to master" (p. 120).

The reform plan included constructivist teaching theory to reach and motivate students and moved away from the behaviorist ideology. "But motivation in humans is far more complex than in rats, and a maze is a far more simple context for rats than the classroom context is for students" (Sarason, 2002, p. 240).

Lower-Class Students

The lower-class students indicator calls attention to the fact that middle-class norms are in conflict with lower-class students. This anomaly must be resolved. The classroom needed to be safe and fair, and students needed to feel safe to notify the teacher when unfair treatment was perceived (Sarason, 2004). Sarason says of the typical student, "When he falls short of expectations (occasionally or frequently) he hopes the teacher will help him and do and say nothing that will humiliate him in the eyes of other students" (p. 82).

Sarason (1993) believes that schools unfortunately deal with problems reactively, instead of developing proactive, preventative policies. Low socioeconomic status students could have developed mental health issues as a result of the poverty, crime, and additional social problems in their communities. The reform plan included significant changes to the structure of school to provide additional assistance to low socioeconomic status students.

Low IQ and Self-Fulfilling Prophecy

The low IQ and self-fulfilling prophecy indicator illuminates the fact that the factory model approach to teaching and learning cannot deal with raw materials who do not mold easily into a finished product. "You start by assuming a group is incapable, you take actions consistent with that assumption, and then you congratulate yourself for demonstrating that indeed they are incapable" (Sarason, 2002, p. 246). The reform plan included a philosophical ideal and specific plans to ensure that all students received learning that stretched them cognitively and expected them to significantly develop.

THE TEACHING PROFESSION

"Teaching is not a science; it is an art fusing ideas, obligations, the personal and interpersonal. The chemistry of that fusion determines whether or how subject matter matters to the student" (Sarason, 2004, p. 199). The rubric's third element organizes Sarason's ideas regarding schools' and school systems' addressing and improving teaching conditions and advancing the teaching profession.

Teacher Development

The teacher development indicator stresses a change in teacher education based on the fact that once a teacher is hired, he or she is not fully trained in teaching and learning and needs additional support and training. Sarason believed that politicians and administrators assumed that they knew what went on in classrooms, but they were mistaken. "Teachers cannot create and sustain contexts of productive learning for students if those conditions do not exist for the teachers" (p. 131). How a reform plan changed the work of teachers was important. The reform plan included significant opportunities for teacher development, for example, 1-year paid sabbaticals (Sarason, 2004), to foster growth in teaching professionals.

The Unlearning Process

The unlearning process indicator requires a method to change minds or at least understand and neutralize differences that teachers may have. Educators had ideas on how schooling was conducted. New theories disproved old theories of learning and teaching, and reform plans created conditions to change ideas. A process of unlearning was vital to assist in necessary paradigm shifts. "Unlearning old attitudes, acquiring new ones, accepting new responsibilities, trying the new and risking failure, unrealistic time perspectives and expectations, limited resources, struggles as a consequence of altered power relationships" (Sarason, 1990, p. 146). The reform plan provided teachers with an unlearning of past ideas that ran counterproductive to the larger aims of the reform.

Teacher Education Programs

The teacher education programs indicator calls for collaboration with schools of education for future hires and staff development for experienced teachers. A method of choosing people to teach who created conditions to allow students to "learn, grow, flourish" was important (p. 198).

The reform plan developed partnerships with schools of education and universities to cultivate future teachers.

Pedagogy

The pedagogy indicator identified the need for taking into account the daily life of teachers. Sarason observes, "We have relatively few studies on what teaching in our schools does to teachers and other personnel" (Sarason, 1990, p. 143). The reform plan included models of effective teaching, and the daily work schedule of teachers was considered.

Productive Teaching Defined

The productive teaching defined indicator involves the development of a definition of good teaching:

> We believe . . . that schools must achieve several goals: (a) to mine, exploit, sustain the motivation to learn; (b) to learn those skills and that knowledge that make the world, past and present, meaningfully comprehensible; (c) to instill the sense of personal competence and social responsibility. (Sarason, 2002, p. 242)

The reform plan contained the goals of student motivation, skill development, and lifelong learning.

SCHOOL POWER AND POLITICS

> The icing on the cake of vexation was provided by my meetings with policymakers and politicians in Washington and elsewhere. I realized that, however sincere their intentions, they knew nothing about schools and why the school culture, honed over many decades, would resist and defeat reforms attempting to alter the status quo. There are no villains. There is a system. You can see and touch villains, you cannot see a system. (Sarason, 1998, p. 141)

The fourth element focuses on macro-educational issues, namely, power issues related to government and the school bureaucracy.

Government Involvement

The government involvement indicator highlights the fact that the government controls education and a reform plan must gain governmental support. "One can change curricula, standards, and a lot of other things by legislation or fiat, but if the regularities of the classroom remain unexamined and unchanged, the failure of the reforms is guaranteed" (Sarason, 1990, p. 88). "In the past half century the federal government . . . has mightily sought to change schools . . . to desegregate them, to 'mainstream' handicapped children, to give poor children a 'head start'" (Sarason, 1993, p. 82). The overarching goals were to change the classroom and spend the money to make the proposals effective. The reform plan garnered local, state, and/or federal government support and financial assistance.

The Middle-Class Ethic

The middle-class ethic indicator asks a question: What should education for lower-class students include? Many students from impoverished backgrounds frustrated teachers because their pace of learning was considered slow (Sarason, 1993). School was where you learned what the teacher said you should learn, and this was different from the cultures of the communities from which lower-class students came. The public school system was set up to Americanize or socialize the poor and the immigrants, and "socialization is the process whereby you become what others want you to become" (Sarason, 1993, p. 29). Issues of tracking and differentiated instruction were included to deal with ingrained ideas and other socioeconomic issues associated with schools.

School Bureaucracy

The school bureaucracy indicator says that the bureaucratic school structure inhibits collaboration and stifles any student or teacher power. Any fundamental reform must have included a restructuring of the entrenched school bureaucracy (Sarason, 2004). The reform plan replaced the top-down structure of school bureaucracy with a horizontal structure that put teachers and parents in important decision-making power roles.

Research and Development

The research and development indicator requires the reform plan to conduct meticulous evaluation and adjustments as necessary. Sarason pointed out that the Food and Drug Administration conducted extensive research to protect the food and drugs that people used. Can one have imagined the FDA never conducting ongoing research (Sarason, 1990)? "Educational reform rarely derives from whatever we mean by theory but rather from opinion, anecdote, an uncritical acceptance of research, or a desperation" (p. 123). The reform plan included government-sponsored or government-funded research and development that enabled tinkering of the reform plan to increase its effectiveness.

Silent Axioms and Educational Policymakers

The silent axioms and educational policymakers indicator states that government and business leaders (the educational policymakers) have ingrained notions of education and that the reform plan must effectively account for this reality. "I have met too many in public officialdom and foundations who do not know how much they do not know . . . they do control the purse strings . . . the educational reformer and researcher cannot run the risk of alienating them" (Sarason, 2002, p. 233). The reform plan recognized threats from educational policymakers and incorporated their mandates without compromising the philosophical underpinnings of the reform.

PLAN SELECTION

I selected school reform plans that were relevant and contained the necessary criteria for comparison to the SDP. I developed criteria for the selection of reform plans and narrowed the choices based on the following: a perceived match to the SDP, richness of the archival data, and historical spread throughout the 200-plus-year existence of the United States.

Each selected reform plan had a theoretical basis to change the status quo of education and operate schools differently. The selected plans came into being at various historical times, and all of the selected plans garnered favorable opinion in their eras. I found that although many novelties existed in modern times—the Internet, cell phones, nuclear proliferation—the concept of raising youth and developing the human mind remained constant.

All of the selected reform plans intended to help better educate the masses. The Lancastrian plan, a transplant from England, was introduced in the United States in 1806 when a Briton, Joseph Lancaster, emigrated to extol the virtues of his plan. The age-graded plan arrived in the United States from Prussia in 1848 at the urging of Horace Mann and top business minds of the emerging industrial revolution.

At the turn of the century, the Gary plan emerged, a creation of Gary, Indiana, school superintendent William A. Wirt, a progressive educator schooled under John Dewey, who dealt with a bourgeoning urban population. The Trump plan was a *Sputnik*-era creation of long-time educator Dr. J. Lloyd Trump that began in 1959 as an answer to the call for increased significance in secondary education. Trump's drive aimed to counter the Soviet Cold War threat by providing a more cognitively significant educational system. The CES plan was the creation of Dr. Theodore Sizer, a result of his quest to rescue students and teachers from what he believed was the warehousing of students in factory model schools that destroyed natural curiosities and stifled critical thinking (Sizer, 1984).

GOALS AND PROCEDURES

The major goal of the research was to find out if Sarason's "failure of school reform" descriptors might predict the success or failure of the SDP. The study proceeded from a history on school reform to the history of school desegregation because the desegregation era served as the sociopolitical and legal context that gave birth to the SDP. I worked to understand the philosophical foundations of the SDP and what Dr. Comer intended to accomplish by creating the SDP. Next, I investigated the histories and philosophical foundations of the selected reform plans. Following the writing of these historiographies, I completed the rubric for each reform plan and analyzed the data.

I proceeded as follows:

1. I studied school reform to find out its history for the past two centuries.
2. I explored the archival data, beginning with the Lancastrian plan, and I wrote a brief historiography for each, including it in the review of the literature.
3. I assessed each reform plan by completing the "failure of school reform" rubric. Analysis included whether the reform plan scored at *effective* or above on the four elements (change theory, teaching theory, the teaching profession, school power and politics). A summary of each plan was included.
4. I compiled a summary of findings (see chapter 3).
5. I answered the following research questions: Did school reform follow a predictable pattern or cycle? Did school reform plans throughout history contain similar factors, patterns, trends, and cycles? Were the most important features of a reform identified and isolated? Was Sarason's "failure of school reform" description confirmed in this study? What significant features must future reform plans contain to make lasting change viable?

The study was conducted to find out if Sarason's descriptors on the "failure of school reform" predicted whether the SDP succeeded as a school reform plan. I developed a rubric of 26 indicators organized in four elements based on Sarason's works and used them to assess five school reform plans. Chapter 3 follows with a completed rubric for the five plans, as well as a completed rubric for the SDP. The last section of the chapter provides a comparative analysis of the results of each plans' rubrics.

3

Autopsy Data From Past Reforms

Many of the difficulties of teachers and principals arise out of the ways in which the pupil population in the United States has changed during this century. . . . The changing demographics, more than philosophical arguments, will force us into a search for school practices designed to accommodate these individual differences without loss of educational quality in schools. More than ever before, the search must be for ways to assure both quality and equity.

—John I. Goodlad & R. H. Anderson (1987, p. xliv)

School reform plans in the late 20th century aimed to improve the process of schooling. The SDP, created by Dr. James Comer, was one such reform plan. I assessed the SDP to determine its efficacy as a school reform plan. I selected five additional reform plans for comparative measurement in predicting the success or failure of the SDP.

I began this study with the belief that the SDP must have constituted the critical features necessary to be considered a successful school reform plan. The narrative in this chapter summarizes the key ingredients that I discovered to have made up the foundational elements of the SDP. I created a rubric based on Sarason's work to provide the comparative analysis of the SDP.

The "failure of school reform" rubric provided a method for gathering qualitative data and the means for comparative analysis of the reform plans. I plugged in the raw data from each reform plan, beginning with the

Lancastrian plan. The other reform plans followed: the age-grade plan, the Gary plan, the Trump plan, the CES plan, and the SDP plan.

The analysis of the data was listed beginning with the Lancastrian plan. I provided analysis of each reform plan, organizing the data by plugging in the data (see Appendixes A–F) to the rubric. I evaluated the data and wrote comparative summaries in this chapter based on the results. The data provided comparative evaluation that enabled me to draw conclusions (see chapter 4).

I studied the body of school reform literature to develop an understanding of the historical legacy of school reform. In this fashion, I determined what had worked and what had not worked, and I identified current research that was deemed effective in school reform.

An investigation of the key ideas of the SDP helped me to identify the foundational features that presumably made the SDP a viable school reform plan. I discovered seven key ideas that strove to guarantee equitable educational opportunities for all students. By identifying this information and including it with the data plugged into the rubric, I intended to prove the worth of the SDP.

The results of the reform plans were analyzed, and each element was given a rating based on the findings from the indicators. For example, the SDP received a *very effective / effective* rating for the teaching theory element. It received this favorable rating because it garnered high scores for each of the variables. The pouring-in knowledge variable received a *medium* rating because the SDP did not significantly address it, instead leaving decision making to individual teachers who were considered the experts. Summary results follow, beginning with a summary of the Lancastrian plan. Each element received an overall rating based on the scores of the variables. A qualitative description of the findings for each variable was included.

NARRATIVE OF THE SDP

The narrative was constructed to provide the foundational components that presumably led to the success of the SDP. The Comer SDP was a product of Dr. Comer's mission to equalize educational opportunities for all children, particularly, the socioeconomically disadvantaged.

The SDP began in the context of increased pressure by the federal government on states and school districts to desegregate all public schools to increase the equality of educational opportunity. I identified seven key features of the SDP: site-based decision making; a mental health team; a plan for parent involvement; consensus in all major decisions; a no-fault ideology practiced by adults; equitable education programs; and schooling based on child development and learning theories of Lewin, Vygotsky, and Dewey. Summary results of each key ingredient follow.

Site-Based Decision Making

Comer developed a site-based management program with the idea that the people most directly affected by decisions should determine what should be done (Comer, 1996). In the public school setting, these stakeholders included parents, teachers, administrators, and other adults in the community. All needed to work together to help in the positive development of children. Comer (1993a) believes in a collaborative relationship between school personnel and parents:

> If parents become involved in school policy and practice, school personnel are sharing power. Most of us do not share power well under any circumstances. Often an unspoken fear is that if power is shared, power is or will eventually be lost. (p. 127)

Federal and state governments created and funded Community Action Programs, spawned from the grassroots civil rights movement. These popularized local control and gave nongovernment-sponsored groups and individuals decision-making power. The historical oppression of African Americans by the federal and state governments created ripe conditions for a grassroots movement calling for civil rights and equality for all, especially, groups that faced historic discrimination.

A Mental Health Team

Comer (1997) created the SDP to provide schooling based on whole-child development for all children—especially, traditionally underserved poor minority children—that could function as a primary prevention social service institution. The mental health team attempted to work "preventively and prescriptively" (Comer et al., 1996, p. 61) in addressing the concerns of individual students and the school community as a whole.

When a teacher discovered unusual behavior in a student, he or she was instructed to send the student to the mental health team for help. This committee documented the issue, which was often disruptive classroom behavior, suspected drug use, suicide talk, or other alarming discourses. The mental health team attempted to work with the student to deal with his or her problems. The team worked to prevent crises from occurring, as opposed to simply reacting to crises that had already developed (Comer et al., 1996).

A Plan for Parent Involvement

Comer theorized that children developed positively when school personnel and parents worked in a collaborative fashion to best promote the needs of the child (Comer et al., 1996). He viewed parent participation as a key ingredient in successfully reaching children, especially, the traditionally underserved poor and minority students:

> The need for parental participation is greatest in low-income and minority communities or wherever parents feel a sense of exclusion, low self-esteem and/or hopelessness. . . . Parents have a knowledge of their children and a relationship on which school personnel can build. . . . The presence of parents could improve accountability and help tie school programs to community needs. . . . If parents themselves are involved in a school program, they will develop a greater interest in program outcomes and will be supportive of budgetary and other school-related economic and political considerations. (p. 126)

The parent team attempted to involve parents in the school to create a stronger link between the home and school (Comer, 1996):

> Many teachers and administrators, regardless of racial or ethnic origin, attribute school problems to a willful failure of youngsters to work hard enough and behave well. . . . Many see the parents as the problem and not part of the solution. (p. 127)

The parent team empowered parents through participation in schoolwide decision making (Comer et al., 1996).

Consensus in all Major Decisions

Comer's plan began in two urban elementary schools in New Haven, Connecticut, at the height of the civil rights era, during the drive for urban renewal. Comer borrowed from the Great Society Community Action Program to involve stakeholders in the decision making process.

The goal of the Community Action Program was "to encourage the 'maximum feasible participation' of the poor themselves in the decisions that affected them" (Boyer et al., 1990, p. 1057). With the decision-making team representative of the entire community, consensus had to be reached on decisions. If members simply voted for or against a plan, this led to a zero-sum game, with winners and losers. Losers would not go along or would attempt to sabotage something they voted against. Consensus meant that all concerned worked toward an agreed solution that was acceptable to everyone (Comer, 1996).

A No-Fault Ideology Practiced by Adults

The principle of no-fault worked to improve personal relationships by diminishing the act of blaming. When people did not feel that they were in a safe environment to express how they felt, they resorted to blaming to express their emotions. The no-fault principle began with the premise that a conflict had arisen from a misinterpretation or misunderstanding. The offensive acts or words were not intended to cause harm (Comer, 1996). Cuban (2001) explains:

> No-fault framing becomes an essential ingredient in stating problems that leave open a more generous range of alternatives to explore a solution. A fault-free definition becomes especially important for the ill-defined problems that most teachers and principals face in their daily work. (p. 9)

Comer described no-fault as an "emergency room" mentality, where time was not wasted on blaming someone for the fact that Johnny could not read. Instead, time was spent teaching Johnny to read (Comer et al., 1996).

Equitable Education Programs

The SDP began in the context of increased pressure by the federal government on states and school districts to desegregate all public schools to increase the equality of educational opportunity for minorities, particularly, African American students. States and school districts succeeded in holding back desegregation until the federal government took strict action in 1969.

Schooling Based on Child Development

Comer framed his program around the ideology of Kurt Lewin's field theory and the writings of other primary prevention psychologists. The SDP use of whole-child development theory as its foundation traced its roots back to early-20th-century progressive education and John Dewey.

Dr. Comer envisioned a school based on whole-child development theory, successfully serving as a primary prevention care system for students, with a healthy school climate conducive to teaching and learning that accomplished goals such as closing the achievement gap. Comer's plan also emphasized human relationship building and stressed the importance of the interaction between teacher and student in accordance with Vygotsky's social–cognitive interactive theory. Comer's reform was school-based and proposed to change the climate of a school that was more responsive to the needs of its underserved students.

SUMMARY OF THE LANCASTRIAN PLAN

Data analysis began with the Lancastrian plan. A score for each element was assigned with a brief explanation. This was followed by a brief narrative about each variable—an analysis of findings—and then a rating level. For example, the Lancastrian plan received a *sometimes effective / not effective* score for the change theory element because it scored *medium* and *low* on most of the indicators under this first element. The encapsulated classroom and school indicator rated low because the Lancastrian plan had a rigid organizational schooling process that seated students in long rows and provided no alternative learning situations.

Table 3.1. Lancastrian Plan

Elements and Indicators	Rating
Change Theory	*Sometimes Effective / Not Effective*
Encapsulated classroom and school	Low
"Unquestioned bedrock assumptions" questioned	High/medium
Axiomatic change	Medium/low
Intractability of schools	Medium/low
Ongoing research and development	Medium
Teachers as reform leaders	Low
Lang's five assumptions	Medium
Past reforms' research	Medium/low
Teaching Theory	*Not Effective*
Productive learning	Low
"Pouring in knowledge" theory	Low
Students as "raw materials"	Low
Personalized learning	Medium/low
Parental inclusion	Low
Student motivation	High/medium
Lower-class students	High/medium
Low IQ and self-fulfilling prophecy	High/medium
Teaching Profession	*Not Effective*
Teacher development	Low
Unlearning process	Low
Teacher education programs	Low
Pedagogy	Low
Productive teaching defined	Low
School power and politics	Sometimes effective
Government involvement	Medium
Middle-class ethic	Medium
School bureaucracy	Low
Research and development	Medium
Silent axioms and educational policymakers	Medium

Change Theory for Lancastrian Plan

Sometime effective / not effective: The reform plan scored *medium* to *low* on the majority of the indicators.

The encapsulated classroom and school. The Lancastrian plan provided no alternatives to the encapsulated classroom, and students sat in rows or stood in semicircles. They were commanded for long periods with military-style regimentation and asked to perform rote low-level cognitive assignments. Rating level: Low—the archival data provided evidence that the reform plan did not include this indicator as a component of the plan.

"Unquestioned bedrock assumptions" questioned. The first education plan that successfully educated the masses, especially, the poor students, by keeping costs low and employing one teacher for up to 1,000 students. Rating level: High/medium—the archival data provided evidence that the indicator was integrated by the reform plan.

Axiomatic change. The teacher had no direct contact with students other than daily lessons given to the selected student monitors. In many ways, however, learning was more personalized than in past schools as students moved to new groupings based on mastery of content. Rating level: Medium/low—the archival data provided little evidence that the reform plan included this indicator.

Intractability of schools. This plan was perhaps not as boring as previous systems, because the majority of students did not sit idle for extremely long periods. There was virtually no teacher development. Lancaster provided a scripted manual that teachers were ordered to follow verbatim. Teacher pay was low. Rating level: Medium/low—the archival data provided little evidence that the reform plan included this indicator.

Ongoing research and development. Lancaster reported statistics that proved the success of his plan; higher numbers of students spelled more words. An audit performed at the African Free School was favorable. The result was a large increase in the number of poor students who attended school. Rating level: Medium—the archival data provided some evidence of integrating the indicator by the reform plan.

Teachers as reform leaders. Teachers did not play a leadership role, and Lancaster provided scripted lessons for all teachers to follow, with instructions ordering them not to deviate from the plans. Rating level: Low—the archival data provided evidence that the reform plan did not include this indicator as a component of the plan.

Lang's five assumptions. Eugene Lang, creator of the "I Have a Dream" Foundation:

Outside agent: Joseph Lancaster brought the plan from England; it was an accepted plan to educate the masses.

Parents and community involvement: The Lancastrian plan provided a better education for the poor, but no significant parental inclusion existed.

Motivation: Lancaster and supporters believed that the schools and his system were necessary components in the upbringing of poor children.

Power relationships altered: Mass education tinkered with the established social order.

Discontinuity lessened: The discipline and military-style regimentation made the school experience unlike a child's daily life outside of the school.

Rating level: Medium—the archival data provided some evidence of integrating the indicator by the reform plan.

Past reforms' research. This was a favorable plan, as compared to some past methods of schooling, but it was acceptable primarily because it was cheap. In time, the inadequacies of student monitors as the day-to-day teachers resulted in its demise. Rating level: Medium/low—the archival data provided little evidence that the reform plan included the indicator.

Teaching Theory for Lancastrian Plan

Not effective: The reform plan consistently scored *low* on the majority of the indicators.

Productive learning. The Lancastrian plan did not include child-centered pedagogy. The plan developed around disciplined, military-style order, and control. Lancaster did not agree with sustained silent reading. Also, sand was used for students to learn to write, and students stood in semicircles around a page of a book posted on a wall. Therefore, one book was purchased rather than 1,000 as a cost-savings measure. Rating level: Low—the archival data provided evidence that the reform plan did not include this indicator as a component of the plan.

"Pouring in knowledge" theory. This involved parrot-like dictation, with lots of memorization and recitation involved. No evidence of cognitively significant learning was found. Rating level: Low—the archival data provided evidence that the reform plan did not include this indicator as a component of the plan.

Students as "raw materials." A rigid school organizational structure was put into place; however, student classification was based on individual achievement. Order and control with mechanistic efficiency was perceived as the proper functioning of the school. The prevailing ideology was to mold students with a militaristic efficiency model. Rating level: Low—the archival data provided evidence that the reform plan did not include this indicator as a component of the plan.

Personalized learning. No teacher–student interaction occurred. Student monitors conducted day-to-day teaching. Promotion to a higher classification was based on individual students' success. Therefore, a student moved at his or her own pace. Peer tutoring was utilized. Homogeneous groupings were positive. Rating level: Medium/low—the archival data provided some evidence that the reform plan included the indicator with the somewhat individualized pace of instruction.

Parental inclusion. The Lancastrian plan did not include parent–teacher collaboration. Poor parents were more or less viewed as the problem, and education was the answer to help the children. Rating level: Low—the archival data provided evidence that the reform plan did not include this indicator as a component of the plan.

Student motivation. Democratic principles were adopted for student discipline. No idle time existed in educational settings during this time (decrease student boredom). Rating level: High/medium—the archival data provided evidence that the reform plan included evidence that the indicator was integrated by the reform plan.

Lower-class students. The Lancastrian plan provided mass schooling for the poor for the first time in history. More poor students enrolled in school than before the Lancastrian plan. Communities went along with the plan because of its low costs. Rating level: High/medium—the archival data provided evidence that the reform plan included this indicator in the reform plan.

Self-fulfilling prophecy and low IQ. Students were moved from one classification (class) to another at an individual pace, once mastery was proven. Classification began with the monitorial plan. Lancaster believed he could positively, cognitively influence poor students. There was no plan in place for mentally deficient students. Rating level: High/medium—the archival data provided evidence that the indicator was integrated by the reform plan.

The Teaching Profession for Lancastrian Plan

Not effective: The reform plan consistently scored *low* on the majority of indicators.

Teacher development. Student monitors received instruction from the teacher in the morning before other students arrived. Rating level: Low—

the archival data provided evidence that the reform plan did not include this indicator as a component of the plan.

The unlearning process. The bulk of the teaching was in the hands of student monitors. No unlearning process was in place for them to assist in moral development. Manuals of instruction did not leave room for creativity. Rating level: Low—the archival data provided evidence that the reform plan did not include this indicator as a component of the plan.

Teacher education programs. Lancaster did not allow intrigued educators to observe him. Scripted lessons allowed illiterate teachers to operate schools. Six weeks of training was the extent of teacher development. Rating level: Low—the archival data provided evidence that the reform plan did not include this indicator as a component of the plan.

Pedagogy. Teachers were forbidden to deviate from the manual of instruction, and it was not the teachers' job to teach. Teaching was the student monitors' job. Effective teaching was equated with following the manual of instruction. Rating level: Low—the archival data provided evidence that the reform plan did not include this indicator as a component of the plan.

Productive teaching defined. Orderly and rigid delivery of knowledge was the definition of productive, efficient teaching. Rating level: Low—the archival data provided evidence that the reform plan did not include this indicator as a component of the plan.

School Power and Politics for Lancastrian Plan

Sometimes effective: The reform plan scored at least *medium* on the majority of the indicators.

Government involvement. Government involvement in education was virtually nonexistent because of the enormous costs associated with such an endeavor. The Lancastrian plan presented a way for local communities to support mass education without a dramatic tax increase. In 18th-century England, religious schooling was implemented for the poor only. Governor Clinton of New York and King George III supported the Lancastrian plan. U.S. representative Thaddeus Stevens also supported it in the United States. Rating level: Medium—the archival data provided some evidence of integrating the indicator by the reform plan.

Middle-class ethic. The ideology behind the Lancastrian plan was socialization of the poor (the Pestalozzian plan was for the middle-class private schools). It was thought that order and moral education were what the poor needed. The Lancastrian plan allowed this to happen. Rating level: Medium—the archival data provided some evidence of integrating the indicator by the reform plan.

School bureaucracy. Parents played no role in the educational system. One teacher controlled the school. He or she reported to local governmental officials. Rating level: Low—the archival data provided evidence that the reform plan did not include this indicator as a component of the plan.

Research and development. This plan seemed beneficial for poor children. Techniques were somewhat archaic, but the plan provided schools for the poor and was better than nothing. Most poor children had no schooling before the plan. Rating level: Medium—the archival data provided some evidence of integrating the indicator by the reform plan.

Silent axioms and educational policymakers. The Friends Society supported this plan. They did not support the monitorial plan development by Bell, Lancaster's rival. Rating level: Medium—the archival data provided some evidence of integrating the indicator by the reform plan.

SUMMARY OF THE AGE-GRADED PLAN

The age-graded plan received a *sometimes effective* rating on the change theory element because it scored a low on the encapsulated classroom indicator and on Lang's five assumptions indicator. Furthermore, the age-graded plan rated *not effective* on the teaching theory element because of low scores on the following indicators: pouring in knowledge theory, students as raw materials, and personalized learning.

Change Theory for Age-Graded Plan

Sometimes effective: The reform plan scored at least a medium on the majority of the indicators.

The encapsulated classroom and school. The age-graded plan formalized the encapsulated classroom and helped create a system of dull, repetitive seat work. Rating level: Low—the archival data provided evidence that the reform plan did not include this indicator as a component of the plan.

Table 3.2.　Age-Graded Plan

Elements and Indicators	Rating
Change Theory	*Sometimes Effective*
Encapsulated classroom and school	Low
"Unquestioned bedrock assumptions" questioned	Low
Axiomatic change	Medium
Intractability of schools	Medium
Ongoing research and development	High/medium
Teachers as reform leaders	Medium
Lang's five assumptions	Low
Past reforms' research	Medium
Teaching Theory	*Not Effective*
Productive learning	Medium
"Pouring in knowledge" theory	Low
Students as "raw materials"	Low
Personalized learning	Low
Parental inclusion	Not applicable
Student Motivation	*Medium/Low*
Lower class students	Low
Low IQ and self-fulfilling prophecy	Medium/low
Teaching Profession	*Not Effective*
Teacher development	Low
Unlearning process	Low
Teacher education programs	High/medium
Pedagogy	High/medium
Productive teaching defined	Medium/low
School Power and Politics	*Sometimes Effective / Not Effective*
Government involvement	High/medium
Middle-class ethic	Medium/low
School bureaucracy	Medium/low
Research and development	Medium/low
Silent axioms and educational policymakers	High/medium

"Unquestioned bedrock assumptions" questioned. A rigid classification of students based on birth year created a dichotomy between retention/promotion and mastery learning. Rating level: Low—the archival data provided evidence that the reform plan did not include this indicator as a component of the plan.

Axiomatic change. This plan changed teaching from the Lancastrian plan to an idea with some teacher–student relationships. A teacher was assigned to every classroom to educate the students. Rating level: Medium—the archival data provided some evidence of integrating the indicator by the reform plan.

Intractability of school. As mass schooling increased, a simple but structured classification of pupils kept things orderly. The teachers liked the specialization. Rating level: Medium—the archival data provided some evidence of integrating the indicator by the reform plan.

Ongoing research and development. Piaget's theories indicated that for cognitive development alone, age-segregation worked. Rating level: High/medium—the archival data provided evidence that the indicator was integrated by the reform plan.

Teachers as reform leaders. Teachers favored specialization and accelerated its development as educators gained power in operating the schools. Rating level: Medium—the archival data provided some evidence of integrating the indicator by the reform plan.

Lang's five assumptions. Eugene Lang, creator of the "I Have a Dream" foundation, five change assumptions:

Outside agent: Horace Mann, a lawyer by trade, introduced the Prussian age-classification scheme, and other government and business leaders supported it.

Parents and community involvement: From a human evolutionary perspective, the age-graded school configuration was not anything close to real life or how humans developed from children into adults.

Motivation: None evident.

Power relationships altered: Older children helped keep order and provided mentorship to younger children in an ungraded classroom. This was eliminated.

Discontinuity lessened: Discontinuity was greatly increased because the age-graded school was unlike real life.

Rating level: Low—the archival data provided evidence that the reform plan did not include this indicator as a component of the plan.

Past reforms' research. More efficient use of time seemed to be evident from research and anecdotes that Mann brought back from Prussia. Rating level: Medium—the archival data provided some evidence of integrating the indicator by the reform plan.

Teaching Theory for Age-Graded Plan

Not effective: The reform plan consistently scored *low* on the majority of the indicators.

Productive learning. In terms of developing intellect, Piaget's theory supported the age-graded classification scheme in terms of promoting harmony and community; however, it made no sense. Rating level: Medium—the archival data provided some evidence of integrating the indicator by the reform plan.

"Pouring in knowledge" theory. The theory of pouring in the knowledge, or specialized teachers' providing all the necessary information, was the predominant theory. Rating level: Low—the archival data provided evidence that the reform plan did not include this indicator as a component of the plan.

Students as "raw materials." Mann promoted the common school for mass learning; foraging societies did not learn this way, and so this system was created based on business model efficiency and the method of production of raw materials. Rating level: Low—the archival data provided evidence that the reform plan did not include this indicator as a component of the plan.

Personalized learning. Teaching content was emphasized over relationship building, and a rigid efficiency method of classifying same-age students and teaching preplanned content was emphasized over adapting to the individual needs of students. Rating level: Low—the archival data provided evidence that the reform plan did not include this indicator as a component of the plan.

Parental inclusion. No evidence existed that showed that parents were included in the decision-making process. Rating level: Not applicable.

Student motivation. Negative competition was increased, and student interests were not tapped. Rating level: Medium/low—the archival data provided little evidence that the reform plan included the indicator.

Lower-class students. System seemed to gear low socioeconomic status students toward failure: Mann wanted to help low socioeconomic status children and provided schooling for them that he believed was more efficient and productive, but the age-graded system disproportionately harmed low socioeconomic status students because they did not keep up with their same-age peers. Rating level: Low—the archival data provided evidence that the reform plan did not include this indicator as a component of the plan.

Self-fulfilling prophecy and low IQ. The spread of mental age was still significant in age-graded classrooms, and the efficiency model had trouble dealing with "retarded" students. Rating level: Medium/low—the archival data provided little evidence that the reform plan included the indicator.

The Teaching Profession for Age-Graded Plan

Not effective: The reform plan consistently scored *low* on the majority of the indicators.

Teacher development. Specialization of teaching was created to help expedite teacher development and training. Rating level: Low—the archival data provided evidence that the reform plan did not include this indicator as a component of the plan.

The unlearning process. No evidence found. Rating level: Low—the archival data provided evidence that the reform plan did not include this indicator as a component of the plan.

Teacher education programs. Normal school development at this time spread the age-graded philosophy. The McGuffey Reader and other textbooks were developed and guided the curriculum and classification systems. Rating level: High/medium—the archival data provided evidence that the indicator was integrated by the reform plan.

Pedagogy. Textbooks guided teachers as they "fit" students into classrooms and curricular decisions. Subjects were divided to improve the daily life of teachers. Rating level: High/medium—the archival data provided evidence that the indicator was integrated by the reform plan.

Productive teaching defined. Orderliness and cognitive accomplishment increased with age classification to the detriment of whole-child development and the individual needs of students. Rating level: Medium/low—the archival data provided little evidence that the reform plan included the indicator.

School Power and Politics for Age-Graded Plan

Sometimes effective / not effective: The reform plan scored *medium* to *low* on the majority of the indicators.

Government involvement. The age-graded plan helped increase governmental involvement as leaders were convinced of the cost effectiveness of this system and its pupil classification scheme. Rating level: High/medium—the archival data provided evidence that the indicator was integrated by the reform plan.

Middle-class ethic. Americanization of immigrants was largely the goal of Mann's school plan. Rating level: Medium/low—the archival data provided little evidence that the reform plan included the indicator.

School bureaucracy. Urban school ideology won over rural one-room schoolhouses. Rating level: Medium/low—the archival data provided little evidence that the reform plan included the indicator.

Research and development. Mann would not have supported the detrimental effects that age grading had on at-risk students, but the system became entrenched. Rating level: Medium/low—the archival data provided little evidence that the reform plan included the indicator.

Silent axioms and educational policymakers. The system maintained the status quo. This plan seemed to be a natural progression that began with the Lancastrian and urban classification of pupils. This plan fit well with the desires of educators. Rating level: High/medium—the archival data provided evidence that the indicator was integrated by the reform plan.

SUMMARY OF THE GARY PLAN

The Gary plan received a *sometimes effective* rating for the change theory element and the teaching theory element, but it also rated *not effective* for the teaching profession element. The Gary plan rated *low* on the unlearning process indicator and on the teacher education programs under the teaching profession element, and it only scored up to *medium/low* on the other three indicators under this element, thus acquiring its low rating.

Change Theory for Gary Plan

Sometimes effective: The reform plan scored at least a *medium* on the majority of the indicators.

The encapsulated classroom and school. The Gary plan changed the school by adding work and play, but the time in the encapsulated classrooms

Table 3.3.   Gary Plan

Elements and Indicators	Rating
Change Theory	*Sometimes Effective*
Encapsulated classroom and school	Medium
"Unquestioned bedrock assumptions" questioned	Medium
Axiomatic change	Medium
Intractability of schools	Medium/low
Ongoing research and development	Medium
Teachers as reform leaders	Low
Lang's five assumptions	Medium
Past reforms' research	Medium/low
Teaching Theory	*Sometimes Effective*
Productive learning	Medium
"Pouring in knowledge" theory	Medium/low
Students as "raw materials"	Low
Personalized learning	Medium
Parental inclusion	Medium/low
Student motivation	Medium/low
Lower class students	Medium
Low IQ and self-fulfilling prophecy	Medium/low
Teaching Profession	*Not Effective*
Teacher development	Medium/low
Unlearning process	Low
Teacher education programs	Low
Pedagogy	Medium/low
Productive teaching defined	Medium/low
School Power and Politics	*Sometimes Effective / Not Effective*
Government involvement	Medium
Middle-class ethic	Medium/low
School bureaucracy	Medium/low
Research and development	Medium/low
Silent axioms and educational policymakers	Low

remained dull, repetitive seat work. Rating level: Medium—the archival data provided some evidence of integrating the indicator by the reform plan.

"Unquestioned bedrock assumptions" questioned. The addition of music, play, work, and community use of facilities changed the focus of school, but the three *R*s remained unchanged, and literacy rates did not significantly improve. Rating level: Medium—the archival data provided some evidence of integrating the indicator by the reform plan.

Axiomatic change. Teachers were still all-knowing in the three-*R* classrooms, and students were not necessarily always passive recipients of knowledge, because of their kinesthetic learning aspects in the work and play of the school. Rating level: Medium—the archival data provided some evidence of integrating the indicator by the reform plan.

Intractability of schools. Teachers were still trained the same way at the university, and this ran contrary to what they were asked to do for children in Gary. After Wirt's death in 1938, the Gary schools reverted to a traditional school system. Rating level: Medium/low—the archival data provided little evidence that the reform plan included the indicator.

Ongoing research and development. Research was conducted by the Rockefeller Foundation, led by Abraham Flexner, and its conclusions were critical of the methods and results of the Gary plan. Wirt made changes based on the results of this study, such as changes to the work aspect of the schools. Rating level: Medium—the archival data provided some evidence of integrating the indicator by the reform plan.

Teachers as reform leaders. The Gary plan contained no significant decision-making power for teachers. In New York City, strong parent and teacher protests against the Gary plan helped lead to its demise. Rating level: Low—the archival data provided evidence that the reform plan did not include this indicator as a component of the plan.

Lang's five assumptions. Eugene Lang, creator of the "I Have a Dream" Foundation, five change assumptions:

Outside agent: Wirt relocated to Gary from a school superintendency in Bluffton, Indiana, prepared to take advantage of a brand-new school system.

Parents and community involvement: No significant parent or community decision-making power existed.

Motivation: Community involvement in the school existed but not in the teaching and learning aspects of the schools.

Power relationships altered: The hierarchical school power relationships remained in place in Gary.

Discontinuity lessened: The community use of facilities helped bridge gaps between the schools and the community. However, as Randolph Bourne (1970) reported, "many of the children and their parents had but the vaguest ideas of the Gary plan goals" (p. xlii).

Rating level: Medium—the archival data provided some evidence of integrating the indicator by the reform plan.

Past reforms' research. Wirt's reform was based in part on Dewey's theories. Wirt was a student of Dewey at the University of Chicago. The major premise of the platoon plan was that it saved money. Rating level: Medium/low—the archival data provided little evidence that the reform plan included the indicator.

Teaching Theory for Gary Plan

Sometimes effective: The reform plan scored at least *medium* on the majority of the indicators.

Productive learning. Gary schools operated on child-centered teaching philosophies, but the three-R classrooms were rigid and rote. Rating level: Medium—the archival data provided some evidence of integrating the indicator by the reform plan.

"Pouring in knowledge" theory. The Rockefeller study found that old-fashioned teaching methods were still in use in Gary. This meant teacher-centered instruction with a large emphasis on memorization. Rating level: Medium/low—the archival data provided little evidence that the reform plan included the indicator.

Students as "raw materials." Wirt and his school system gained credibility by promoting scientific management and business efficiency. With a business model, there was no way to categorize students other than as raw materials. Rating level: Low—the archival data provided evidence that the reform plan did not include this indicator as a component of the plan.

Personalized learning. Dewey's "school is life" philosophy adapted but did not seem to translate into significant differences in the three-R classrooms. Rating level: Medium—the archival data provided some evidence of integrating the indicator by the reform plan.

Parental inclusion. The school served as a social center and offered night classes for adults, but no authentic parent–teacher collaboration on the work of schooling existed. Rating level: Medium/low—the archival data provided little evidence that the reform plan included the indicator.

Student motivation. Democratic principles were adopted for student discipline. Rating level: Medium/low—the archival data provided little evidence that the reform plan included the indicator.

Lower-class students. Bourne reported that the work-and-play aspects of the Gary system helped reach students with "diverse interests and aptitudes." Rating level: Medium—the archival data provided some evidence of integrating the indicator by the reform plan.

Self-fulfilling prophecy and low IQ. The use of IQ and other intelligence tests were used to categorize students in school. Gary and other school systems adopted this method for tracking. Rating level: Medium/low—the archival data provided little evidence that the reform plan included the indicator.

The Teaching Profession for Gary Plan

Not effective: The reform plan consistently scored *low* on the majority of the indicators.

Teacher development. Departmentalization was the only method for improving the work of teachers. Teachers were no longer required to teach all subjects; they specialized, and this led to curricular fragmentation and a movement away from student-centered instruction. Rating level: Medium/low—the archival data provided little evidence that the reform plan included the indicator.

The unlearning process. No system was in place to assist teachers in making the necessary personal paradigm shifts to fulfill the teaching requirements of the Gary plan. Rating level: Low—the archival data provided evidence that the reform plan did not include this indicator as a component of the plan.

Teacher education programs. The Gary plan contained no collaborative teacher training program with any university schools of education. Rating level: Low—the archival data provided evidence that the reform plan did not include this indicator as a component of the plan.

Pedagogy. Three-*R* teachers still used old-fashioned methods. Teacher specialization seemed to diminish student-centered classrooms. The Gary plan offered ideas for teachers to use in their teaching but contained no systematic way of ensuring that they did. Rating level: Medium/low—the archival data provided little evidence that the reform plan included the indicator.

Productive teaching defined. The work-and-play aspects of the platoon plan were used to improve student motivation. Overall, teachers were left to develop their teaching styles in their own ways (Bourne, 1970, p. 222). Rating level: Medium/low—the archival data provided little evidence that the reform plan included the indicator.

School Power and Politics for Gary Plan

Sometimes effective / not effective: The reform plan scored *medium* to *low* on the majority of the indicators.

Government involvement. The Gary plan became successful because it claimed to be able to educate more students, at less cost, and with more pedagogical significance. The platoon system of rotating three groups of students throughout a school building was adopted by thousands of schools throughout the nation in the early 20th century as mass immigration from Europe reached its height. Rating level: Medium—the archival data provided some evidence of integrating the indicator by the reform plan.

Middle-class ethic. Americanization of immigrants was the standard operating procedure in the Gary schools. Also, Gary provided separate schools for its African American children. Rating level: Medium/low—the archival data provided little evidence that the reform plan included the indicator.

School bureaucracy. The bureaucracy of Gary was less hierarchical, with no large central office, but Wirt stood firmly at the top as the key decision maker. Teachers and parents were afforded little decision-making power. Rating level: Medium/low—the archival data provided little evidence that the reform plan included the indicator.

Research and development. Wirt presented a plan that seemed more significant for learning and cheaper at the same time. No research supported its claim of significance. Rating level: Medium/low—the archival data provided little evidence that the reform plan included the indicator.

Silent axioms and educational policymakers. The Gary plan was adopted by government leaders because of its cost-savings measures. Educational researchers questioned its effectiveness and were even critical of the work time because of the dangers and unproductiveness. They thought of play time as being too unstructured and study time as more of the same, rote, cognitively insignificant learning. Rating level: Low—the archival data provided evidence that the reform plan did not include this indicator as a component of the plan.

SUMMARY OF THE TRUMP PLAN

The Trump plan received a *sometimes effective* rating for the change theory element, the teaching theory element, and the teaching profession element and a *sometimes effective / not effective* rating for the school power and politics element. Although the Trump plan received high ratings on the unquestioned bedrock assumptions questioned indicator, the axiomatic change indicator, and the teachers-as-reform-leaders indicator, it rated *medium/low* on the intractability of schools indicator, Lang's five

Table 3.4.   Trump Plan

Elements and Indicators	Rating
Change Theory	*Sometimes Effective*
Encapsulated classroom and school	High/medium
"Unquestioned bedrock assumptions" questioned	High
Axiomatic change	High
Intractability of schools	Medium/low
Ongoing research and development	Medium
Teachers as reform leaders	High
Lang's five assumptions	Medium/low
Past reforms' research	Medium/low
Teaching Theory	*Sometimes Effective*
Productive learning	High
"Pouring in knowledge" theory	High
Students as "raw materials"	High
Personalized learning	High
Parental inclusion	Low
Student motivation	Medium
Lower class students	Low
Low IQ and self-fulfilling prophecy	Medium
Teaching Profession	*Sometimes Effective*
Teacher development	High/medium
Unlearning process	Medium/low
Teacher education programs	Low
Pedagogy	High
Productive teaching defined	High
School Power and Politics	*Sometimes Effective / Not Effective*
Government involvement	Medium
Middle-class ethic	Medium
School bureaucracy	Low
Research and development	Medium
Silent axioms and educational policymakers	Low

assumptions indicator, and the past reforms' researched indicator. This split result caused the average rating on the change theory element.

Change Theory for Trump Plan

Sometimes effective: The reform plan scored at least *medium* or higher on five of the eight indicators.

The encapsulated classroom and school. The Trump plan changed the duration and rigidity of the encapsulated classroom with large-group, medium-group, and small-group instruction, as well as independent study time. However, students still spent a great deal of time in reconfigured but still encapsulated classrooms. Rating level: High/medium—the archival data provided evidence that the indicator was integrated by the reform plan.

"Unquestioned bedrock assumptions" questioned. The implementation of individualized student and teacher schedules that varied weekly with opportunities for independent study, student collaboration, and student-centered pedagogy reshaped the curriculum and pedagogy because it challenged the fundamental structure of all classes being taught in encapsulated classrooms with the same duration, at the same time each day. Rating level: High—the archival data provided compelling evidence that this indicator was fully integrated by the reform plan.

Axiomatic change. The emphasis shifted to the student as worker and placed responsibility for learning in the hands of individual students. Seminars allowed students to lead in collaborative dialogue, whereas learning labs promoted individualized student and teacher interactions. Rating level: High—the archival data provided compelling evidence that this indicator was fully integrated by the reform plan.

Intractability of schools. In Decatur, Illinois, the reform allowed for all decision making to come from the school building level. In Norridge, Illinois, Ridgewood High School opened, implementing the Trump plan at the outset. In fact, the plan determined the physical construction of the building. At the same time, at Wayland High School in Massachusetts, a determined principal pushed for reform. Over time, new administrators and teachers who were never trained according to the Trump plan principles contributed to the plan's erosion and ultimate demise. Rating level: Medium/low—the archival data provided little evidence that the reform plan included the indicator.

Ongoing research and development. Data sets and experimentation of ideas were used to determine if specific practices were successful. Teachers reported that what sounded good in theory was often good enough for the implementation, regardless of what the educational research said. Rating level: Medium—the archival data provided some evidence of integrating the indicator by the reform plan.

Teachers as reform leaders. The Trump plan provided a significant leadership role for teachers. Rating level: High—the archival data provided compelling evidence that this indicator was fully integrated by the reform plan.

Lang's five assumptions. Eugene Lang, creator of the "I Have a Dream" Foundation, five change assumptions. Dr. J. Lloyd Trump created the Trump plan while serving as president of the National Association for Secondary School Principals. Under his plan, community members were called on to serve as specialist consultants or instructional assistants. Decision-making bodies included community members as participants. A more collaborative relationship between a school and its community was established. There was no significant motivation for students or their families. Rating level: Medium/low—the archival data provided little evidence that the reform plan included the indicator.

Past reforms research. No evidence could be found showing that Trump utilized any educational research in designing his reform plan. It appears that he relied largely on his own experience. Trump served as a principal in the Gary, Indiana, public schools early in his career. Rating level: Medium/low—the archival data provided little evidence that the reform plan included the indicator.

Teaching Theory for Trump Plan

Sometimes effective: The reform plan scored at least *medium* on the majority of the indicators.

Productive learning. The Trump plan advocated a student-centered and inquiry-based approach to student learning with use of learning laboratories, seminars, and various groupings for classroom presentations. Rating level: High—the archival data provided compelling evidence that this indicator was fully integrated by the reform plan.

"Pouring in knowledge" theory. The Trump plan learning theory moved away from the "muscle theory" of cognitive development and toward developmental theories more in line with constructivist teaching. Rating level: High—the archival data provided compelling evidence that this indicator was fully integrated by the reform plan.

Students as "raw materials." The development of learning laboratories, various types of student groupings, independent study, and seminars were all strategies used to move teaching and learning away from the assembly-line process into more cognitively significant learning situations. Rating level: High—the archival data provided compelling evidence that this indicator was fully integrated by the reform plan.

Personalized learning. The Trump plan personalized learning with student and teacher schedules that permitted time for individual conferencing, learning labs for individual-paced learning, large and small class sizes for lectures and seminars, and new technologies to assist in student cognitive development. Rating level: High—the archival data provided compelling evidence that this indicator was fully integrated by the reform plan.

Parental inclusion. The Trump plan provided no significant process for parent–teacher collaboration. Rating level: Low—the archival data provided evidence that the reform plan did not include this indicator as a component of the plan.

Student motivation. Students were permitted to develop their own learning with independent study time, leading to some degree of self-motivation. Rating level: Medium—the archival data provided some evidence of integrating the indicator by the reform plan.

Lower-class students. More guidance counselors were placed in schools to help keep students in school. There was no specific plan or structure in place to address the unique needs of low socioeconomic status students. Rating level: Low—the archival data provided evidence that the reform plan did not include this indicator as a component of the plan.

Self-fulfilling prophecy and low IQ. The use of seminars was a tool to engage and make all students active in their learning. Rating level: Medium—the archival data provided some evidence of integrating the indicator by the reform plan.

The Teaching Profession for Trump Plan

Sometimes effective: The reform plan scored at least a medium on the majority of the indicators.

Teacher development. More planning time and a collaborative work environment—in addition to a differentiated pay scale—contributed to positive development of teachers. Rating level: High/medium—the archival data provided evidence that the indicator was integrated by the reform plan.

The unlearning process. Team teaching created a collaborative learning situation for teachers that gave them space to consider personal learning and teaching theories. Rating level: Medium/low—the archival data provided little evidence that the reform plan included the indicator.

Teacher education programs. The Trump plan advocated collaboration with teacher education programs, but no significant plan was developed. Rating level: Low—the archival data provided evidence that the reform plan did not include this indicator as a component of the plan.

Pedagogy. Consideration was given to the daily workload of teachers. Thus, more time was allotted for teachers to plan and evaluate student work. Team teaching created a collaborative working environment, and the variety of class instruction groupings allowed for a decrease in teacher workloads. Rating level: High—the archival data provided compelling evidence that this indicator was fully integrated by the reform plan.

Productive teaching defined. The teacher played the role of facilitator instead of the more traditional teacher as conveyor of all knowledge. Rating level: High—the archival data provided compelling evidence that this indicator was fully integrated by the reform plan.

School Power and Politics for Trump Plan

Sometimes effective / not effective: The reform plan scored *medium* or *low* on the indicators.

Government involvement. The town of Wayland, Massachusetts, for example, built its high school's physical plant to accommodate the large-group, small-group, and individual learning scheduling of the Trump plan.

Rating level: Medium—the archival data provided some evidence of integrating the indicator by the reform plan.

Middle-class ethic. Independent study time was allotted, and smaller classes were designed for discussion, to permit more significant cognitive interaction with the content, as well as differentiated instruction. Rating level: Medium—the archival data provided some evidence of integrating the indicator by the reform plan.

School bureaucracy. Archival data suggested that as a new school leader replaced the last, the Trump plan waned. A typical school bureaucracy placed power in the hands of the principal. If the principal did not support the Trump plan or was not required to adhere to its principles, then it did not last. Rating level: Low—the archival data provided evidence that the reform plan did not include this indicator as a component of the plan.

Research and development. Programs and procedures were rated and changed. The Ford Foundation provided funding for assistants to staff the learning laboratory. When grant money was withdrawn, so too was the reform plan. Rating level: Medium—the archival data provided some evidence of integrating the indicator by the reform plan.

Silent axioms and educational policymakers. Not addressed. Rating level: Low—the archival data provided evidence that the reform plan did not include this indicator as a component of the plan.

SUMMARY OF THE CES PLAN

The CES plan received a *very effective* rating on the teaching theory element because it rated high on all of the indicators. Ratings of *medium/low* on the past reforms' researched indicator lowered the change theory element to a *sometimes effective*, and a *medium/low* on the government involvement indicator kept the school power and politics element at a *sometimes effective.*

Change Theory for CES Plan

Sometimes effective: The reform plan scored *medium* or *higher* on the majority of the indicators.

Table 3.5. Coalition of Essential Schools Plan

Elements and Indicators	Rating
Change Theory	*Sometimes Effective*
Encapsulated classroom and school	High/medium
"Unquestioned bedrock assumptions" questioned	High
Axiomatic change	High
Intractability of schools	High
Ongoing research and development	High
Teachers as reform leaders	High
Lang's five assumptions	Medium
Past reforms' research	Medium/low
Teaching Theory	*Very Effective*
Productive learning	High
"Pouring in knowledge" theory	High
Students as "raw materials"	High
Personalized learning	High
Parental inclusion	High
Student motivation	High
Lower class students	High
Low IQ and self-fulfilling prophecy	High
Teaching Profession	*Sometimes Effective*
Teacher development	High/medium
Unlearning process	Medium
Teacher education programs	Medium
Pedagogy	High
Productive teaching defined	Medium
School Power and Politics	*Sometimes Effective*
Government involvement	Medium/low
Middle-class ethic	High/medium
School bureaucracy	Medium
Research and development	Medium
Silent axioms and educational policymakers	High

The encapsulated classroom and school. The reform changed the encapsulated classroom by converting student interest and mastery of content into the goals themselves rather than the traditional "coverage of content" ideal. No plan was implemented to end the encapsulated classroom. It was left to each school to figure that out in its own way. Rating level: High/medium—the archival data provided evidence that the indicator was integrated by the reform plan.

"Unquestioned bedrock assumptions" questioned. CES questioned the 19th-century school structure and proposed a new way for teaching and

learning in schools. Rating level: High—the archival data provided compelling evidence that this indicator was fully integrated by the reform plan.

Axiomatic change. The student-as-worker method allowed students to perform exhibitions to prove mastery of learning. Teachers were not all-knowing, and students were no longer passive recipients. Rating level: High—the archival data provided compelling evidence that this indicator was fully integrated by the reform plan.

Intractability of schools. CES provided no preset model or method to follow. The core principles led school reform. Rating level: High—the archival data provided compelling evidence that this indicator was fully integrated by the reform plan.

Ongoing research and development. The 1979–1984 study of high schools by Sizer and colleagues culminated with the publishing of *Horace's Compromise* and the creation of CES. Rating level: High—the archival data provided compelling evidence that this indicator was fully integrated by the reform plan.

Teachers as reform leaders. CES posited that if teachers were not involved with the reform from the beginning, the plan would ultimately fail. Rating level: High—the archival data provided compelling evidence that this indicator was fully integrated by the reform plan.

Lang's five assumptions. Eugene Lang, creator of the "I Have a Dream" Foundation, five change assumptions:

Outside agent: Sizer and the CES National office provided structure, but the "no two schools are alike" belief led each school to develop the CES reform according to its unique needs.

Parents and community involvement: Principle 10 of the common principles held that inclusive democratic practices that honored diversity had to be included.

Motivation: The "all children can" philosophy of CES required significant and substantial connections with families.

Power relationships altered: Principle 4 placed time decisions and pedagogical decisions in the hands of administrators and teachers.

Discontinuity lessened: Principle 10 held that diversity must be honored and community inequities must be challenged.

Rating level: Medium—the archival data provided some evidence of integrating the indicator by the reform plan.

Past Reforms' Research

The roots of CES were planted when Sizer and other researchers concluded that high schools were failing because the curriculum emphasized coverage at the expense of in-depth thinking. Active learning was not important, and there was no structure to allow teachers to effectively collaborate. These problems had been singled out in past reform plans. There were no indications, however, that CES investigated prior reform plans to help change the decision-making process. Rating level: Medium/low—the archival data provided little evidence that the reform plan included the indicator.

Teaching Theory for CES Plan

Very effective: The reform plan provided a comprehensive inclusion of the indicators. The plan scored a high rating for each indicator.

Productive learning. The CES core belief was that teachers had to help students use their minds well, and exhibitions constituted the sound method for students to exhibit individual learning and mastery of content. Rating level: High—the archival data provided compelling evidence that this indicator was fully integrated by the reform plan.

"Pouring in knowledge" theory. The student-as-worker philosophy (Principle 5) meant that a diploma was earned from the exhibition of mastery rather than from an exam that tested content knowledge based on coverage of material. Rating level: High—the archival data provided compelling evidence that this indicator was fully integrated by the reform plan.

Students as "raw materials." The teacher was the deliverer of instructional services while students worked. Students were no longer clay to be molded. Rating level: High—the archival data provided compelling evidence that this indicator was fully integrated by the reform plan.

Personalized learning. Learning was tailored to meet the individual needs of each student, and staff members served many roles, including teacher–counselor–manager (Principle 8). The student as worker (Principle 5), personalization (Principle 4), and exhibitions (Principle 6) increased the level of personalization for students. Rating level: High—the archival data provided compelling evidence that this indicator was fully integrated by the reform plan.

Parental inclusion. Principle 7 posited that parents played a key role in the educational process and were included in decision making. Rating level: High—the archival data provided compelling evidence that this indicator was fully integrated by the reform plan.

Student motivation. The "less is more" adage from Principle 2, along with smaller classes for personalization and the "tone of the school . . . unanxious expectation" (Principle 7) appropriately considered human development and motivational theories. This constituted a departure from the traditional rat theory of motivation. Rating level: High—the archival data provided compelling evidence that this indicator was fully integrated by the reform plan.

Lower-class students. Principles 3, 7, and 10 stressed the need for inclusive educational practices that were adapted to the needs of individual students, with a trusting and fair environment for all students. Rating level: High—the archival data provided compelling evidence that this indicator was fully integrated by the reform plan.

Self-fulfilling prophecy and low IQ. A "one best curriculum" theory was discriminatory because the CES theorized that people do not all learn in the same manner. Principle 3 of the common principles prescribed tailor-made school practices to meet the needs of every group or class. Rating level: High—the archival data provided compelling evidence that this indicator was fully integrated by the reform plan.

The Teaching Profession for CES Plan

Sometimes effective: The reform plan scored at least *medium* on the majority of the indicators.

Teacher development. A reduced class load, coupled with collective planning time for teachers and competitive salaries (Principle 9), established the necessary conditions for productive teaching. Rating level: High/medium—the archival data provided evidence that the indicator was integrated by the reform plan.

The unlearning process. Faithful adherence to the common principles required teachers to unlearn past ideologies about teaching and learning and make the intellectual development of the students the priority via mastery proven through exhibitions, in-depth focus on smaller amounts of content, the student-as-worker philosophy, and a personal relationship between teachers and students. Rating level: Medium—the archival data provided some evidence of integrating the indicator by the reform plan.

Teacher education programs. University teacher education programs trained teachers as specialists instead of the more-needed generalists. Rating level: Medium—the archival data provided some evidence of integrating the indicator by the reform plan.

Pedagogy. CES included a plan to reduce class loads to 80 students per teacher (20 students for elementary school), include common planning time, and change teachers from specialists to generalists. Rating level: High—the archival data provided compelling evidence that this indicator was fully integrated by the reform plan.

Productive teaching defined. CES defined productive teachers as generalists who emphasized a more in-depth analysis of less content and coached students at their own pace. This ideology lacked a research-based foundation. Rating level: Medium—the archival data provided some evidence of integrating the indicator by the reform plan.

School Power and Politics for the CES Plan

Sometimes effective: The reform plan scored at least *medium* on the majority of the indicators.

Government involvement. The CES plan proposed a role for government as financier of education but recommended that the government not play a large role in directing educational policy. In an era of high-stakes accountability, the CES principles of "less is more" and exhibitions ran contrary to state and federal testing philosophies. Rating level: Medium/low—the archival data provided little evidence that the reform plan included the indicator.

Middle-class ethic. The "all children can learn" philosophy and ideals of multiculturalism were stressed to help schools grapple with equity issues. Rating level: High/medium—the archival data provided evidence that the indicator was integrated by the reform plan.

School bureaucracy. More power for the day-to-day decisions about pedagogy, supplies, staffing, and student and teacher needs were made at the school level. The CES reform did not include all stakeholders—including parents—in curriculum decision making. Rating level: Medium— the archival data provided some evidence of integrating the indicator by the reform plan.

Research and development. CES gained funding from the Annenberg Corporation and Gates Foundation to explore smaller school settings that could have improved high school education. Rating level: Medium—the archival data provided some evidence of integrating the indicator by the reform plan.

Silent axioms and educational policymakers. As the small school movement swept the nation, the CES reform did not have to compromise its core values. The 10 common principles were easily adapted to the goals of major funding sources, such as the Gates Foundation. Rating level: High—the archival data provided compelling evidence that this indicator was fully integrated by the reform plan.

SUMMARY OF THE SDP PLAN

The SDP was most successful with the teaching theory element with a *very effective/effective* rating. A *medium* rating on the pouring-in knowledge theory indicator prevented it from receiving a *very effective* rating. Also, this reform was least effective on the teaching profession element and the school power and politics element because it received a *sometimes effective* rating on these two elements.

Change Theory for SDP Plan

Effective: The reform plan included most of the indicators. The plan scored *high* on most of the indicators and nothing lower than *medium*.

The encapsulated classroom and school. The SDP plan changed the theory of the encapsulated classroom and created a partnership between teachers and parents. The physical setup of the encapsulated classroom remained unchanged, but the minds of teachers were modified to holistically focus, rather than narrowly and cognitively focus, on the needs of

Table 3.6. School Development Plan

Elements and Indicators	Rating
Change Theory	*Effective*
Encapsulated classroom and school	High/medium
"Unquestioned bedrock assumptions" questioned	High
Axiomatic change	Medium
Intractability of schools	High
Ongoing research and development	High
Teachers as reform leaders	High
Lang's five assumptions	High
Past reforms' research	High/medium
Teaching Theory	*Very Effective / Effective*
Productive learning	High
"Pouring in knowledge" theory	Medium
Students as "raw materials"	High
Personalized learning	High
Parental inclusion	High
Student motivation	High
Lower class students	High
Low IQ and self-fulfilling prophecy	High
Teaching Profession	*Sometimes Effective*
Teacher development	Medium
Unlearning process	High/medium
Teacher education programs	Medium
Pedagogy	Medium/low
Productive teaching defined	High/medium
School Power and Politics	*Sometimes Effective*
Government involvement	Medium/low
Middle-class ethic	High
School bureaucracy	High/medium
Research and development	High
Silent axioms and educational policymakers	Medium

students. Rating level: High/medium—the archival data provided evidence that the indicator was integrated by the reform plan.

"Unquestioned bedrock assumptions" questioned. The SDP rejected common assumptions about schooling and based all decision making on positive child development theory. Rating level: High—the archival data provided compelling evidence that this indicator was fully integrated by the reform plan.

Axiomatic change. The teacher–student relationship was the vital element of schooling, and the SDP focused the teachers' attention on the whole child. The social action model was part of the theoretical framework of the SDP. Comer termed a school a *social system*, and all social systems must address socioeconomic issues and the fact that different environments cause humans to behave differently (Reiff, 1966). Rating level: Medium—the archival data provided some evidence of integrating the indicator by the reform plan.

Intractability of schools. The SDP included stakeholder involvement in decision making and consensus voting for all major decisions. In researching organizational behavior, Comer determined that change could occur only from within and not from the outside. Rating level: High—the archival data provided compelling evidence that this indicator was fully integrated by the reform plan.

Ongoing research and development. The SDP staff worked to measure school climate from the perspective of all stakeholders, including parents, teachers, students, and others. Rating level: High—the archival data provided compelling evidence that this indicator was fully integrated by the reform plan.

Teachers as reform leaders. All stakeholders were included in decision making, and teachers were at the forefront of reform. Rating level: High—the archival data provided compelling evidence that this indicator was fully integrated by the reform plan.

Lang's five assumptions. Eugene Lang, creator of the "I Have a Dream" Foundation:

Outside agent: Comer developed a theoretically sound plan to address the mental health issues that had to be addressed for positive development.

Parents and community involvement: The parent team group promoted parent involvement as a key component of the plan.

Motivation: Not applicable.

Power relationships altered: Stakeholders were given decision-making power, and consensus voting was needed for all major decisions.

Discontinuity lessened: Significant collaboration was established between the home and school.

Rating level: High—the archival data provided compelling evidence that this indicator was fully integrated by the reform plan.

Past reforms' research. Comer relied on research of human social systems and child development theory to create the reform plan. Rating level: High/medium—the archival data provided evidence that the indicator was integrated by the reform plan.

Teaching Theory for SDP Plan

Very effective / effective: The reform plan scored a *high* rating on most of the indicators and nothing lower than *high/medium.*

Productive learning. The emphasis was on whole child development—the six developmental pathways—instead of cognitive development. A structured classroom promoted student creativity and total development. Rating level: High—the archival data provided compelling evidence that this indicator was fully integrated by the reform plan.

"Pouring in knowledge" theory. The SDP promoted a problem-centered approach to teaching but also left much of the teaching theory to teachers, whom the SDP considered as experts. Rating level: Medium—the archival data provided some evidence of integrating the indicator by the reform plan.

Students as "raw materials." The student and staff support team was an example of how the SDP worked to prevent and prescribe in addressing the individual needs of students. Rating level: High—the archival data provided compelling evidence that this indicator was fully integrated by the reform plan.

Personalized learning. The SDP charged educators with the task of understanding each child's background to create developmentally appropriate learning. Rating level: High—the archival data provided compelling evidence that this indicator was fully integrated by the reform plan.

Parental inclusion. The parent–teacher relationship was a cornerstone of the SDP plan. Rating level: High—the archival data provided compelling evidence that this indicator was fully integrated by the reform plan.

Student motivation. The SDP was based on Lewin's field theory—students felt good about themselves as they gained competence and a sense of self-determination. Rating level: High—the archival data provided compelling evidence that this indicator was fully integrated by the reform plan.

Lower-class students. The heart of the SDP lay in the quest to create a developmentally appropriate educational setting to help poor and minority students who were stuck in seemingly hopeless school situations. Rating level: High—the archival data provided compelling evidence that this indicator was fully integrated by the reform plan.

Self-fulfilling prophecy and low IQ. The SDP viewed teaching from an emergency-room perspective: Teach the child from the place where he or she is, instead of from a deficit perspective that deemed a child hopelessly behind his or her peers. Rating level: High—the archival data provided compelling evidence that this indicator was fully integrated by the reform plan.

The Teaching Profession for SDP Plan

Sometimes effective: The reform plan scored at least *medium* on the majority of the indicators.

Teacher development. The SDP provided training and advice for teachers when dealing with nonmainstream students and parents. However, no structural teacher development plan was implemented. Rating level: Medium—the archival data provided some evidence of integrating the indicator by the reform plan.

The unlearning process. The SDP challenged traditional theories of education and held that with time and training staff members would embrace theories that all children could learn and be successful. No specific process was put in place to facilitate paradigm shifts. Rating level: High/medium—the archival data provided evidence that the indicator was integrated by the reform plan.

Teacher education programs. The New Orleans public school system partnered with Southern University to further promote teacher development. The purpose of the partnership was to train teachers who were not adequately prepared for the realities of the classroom in traditional university teacher preparation programs. Rating level: Medium—the archival data provided some evidence of integrating the indicator by the reform plan.

Pedagogy. The SDP considered the daily realities of the classroom and proposed mental health assistance for maladjusted students. Day-to-day curriculum plans were not addressed. Rating level: Medium/low—the archival data provided little evidence that the reform plan included the indicator.

Productive teaching defined. The SDP focused on relationship building, mental health issues, and whole child development theory to create the conditions in the classroom that could motivate and develop all students. Rating level: High/medium—the archival data provided evidence that the indicator was integrated by the reform plan.

School Power and Politics for SDP Plan

Sometimes effective: The reform plan scored at least *medium* on the majority of indicators.

Government involvement. Prince George's County, for example, ended court-ordered busing with the promise of implementing a districtwide SDP program to ensure equity for all students. Over time, however, the district moved away from the SDP reform. Rating level: Medium/low—the archival data provided little evidence that the reform plan included the indicator.

Middle-class ethic. The SDP theoretical framework focused on assisting students who were not middle class and did not know or understand the middle-class norms of schooling. The blame game was not allowed, and school staff was charged with changing ideologies and helping all students to develop and succeed, especially, poor students who had the will but not the skills. Rating level: High—the archival data provided compelling evidence that this indicator was fully integrated by the reform plan.

School bureaucracy. The SDP recognized the entrenched school bureaucracy and attempted to modify it with the inclusion of consensus decision making from all stakeholders and the school planning and management team.

Rating level: High/medium—the archival data provided evidence that the indicator was integrated by the reform plan.

Research and development. The SDP was created using a solid research-based foundation by Comer. The plan was developmentally appropriate for all children, had a method for addressing the mental health needs for all, included stakeholders in decision making, and contained a change process from the inside out. Ongoing tinkering and the provision of literacy development ensured that the SDP continued as a viable reform plan. It received Rockefeller Foundation funding to help foster its growth. Rating level: High—the archival data provided compelling evidence that this indicator was fully integrated by the reform plan.

Silent axioms and educational policymakers. Comer challenged the status quo because he believed that middle-class Americans did not understand the complexity of the problem that poor and minority people faced in their daily lives. The SDP was developmentally appropriate for all. However, many believed that the plan was useful for only inner-city, high-poverty schools. Rating level: Medium—the archival data provided some evidence of integrating the indicator by the reform plan.

ANALYSIS OF THE RESULTS

Descriptive analysis of the results follows (Tables 3.7–3.9) as I compared the performance results of the reform plans for each indicator. For example, under change theory, none of the reform plans received a high rating for the past reforms variable, because none of the reform plans used the failures of past reforms to a high degree to guide in the development of the new plan.

Table 3.7.   Summary Rubric Results for Change Theory Element

	Lancastrian	Age-Graded	Gary	Trump	CES	SDP
Change theory	SE/NE	SE	SE	SE	SE	E
Encapsulated classroom	L	L	M	H/M	H/M	H/M
Unquestioned bedrock assumptions	H/M	L	M	H	H	H
Axiomatic change	M/L	M	M	H	H	M
Intractability of schools	M/L	M	M/L	M/L	H	H
Ongoing R&D	M	H/M	M	M	H	H
Teacher leaders	L	M	L	H	H	H
Lang's five assumptions	M	L	M	M/L	M	H
Past reforms	M/L	M	M/L	M/L	M/L	H/M

Note. CES = Coalition of Essential Schools; SDP = School Development Plan. VE = very effective, E = effective, SE = sometimes effective, NE = not effective, H = high, M = medium, L = low.

Table 3.8. Summary Rubric Results for Teaching Theory Element

	Lancastrian	Age-Graded	Gary	Trump	CES	SDP
Teaching theory	NE	NE	SE	SE	VE	VE/E
Productive learning	L	M	M	H	H	H
"Pouring in knowledge"	L	L	M/L	H	H	M
Students as "raw materials"	L	L	L	H	H	H
Personalized learning	M/L	L	M	H	H	H
Parental inclusion	L	N/A	M/L	L	H	H
Student motivation	H/M	M/L	M/L	M	H	H
Lower-class students	H/M	L	M	L	H	H
Low IQ and self-fulfilling prophecy	H/M	M/L	M/L	M	H	H

Note. CES = Coalition of Essential Schools; SDP = School Development Plan. VE = very effective, E = effective, SE = sometimes effective, NE = not effective, H = high, M = medium, L = low.

Change Theory

Encapsulated classroom. The encapsulated classroom still dominated teaching and learning in school, during all of the reforms discussed in this work, with the exception of two. The CES plan and the SDP changed the mind-set of teachers and students in the encapsulated classrooms. Students and teachers moved outside of the walls, in a creative sense. The Trump plan included more independent study time for students, whereas the Gary plan included work and play time. Both of these plans, however,

Table 3.9. Summary Rubric Results for the Teaching Profession Element and the School Power and Politics Element

	Lancastrian	Age-Graded	Gary	Trump	CES	SDP
Teaching profession	NE	NE	NE	SE	SE	SE
Teacher development	L	L	M/L	H/M	H/M	M
Unlearning process	L	L	L	M/L	M	H/M
Teacher education	L	H/M	L	L	M	M
Pedagogy	L	H/M	M/L	H	H	M/L
Productive teaching	L	M/L	M/L	H	M	H/M
School power and politics	SE	SE/NE	SE/NE	SE/NE	SE	SE
Government involvement	M	H/M	M	M	M/L	M/L
Middle-class ethic	M	M/L	M/L	M	H/M	H
School bureaucracy	L	M/L	M/L	L	M	H/M
R&D	M	M/L	M/L	M	M	H
Silent axioms	M	H/M	L	L	H	H

Note. CES = Coalition of Essential Schools; SDP = School Development Plan. VE = very effective, E = effective, SE = sometimes effective, NE = not effective, H = high, M = medium, L = low.

employed encapsulated classrooms with rote learning. The Lancastrian plan and age-graded plan believed in rigid and structured learning as good training and discipline development for students.

Unquestioned bedrock assumptions. Fundamental beliefs about the conduct of schooling were challenged. The Lancastrian plan was historic in that it was the first method in history that successfully provided a system for educating the masses. The Gary plan, Trump plan, SDP, and CES all challenged long-held beliefs about schooling and attempted to forge a new way. The Gary plan added work and play, but the rigidity of academic learning was not changed. The Trump plan added individual study time and time for student-to-student and teacher-to-teacher collaboration. The CES plan challenged the "course and credit" Committee of Ten system, and the SDP based all decision making on child development theory. The age-graded plan simply adopted the prevailing business theme of efficiency and believed that this was accomplished with a rigid student classification system.

Axiomatic change. In the Trump plan and the CES plan, axiomatic change occurred as students became workers. The SDP concentrated on developing good student–teacher relationships by improving the "home training" and mental health aspects of student development, but the cognitive dimensions of learning were still traditional. The Gary plan gave students a kinesthetic mode of learning, whereas the age-graded and Lancastrian plans offered little axiomatic change because teachers played the role of all-knowing dispensers of knowledge.

Intractability of schools. The SDP and CES plans both placed school change decision-making power into the hands of stakeholders, especially, teachers. The Lancastrian plan gave no power to teachers. Many teachers favored the age-graded plan because of its teacher specialization component. The Gary plan gave no decision-making power to teachers, whereas the Trump plan provided limited power. Both reforms evolved over time: Neither enjoyed sustained teacher support. Teacher training was traditional and at odds with the goals of both Gary and Trump plans.

Ongoing research and development. Based on Piaget's cognitive development theory, the age-graded system of classification was appropriate for student learning. The Lancastrian plan never evolved from a mass education warehouse to a cognitively significant educational operation. The Gary plan and Trump plan made some changes based on research, whereas the SDP launched an ambitious plan to measure school climate. The basis of the CES plan was Sizer's book *Horace's Compromise*, and the plan added a 10th common principle to promote democracy in schools.

Teacher leaders. The Trump, SDP, and CES plans included teachers at the forefront of reform. The other plans did not include teacher leadership in school reform.

Lang's five assumptions. The SDP was the only reform that successfully measured up to Lang's five assumptions regarding school reform. The Lancastrian plan radically improved educational opportunities for the poor, but discontinuity between home and school persisted. The age-graded plan was unlike human evolutionary experience. Human beings had never learned in such a rigid classification structure. It was not like the real world that students came from. The Gary plan provided no decision-making power for parents, and the disconnectedness between homes and schools persisted. The Trump plan provided no significant motivation for families and students, whereas the CES plan honored diversity and placed decision making at the school level. The SDP provided significant collaboration between home and school.

Past reforms. The Lancastrian plan used the English monitorial plan and expanded it to teach large numbers of poor students. The age-graded plan relied on the efficiency ideology that swept the world during the industrial revolution. The Gary plan was based on efficiency and whole-child development theory. Trump had been a school principal in Gary, Indiana public schools before the development of the Trump plan. Comer researched human social systems and child development theory before the creation of the SDP. The CES plan contained no significant research of past school reforms.

Teaching Theory

Productive learning. The Lancastrian plan defined an orderly and controlled climate as a good teaching and learning environment. The age-graded plan's classification system was found to have merit based on Piaget's cognitive development theory—it helped students in their cognitive development—but the rest of child development was neglected. The Gary plan was based on Dewey's child development theories, but classrooms were still rote and rigid. Trump's ideal was student centered and inquiry based, tapping the interests of students individually. The CES plan's core belief was exhibition of mastery, whereas the SDP utilized teaching and learning based on its developmental pathways.

"Pouring in knowledge" theory. The Lancastrian, age-graded, and Gary plans relied on rote teacher-centered instruction. The Trump plan addressed various learning theories and was more in accord with constructivist learning theories, as was the CES plan. The SDP left much of the teaching theory decision making in the hands of teachers who, in turn, taught the way that they were trained, not necessarily in accordance with Comer principles.

Students as "raw materials." The Lancastrian, age-graded, and Gary plans relied on an efficiency model styled after the military or business world, and students were clay to be molded. The Trump plan moved away from the assembly-line process of education and provided individual study time and small-group, student-led seminars. A CES common principle was student as worker, whereas the SDP was a social service institution that catered to the individual needs of its clients (the students).

Personalized learning. In the Lancastrian plan, students moved from one classification to the next based on individual mastery; however, there was virtually no teacher–student interaction—the teaching was performed by student monitors. The age-graded plan created a rigid classification system and included teacher specialization—both depersonalized learning. The Gary plan attempted to fulfill Dewey's "school is life" philosophy with the work–study–play plan, but its three-*R* classrooms were rigid, graded, and rote. The Trump, SDP, and CES plans always personalized learning for students: Trump emphasized individual study and learning time; the SDP emphasized relationships; and the CES plan emphasized the student as worker and personalization of learning.

Parental inclusion. The Lancastrian, age-graded, Gary, and Trump plans did not include parents, and poor parents were oftentimes viewed as a problem, especially in the Lancastrian and age-graded plans. Schools operated under the guise of raising indigent children because the parents were not able to effectively raise their own children. Under this ideology, it was the schools' job to properly raise and educate the children. On the contrary, parental inclusion was a cornerstone of the SDP as well as the CES plans. Principle 7 in the CES plan held that the inclusion of parents in the decision-making process was important.

Student motivation. The Lancastrian plan adopted democratic principles for student discipline. The plan focused on keeping kids busy instead
of creating a great deal of idle time. This was a sharp break from past
schooling efforts, where students sat idle and bored for long periods. The
age-graded plan led to an increase in negative competition among same-
age peers, and student interest was not the focus of lessons. The Gary
plan relied on democratic principles for student discipline, and the Trump
plan made a student responsible for his or her own learning through independent study time. The CES plan adage of "less is more" required students to study a particular topic in-depth in a climate of unanxious expectation. The SDP motivated students by accounting for each student's
mental health status and assisting the psychologically and emotionally
unstable.

Lower-class students. The Lancastrian plan provided a schooling idea
for masses of children for the first time in human history. The age-graded
plan's rigid classification system harmed poor "at-risk" students because
these students were disproportionately not able to keep up with their
same-age peers. The Gary plan provided work and play to meet the diverse interests of all students. The Trump plan contained nothing extraordinary for poor students. The heart of the CES plan and the SDP was to
help poor and minority students succeed in school.

Low IQ and self-fulfilling prophecy. The Lancastrian plan contained no
method for appropriately educating the mentally deficient. Slower students were a drag in the age-graded plan because they made the plan less
efficient. The Gary plan relied on intelligence testing and classified students according to test scores, whereas the Trump plan employed seminars and a student worker focus but no significant plan for the mentally
deficient. The CES plan prescribed a tailor-made school practice for each
student, whereas the SDP took an emergency-room approach to meeting
the needs of all students, instead of a deficit perspective.

The Teaching Profession

Teacher development. The Lancastrian plan placed teaching into the hands
of student monitors, who received instruction from a teacher in the morning before the other students arrived. The age-graded plan provided specialization to help expedite teacher training, whereas the Gary plan provided

departmentalization as the method for teacher development. The Trump plan provided more planning and collaboration time, a differentiated pay scale, and paraprofessionals to handle nonteaching duties. The CES plan prescribed a reduced teacher class load, collective planning time, and competitive teacher salaries. The SDP helped teachers in dealing with nonmainstream parents and students, but it provided no structured development plan for teachers.

The unlearning process. The Lancastrian, age-graded, and Gary plans contained no significant unlearning process for teachers. The Trump plan provided a method that could have enabled unlearning through team teaching and a common planning time. The CES plan believed that faithful adherence to common principles would foster an unlearning process. The SDP provided theoretical shifts in the philosophy of teaching, but there was no specific indoctrination process that guaranteed adoption of the SDP philosophy (no-fault, e.g.).

Teacher education programs. The Lancastrian plan provided a manual of instruction, whereas the rise of normal teacher colleges developed as a result of the age-graded plan. The Gary and Trump plans provided no teacher education programs. The CES plan trained teachers as generalists instead of specialists; however, universities still trained teachers as specialists during the era of the CES plan. The SDP built partnerships with colleges of education; not all staff were trained in these partnerships, however.

Pedagogy. The Lancastrian plan called for faithful adherence to the manual of instruction. The age-graded plan used textbooks to fit students into the curriculum. It also provided specialization for teachers. The Gary plan contained rote teaching in the three-*R* rooms. It offered new pedagogy, but these offerings were only suggestions and were not enforced. The Trump plan altered teacher schedules and provided more time for planning, collaboration, and teaching fewer students. The CES plan provided a small teaching class load and teachers as generalists. The SDP helped with maladjusted students.

Productive teaching defined. The Lancastrian plan called for order and a rigid delivery of knowledge by student monitors. This method was deemed both productive and efficient. The age-graded plan allowed individual needs to suffer as a result of the quest for order for cognitive accomplishment. The Gary plan improved motivation by adding work and play to the day of each student's schedule. However, no plan was implemented for significant development. The CES plan lacked a research base for teachers to be generalists. The SDP prescribed relationship building, whole-child development, and a focus on addressing mental health issues.

School Power and Politics

Government involvement. The Lancastrian plan was supported because of its low cost. It received commendations from King George III and Governor Clinton of New York. Over time, it lost its support as the student-as-teacher aspect of it came into question. The age-graded plan convinced governments that it was cost-effective and efficient. These two variables were among the reasons that it became part of the permanent school structure. The Gary plan convinced governments that it was educating more students at a lower cost and was more cognitively significant. Most support was the result of the cost-effectiveness variable. The Trump plan gained so much favor that some school plants were built to accommodate large, medium, and small grouping. The CES plan existed in an era of high-stakes testing, and its philosophy ran contrary to the government's accountability approach. The SDP was mandated for all schools in Prince George's County, Maryland, as part of a federal judge's ruling on ending court-ordered desegregation efforts.

Middle-class ethic. The Lancastrian plan socialized the poor; order and moral education were what they needed, it was believed. The age-graded plan sought to Americanize immigrants. The Gary plan sought to Americanize immigrants, while maintaining segregated schools based on ethnicity. The Trump plan provided differentiated instruction through independent study time. The CES plan's motto was "all children can learn." The SDP assisted in the development of nonmainstream students utilizing a theory of no-fault.

School bureaucracy. The Lancastrian plan gave no power to parents or the community, and each school employed one teacher who reported to local government officials. The age-graded plan signaled that the urban school bureaucracy won over the rural one-room schoolhouse organization. The Gary plan was set up to be less hierarchical, but Wirt, its creator, still stood at the top and firmly in control. The Trump plan was not able to stave off the traditional school bureaucracy, and the plan waned over time. The CES plan was site based, and the SDP recognized the bureaucracy and tried to alter it with site-based, consensus decision making.

Research and development. The Lancastrian plan seemed good for poor students because it was better than no school at all. The teaching was not so great. In the long run, the age-graded plan harmed at-risk students the most. They fell behind and could not catch up. Mann would not have supported it. No research supported the lack of significance in the three-*R* classrooms or the other aspects of the plan. The CES plan fit with the small schools movement that received Gates Foundation money, and the SDP conducted ongoing research about school climate to further develop mental health approach.

Silent axioms. The Lancastrian plan had support from power players. The age-graded plan fit well with what policymakers wanted. The Gary plan was liked by government officials because it saved money. They were not concerned with its purported whole-child development significance. The Trump plan found support because of Cold War fears. The CES plan rode the wave of the small schools movement and Gates Foundation money. The SDP challenged the status quo during a politically liberal time but was stigmatized as an inner-city reform plan.

SDP Conclusions

The SDP did not significantly address all of the elements and variables that Sarason identified as being vital. The SDP was most successful with the teaching theory element. It received an overall rating of *very effective / effective*. Also, it received an *effective* rating for the change theory element. However, the SDP did not receive high scores on several of the variables under the teaching profession element nor under the school power and politics element. The SDP received a *sometimes effective* rating for each of these elements.

The SDP rated *effective* instead of *very effective* on the change theory element because it scored *high/medium* on the encapsulated classroom and past reforms research and *medium* on axiomatic change. Comer researched child development theory to improve schooling but did not necessarily research past school reforms, nor did the SDP change the physical arrangement of the encapsulated classroom. The SDP did seek change in the minds of the teachers to improve the encapsulated classroom and make it a holistic educational experience. Although the SDP sought change to address the mental health of students, it received a *medium* score on the axiomatic change variable because the SDP worked to improve student–teacher relationships, but it did not address and improve the teaching and learning method in classrooms.

The SDP rated highest on the teaching theory element, with a *very effective / effective* rating. It received a *medium* score for the pouring-in knowledge theory indicator because it did not significantly alter curiosity-stifling classroom pedagogy. Teachers in Comer schools could still teach students as though they were vessels to be filled up with knowledge.

The SDP received a *sometimes effective* rating on the teaching profession element and the school power and politics element because of *high/medium* or lower scores on eight indicators. For the teaching profession element, the SDP received a *high/medium* score on the unlearning process and productive teaching, a *medium* score on teacher development and teacher education programs, and a *medium/low* score on the pedagogy indicator. The SDP received a *high/medium* score on the school bureaucracy indicator, a *medium* score on the silent axioms and educational policymakers indicators, and a *medium/low* score on the government involvement indicator.

The SDP received a *high/medium* score on the unlearning process and productive teaching defined indicators. The SDP challenged traditional theories of teaching and learning and focused on relationship building and mental health issues in offering an unlearning process and teaching ideology to help all students find success.

The SDP was less successful with the teacher development indicator, teacher education programs indicator, and pedagogy indicator by scoring a *medium* on the first two and a *medium/low* on the last mentioned indicator. The SDP did not provide a structured program to develop teachers in schools or for future teachers in universities. Occasional instances of SDP-based teacher education programs existed, for example, at Southern University in Louisiana, but the SDP could not guarantee that all teachers in Comer schools would have the requisite training necessary to follow the Comer principles. As a result, the day-to-day regularities of teaching and curriculum transmission were not significantly improved; thus, the SDP received the unfavorable score on the pedagogy indicator.

In the school power and politics element, the SDP did not find success with the government involvement indicator, scoring a *medium/low*, but was somewhat more successful with the silent axioms and educational policymakers indicator, scoring *medium*, and with the school bureaucracy indicator, scoring a *high/medium*. The SDP never gained government, business, or policymaker support, but in some instances it was able to alter the top-down school bureaucracy when schools successfully implemented its collaborative, consensus-seeking, site-based management style that included teachers and parents in the official decision-making process. Comparative reform plan results follow.

4

Initiatives That May Break the Cycle of Failed Reforms

School is not easy and for the most part not very much fun, but then, if you are very lucky, you may find a teacher. Three real teachers in a lifetime is the very best of luck. I have come to believe that a great teacher is a great artist, and that there are as few as there are any other great artists. Teaching might even be the greatest of the arts since the medium is the human mind and spirit. My three had these in common—they loved what they were doing. They did not tell—they catalyzed a burning desire to know. Under their influence, the horizons sprung wide and fear went away and the unknown became knowable. But most important of all, the truth, that dangerous stuff, became beautiful and precious.

—John Steinbeck, from Crossroads,
College of Holy Cross, March/April 1991

After an examination of the earlier failed school reform plans, it became clear that the SDP, proffered by James Comer, was going to be another such effort. Each of the reform plans studied failed to improve the teaching profession element, and none addressed the school power and politics element in a significant way.

ANALYSIS OF THE DATA

Did School Reform Follow a Predictable Pattern or Cycle?

Each of the earlier reform plans contained similar features. The entrenched structure of traditional schooling and the encapsulated classroom led to predictable patterns. Each plan was developed by a figurehead who provided the leadership that gave each plan thrust for takeoff. Each plan sounded good in theory, gained recognition, and spread into school districts and schools throughout the United States. Over time, however, weaknesses in each plan manifested, and the significant change that had been sought did not occur. In time, new national concerns fostered new school reform plans, and a wave of new reforms took the place of old plans. The cycle repeated.

A comparative analysis of the completed analytical rubrics showed similar shortcomings in all of the plans. All of the reform plans struggled with the school power and politics element and, specifically, the following indicators: government involvement, school bureaucracy, and research and development (Table 4.1).

The government involvement indicator stated that "the reform plan garnered local, state, and/or federal government support and financial assistance." The reform plans gained government support only if they promised a significant money-savings approach to reform. The Lancastrian plan was less popular for its altruistic ideal of educating the masses than for its low cost of educating large numbers of students. Likewise, the Gary plan found favor with government officials because of its platoon system of educating more students without building new and expensive schools.

Table 4.1. Each Plan Struggled With Three Indicators From School Power and Politics

Indicator	Description
Government involvement	The reform plan garnered local, state, and/or federal government support and financial assistance.
School bureaucracy	The reform plan replaced the top-down structure of school bureaucracy with a horizontal structure that put teachers and parents in important decision-making power roles.
Research and development	The reform plan included government-sponsored or government-funded research and development that enabled tinkering of the reform plan to increase its effectiveness.

The school bureaucracy indicator stated that "the reform plan replaced the top-down structure of school bureaucracy with a horizontal structure that put teachers and parents in important decision-making power roles." None of the 20th-century reform plans were able to circumvent, alter, or disrupt the entrenched school bureaucracy. The Lancastrian plan operated in a time before the large school bureaucracy, but it had its own top-down decision-making structure. One teacher made the decisions and reported only to local government officials.

The research and development indicator stated that "the reform plan included government-sponsored or government-funded research and development that enabled tinkering of the reform plan to increase its effectiveness." School reform plans did not take into account past reforms' successes and failings when making considerations for implementing change. The "burying our heads in the sand" mentality to school reform ensured that history repeated itself as reform plans failed to develop a method for implementing their thoughtful approach to changing teaching and learning in schools.

Each reform plan was successful with the following indicators under the change theory element: axiomatic change, unquestioned bedrock assumptions questioned, ongoing research and development, productive learning, and low IQ and self-fulfilling prophecy indicator under the teaching theory element (Table 4.2).

The axiomatic change indicator stated that "the reform plan confronted accepted norms and proposed significant 'out of the box' changes in school, such as 'teacher as all-knowing' and 'student as passive recipient' into a more collaborative and inquiring teacher and student relationship." Although the Trump plan and CES plan included significant measures to change teachers from all-knowing dispensers of knowledge, teachers relied on their own instincts in the classroom. The largest influences on teaching methodology were individual teachers' own classroom experiences as students, as student teachers, and as teachers. Reform plans that sought to help practicing teachers "find a new way" were not successful.

The unquestioned bedrock assumptions questioned indicator required that basic school structures that had been in place for over 100 years had to be questioned, critiqued, and, in most instances, radically changed. The reform plans challenged fundamental beliefs about schooling and reshaped

Table 4.2.   Each Reform Plan Was Successful With the Following Indicators for Change Theory and Teaching Theory

Indicator	Description
Axiomatic change	The reform plan confronted accepted norms and proposed significant "out of the box" changes in school, such as "teacher as all-knowing" and "student as passive recipient" into a more collaborative and inquiring teacher and student relationship.
Unquestioned bedrock assumptions	The reform plan challenged fundamental beliefs about schooling, for example, the notion that all students needed math, and reshaped schooling based on researched theory.
	The reform plan replaced the top-down structure of school bureaucracy with a horizontal structure that put teachers and parents in important decision-making power roles.
Ongoing research and development	Research and development was a significant part of the reform plan and was included with the funding source, to provide ongoing measurement of the reform.
Productive learning	The reform plan provided a definition for the concept of productive learning that included whole-child development theory. The definition was at once cognitive, affective, emotional, motivational, and attitudinal.
Low IQ and self-fulfilling prophecy	The reform plan included philosophical ideal and specific plans that ensured that all students received learning that stretched them cognitively and expected them to significantly develop.

schooling based on researched theory. All of the reform plans—except for the age-graded plan—included changes to basic schooling theories.

The ongoing research and development indicator held that "research and development was a significant part of the reform plan and was included with the funding source, to provide ongoing measurement of the reform." The SDP included inside auditors to measure the effectiveness of improving school climate. In the long run, none of the reform plans proved to be meritorious by educational researchers, policymakers, the public, or school practitioners.

The productive learning indicator called for reform plans to provide a definition for the concept of productive learning that included whole-child development theory. The Trump and CES plans outlined methods to make learning meaningful for the students, and the SDP emphasized whole-child development as a way to make learning beneficial for all students.

The low IQ and self-fulfilling prophecy indicator posited that the "reform plan included philosophical ideal and specific plans that ensured that all students received learning that stretched them cognitively and expected them to significantly develop." Spring's "sorting machine" identification of schooling in America (1976) envisioned school reform plans that worked outside of the public school system to effectively help all children, regardless of measured cognitive ability development. All of the reform plans attempted to change the system from within.

All of the reform plans struggled with the teaching profession element. An effective method of unlearning theories and methodologies never emerged from the plans. Each plan proposed a new ideology and/or methodology to change the status quo. Each failed to help all teachers unlearn past theory and adopt the new ideology or methodology. Although the Trump and CES plans included some significant teacher development training, Gary and SDP did not address pedagogical issues, and the age-graded plan contained no strategy—it left teacher training up to the normal schools—and the Lancastrian plan placed daily teaching into the hands of older students. The CES plan included an ideological shift from teachers as specialists to teachers as generalists—in the age of high-stakes testing. This went against most teacher certification programs and NCLB federal laws that required specialized training.

Although the reform plans experienced varying degrees of success in several of the change theory indicators, none experienced an *effective* rating in the more macro-educational school power and politics element. The reform plans also failed to obtain an *effective* rating in the teacher-centered teaching profession element that contained the unlearning process indicator as well as the pedagogy indicator (Table 4.3).

Did School Reform Plans Throughout History Contain Similar Factors, Patterns, Trends, and Cycles?

After spawning in select locales, the reform plans spread nationally. Their creation was often the result of a current issue or event that the public at large—and, in turn, politicians—connected to public schooling. The Lancastrian plan emerged as the need for mass education presented itself in the new democracy. The age-graded plan answered the call for an efficient

Chapter 4

Table 4.3.   Mixed Results on the Teaching Profession Element

Indicator	Description
Teacher development	The reform plan included significant opportunities for teacher development to foster growth for teaching professionals.
Unlearning process	The reform plan provided teachers with an unlearning of past ideas that ran counterproductive to the larger aims of the reform.
Teacher education programs	The reform plan developed partnerships with schools of education and universities to cultivate future teachers.
Pedagogy	The reform plan included models of effective teaching and the daily work schedule of teachers was considered.
Productive teaching defined	The reform plan contained the specific goals of student motivation, skill development, and life-long learning.

plan to Americanize immigrants. The Gary plan allowed communities to continue providing education to the masses without building new school facilities. The Trump plan emerged out of Cold War fears and hostilities. The SDP plan was proposed as a means of educating poor and minority children in the slow-moving desegregation era. Finally, the CES plan rode the wave of a small schools movement to personalize and then better educate students.

All of the reform plans were founded and spread with great promise and fanfare, and their effects were felt for decades before their influence waned and died. Their creators sought to influence teaching and learning in a positive manner, but as the plans faded, the old convention of rote recitation—never permanently extinguished—revived. Little of the plans survived the test of time, with the exception of the age-graded plan, which became a permanent feature of schooling.

All of the reform plans seemed poised to make a positive difference in schooling, and all did make changes. However, the changes consistently transformed educational features indirectly related to classroom practices. No reform significantly revolutionized the teaching practice, nor did any accept learning theory based on millions-year-old human growth, development, and socialization ideas (Bernhard, 1988).

Were the Most Important Features
of a Reform Identified and Isolated?

The most important features of each reform plan are listed as follows. The characteristics presumably made each plan distinctive and successful.

> *Lancastrian plan*—equity, mass education, manual of instruction, one teacher and student monitors for up to 1,000 students. It was mass education at an inexpensive price.
>
> *Age-graded plan*—excellence, efficiency, specialization of teachers, same-age classification. The age-graded plan was efficient and cheap.
>
> *Gary plan*—excellence, work, study, play, efficiency. The Gary plan ensured communities that a massive increase in immigrant children would not mean more school buildings and more taxpayer money with the platoon plan in place.
>
> *Trump plan*—excellence; large-group, small-group, and individual learning; cognitive significance. The Cold War fear of Soviet domination resulted in the rise of school reforms, such as the Trump plan. The promise of Trump involved more cognitively significant learning experiences for students.
>
> *CES plan*—excellence and equity, 10 common principles, cognitive significance. The CES plan strove to restructure schooling to add cognitive significance and real-world experience to the life of school-age students.
>
> *SDP*—Equity, help for the poor and maladjusted, consensus, collaboration, no-fault, student and staff support team, school planning and management team, parent team, site-based decision making. The SDP promised to help parents and teachers work together to best benefit the needs of the students. It also affected the school climate in a positive way by addressing the mental health needs of disruptive students.

Was Sarason's Idea That All School Reforms
Predictably Fail Confirmed in This Study?

None of the reform plans lived up to criteria outlined on the failure of school reform rubric. Sarason's prophecy (1990, 1993, 2002, 2004) about the predictable failure of school reform (see Sarason, 1990) was confirmed.

As Sarason believed, until society as a whole reevaluates the manner in which it attempts school reform, it will go nowhere. The school reforms analyzed in this study never cracked the entrenched structure of American public schools. That ingrained structure is like a black hole that swallows up all reform ideas, seemingly erasing any collective memory of them, only to churn them out decades later as reform ideas recast in new clothing.

The reforms studied in this report all sought to improve teaching and learning for masses of students. All found some success. Only the age-graded plan achieved permanence. The unintended consequences of its permanence, however, would have been distained by its originator, Horace Mann. He never lived to see the sort-and-sift warehousing of children in schools that his plan created.

The permanent feature of the age-graded plan itself answered the question of what needed to be changed in the early 21st century to achieve meaningful reform.

What Significant Elements Must Future Reform Plans Contain to Make Lasting Change Viable?

Although the failure of the school reform rubric arranged what Sarason believed was needed to make schooling significant and productive for all students, the reality was that Sarason's descriptors did not necessarily matter. The age-graded plan did not pass the muster of the rubric, yet it did become a permanent part of the American school structure. Sarason's work came long after the age-graded plan. All of the selected plans came before Sarason's theory, except for the CES plan. This fact indicated that there were other conditions that led to the success or failure of school reform plans. It did not matter how altruistic, theoretically sound, or cognitively significant a reform plan was. What mattered were the conditions in the society at the time of the reform needed to be aligned with what the reform plan had to offer.

I concluded that the following conditions and variables coexisted and so allowed the age-graded plan to take root in mid-19th-century America:

Textbooks were the tool for teachers to convey knowledge to students.
A classification system was becoming established—for example, pupils finished one spelling book and moved to the next.

The physical building structure, following the lead in Boston, created the "egg crate" design that led to the encapsulated classroom.

Educational leaders and researchers of the time supported the age-graded plan.

Political support from government leaders and the public followed.

Age-grading was a philosophy of the industrial revolution, rooted in efficiency, and that fit well with the assembly-line model theory.

Control and Americanization were important in the minds of Americans who worried about the large influx of immigrants.

On this last point, Gumbert and Spring (1974) say that "an anti-immigrant feeling [was] prevalent among native Americans. . . . The school was viewed as a protective shield . . . and as a means of protecting American values by Americanizing the immigrants from Europe" (p. 117). M. S. Katz (1976) says: "new waves of eastern and southern European immigrants raised fears of crime, vagrancy, and a foreign-speaking pauper class. . . . In response to these fears, schools were promoted as agencies of social control and assimilation" (p. 23).

This study examined the SDP by comparing it to five other reform plans according to Sarason's "failure of school reform" descriptors. The SDP, like virtually all other reform plans and ideas, was not able to achieve what it intended, because it was not able to change the deep-rooted system of schooling.

Comer theorized that improving a social system like a school, for example, by emphasizing primary prevention care, led to all children's receiving quality care and education. Problems such as the minority achievement gap, for example, then became a thing of the past. Comer's philosophy agreed with Dewey's in terms of whole-child development. In this regard, Comer's educational theories were based in Dewey's student-centered teaching and learning ideas, Vygotsky's social–cognitive interactive process, and Lewin's child psychology theories.

The SDP failed to adequately achieve results with the teaching profession element and the school power and politics element. For example, the SDP contained no significant pedagogical changes to improve teaching (see Table 4.4). It believed that teachers must not subscribe to the deficit perspective of teaching and learning, but it provided no transformational unlearning process to help all teachers find a better way. Two other

Table 4.4. School Development Plan Did Not Live Up to All of the Indicators

Indicator	Rating
Axiomatic change	Medium
"Pouring in knowledge" theory	Medium
Teacher development	Medium
Teacher education programs	Medium
Pedagogy	Medium/low
Government involvement	Medium/low
Silent axioms and educational policymakers	Medium

examples—the SDP was not able to adequately improve the pouring-in knowledge teaching theory nor the axiomatic change indicator.

The SDP promoted progressive teaching strategies but believed the teachers to be the experts and did not end all practices of rote mindless pedagogical practice—the pedagogy indicator. Similarly, the SDP promoted significant changes to the treatment of low socioeconomic status students, but it still rated *medium* on the axiomatic change indicator because the traditional student–teacher relationship in the modal classroom remained unchanged. Also, the SDP did not rate high on the government involvement indicator, the teacher development or teacher education program indicator, or the silent axioms indicator. The improvements promised by the SDP were weakened by the rigid, exploitative, hierarchical school system.

DISCUSSION

The SDP relied on child development theory and emphasized whole-child development as the key to raising children to survive independently. As adults, people who received good development positively contributed to democratic society.

The SDP challenged some of the basic structures of public education, such as bureaucracy, with a site-based decision-making process; class bias, with a philosophy of no-fault teaching; and racism, by providing a collaborative framework for all adult stakeholders to work together to help all students. M. B. Katz (1971) reports on the basic structures that the SDP was up against:

Acceptance of the proposition that the basic structure of American education has remained unchanged rests, quite obviously, on the definition of "basic." I mean by the term that certain characteristics of American education
today were also characteristic nearly a century ago: it is, and was, universal,
tax-supported, free, compulsory, bureaucratic, racist, and class-biased.
Those features marked some educational systems by 1880; they diffused
throughout the rest of the country. (p. xx)

The SDP was not able to significantly alter the entrenched schooling
structure. It was not able to improve the pedagogy indicator or gain government approval (the government involvement indicator). For Sarason,
the root of the problem in education was the method of day-to-day instruction. This meant that most daily teacher-to-student interactions did
not live up to the curiosity-seeking needs of the pupils. Comer (1993a) believed that the hierarchical structure of public education contributed to
this: "I concluded that teacher powerlessness was more the problem than
ineffective teaching methods or negative attitudes" (p. 149). However, the
SDP was not able to significantly improve the structure of schooling to
positively influence and change the daily life of teachers. Therefore, pedagogical innovation remained low.

Similarly, the SDP did not gain government support financially or otherwise, other than in isolated instances (e.g., Prince George's County,
Maryland, was court ordered to implement the SDP districtwide in the
1980s).

I discovered that the structure of public education in 2007 did not enable the comprehensive change proposed by the SDP or by other reform
plans. The structure of schooling as well as the manner of thinking about
education needed to change in more powerful entities—namely, in the
minds of federal and state government representatives who set educational
policy. Sarason (1997) wrote that schools "arose largely as a way to tame
and socialize the children of scores of millions of immigrant children" (p.
35). The SDP was not able to change the traditional delivery of knowledge
via textbooks, the conveyance of schooling in school buildings with age-
graded classification, and decision making from an entrenched and hierarchical school bureaucracy.

I viewed the rise in personal computers and additional technology as a
possible road to ending the monopoly that textbooks, egg-crate school

buildings, graded school classification, and school bureaucracy have on the schooling of children and teenagers. The new ultrasophisticated technology can be utilized to provide a new educational delivery system and allow for the evolution of a new kind of schooling.

RECOMMENDATIONS FOR PUBLIC POLICYMAKERS WHO WANT TO BREAK THE CYCLE OF FAILED SCHOOL REFORMS

The goal of the educational enterprise in the United States has been to create a literate citizenry capable of governing the country. In the past, public education sought to Americanize immigrants and prepare the majority of students for low-skill factory labor. Now in the 21st century, new immigrants are Americanized long before they arrive in the country. Mass communication devices and the media spread popular American culture and socialize immigrants long before they arrive in the United States. Also, low-skill factory jobs are no longer as plentiful in the United States as in the past. Immigrant students today still need English-language skills; all students need higher levels of education to meet the needs of the 21st-century postindustrial economy and its ultrasophisticated technological advances.

Lessons from this study led to the conclusion that school reform in 2007 is failing just as past reform plans failed. The encapsulated classroom is an outmoded form of education, and as Sarason pointed out long ago, true reform will require a remodeling of the educational enterprise.

Data from this study show that school reform plans to date have failed to significantly address two indicators of observable characteristics from the rubric: the development of teachers and the unlearning process. Teacher education programs must provide pedagogical skills beyond those used to maintain the norms of the traditional encapsulated classroom. Students in 2007 sit passively disengaged at their desks, in rows, in four-walled classrooms while a teacher stands at the front of the classroom telling them what is important based on a textbook and a prescribed fragmented curriculum.

Past reform plans struggled most with the teaching profession element as well as with the school power and politics element of the rubric. The highest rating achieved by any of the reform plans on these two elements was *sometimes effective* (see Tables 3.7–3.9). The Trump plan, CES plan, and SDP scored *high* on only two of the indicators, whereas the other plans failed to attain a *high* on any indicators from these elements.

The reform plans struggled just as profoundly with the unlearning process and teacher education programs indicators. These two indicators tallied three *low* ratings from the historical reform plans, and the highest rating noted was a *high/medium* by the SDP on the unlearning process indicator and a *high/medium* by the age-graded plan on the teacher education programs indicator.

If Sarason is correct about school reform, then launching an intensive study to document contexts of productive and unproductive learning must occur. Glazek and Sarason (2007) believe that the concept of productive learning has never been adequately researched and defined. School reform will never succeed until productive and unproductive teaching and learning definitions are established.

Glazek and Sarason (2007) compare the school reform quagmire to understanding Einstein's theory of relativity. They posited that people are conditioned into believing that only a small minority of people possess the necessary cognitive ability to understand Einstein's theory:

> One way to put it is to say that we have been socialized to believe that what he did is so abstract, complex, and mathematical, that it requires a special kind of mind to grasp its content and its consequences. So, they perform an act of faith in accepting the message that what he did cannot be understood by ordinary mortals. We disagree with that sweeping conclusion. (p. 152)

To comprehend $E = mc^2$, a person must conceive of time, mass, and the speed of light as one variable instead of separate variables (Glazek & Sarason, 2007). In educational terms, people must think of teaching, learning, and schooling in a fundamentally new way.

To effect true school reform, citizens and policymakers must transform their thinking about schooling. "The modal American classroom reflects a conception of learning that is self-defeating to the goals of reform. . . . There is something wrong with the concept of learning that the system perpetuates" (Glazek & Sarason, 2007, p. 152). For Sarason, a new concept of teaching and learning will naturally lead to a reconfiguration of the schooling enterprise.

The results of this analysis of failed school reforms should reveal to policymakers that additional time, money, and effort should not be spent on school reform initiatives. Serious consideration should be given to a reform plan that can live up to all the elements and indicators of the failure of school reform analytical rubric. The reality appears to be that no reform plan will satisfy all the criteria outlined in the rubric.

M. Mann's assertion (1986) on the developmental power and influence of the major world religions that "no laws are possible in sociology" leads me to conclude that even significantly addressing all the elements of the failure of the school reform rubric will not guarantee successful school reform. Mann wrote:

> No laws are possible in sociology. We may begin to search for general formulas of the form "if *x*, then *y*," where *y* is the rise of ideological power; but we realize fairly quickly that ideological power on the scale of early Christianity is rare. . . . Each of the four world religions or philosophies that rose to power in that period was unique in various ways. On that empirical basis we cannot build social-science laws, for the number of cases is far smaller than the number of variables affecting the outcome. A tentative description . . . is all we can aim for. (p. 341)

The number of factors that must be given consideration in reforming schooling far exceeds those included in reform initiatives. The lesson from this study is that no school reform plan has yet been translated into significant or lasting school change.

Reform plans in 2007 and beyond must pay attention to conditions of the moment to succeed. Just as features of the age-graded plan managed to become entrenched in mid-19th-century school structure because conditions necessitated embracement of such features—textbooks, development of a classification system, governmental endorsement—policymakers today must pay close attention to those features of proposed school reform plans that present conditions demand. In 2007, the postindustrial economy demands high-skilled workers who are innovative, original thinkers. The schooling system educating these workers was unfortunately designed for a past industrial era.

A two-pronged approach to school reform is proposed to end the stranglehold that traditional schooling has on education and learning. First, the launching of an intensive study to document contexts of productive and unproductive learning must occur to develop appropriate learning opportunities. Ultimately, a comprehensive study of productive learning will lead to a fundamental reform in the preparation of teachers (Sarason, 1990, 1993, 2002, 2004) and provide revolutionary change in the schooling enterprise. However, educational policymakers have yet to come to terms with this. The immediate future calls for some new initiatives to crack open the traditional egg-crate school to help initiate teaching reform.

The education of children must be taken out of the hands of government agencies and placed back into the hands of families, with the caveat that public or private community assistance will be needed for children from dysfunctional homes. This assertion is made with the understanding that governmental and business entities will have to engage themselves in societal changes to support families who choose childrearing over working outside the home.

In crafting future school reform plans, policymakers must give more consideration to the family as well as to difficult indicators from the teaching profession element and the school power and politics element. Schooling will change as the public continues to voice opposition to the status quo. Whether the changes that schools experience will be seen as improvements based on the ideas expressed by Sarason (1990, 1993, 2002, 2004) and this study remains to be seen.

If the rubrics from this analysis provide a true assessment of schooling, then the following recommendations to public policymakers appear warranted; that is, public policymakers should give serious consideration to the following five initiatives: individualized learning from home, small school / alternative school arrangements, new school ventures such as virtual learning, national curriculum standards, and criterion-referenced mastery tests (see Table 4.5). Policymakers should support these initiatives because they provide students with alternatives to traditional schooling and help create the necessary conditions to move education beyond the 19th-century factory model schooling concept.

The warehousing of students stifles learning, and a new model of schooling that promotes productive learning is needed. If a reform idea not mentioned here is found that measures up to the indicators and elements from the "failure of school reform" rubric, then policymakers should contemplate its success potential.

Table 4.5. New School Reform Recommendations for Public Policymakers

Reform Idea	*Rationale*
Individualized learning	Allow millions-year-old child development theories (Bernhard, 1988) to be reestablished as parents raise and educate their progeny.
Small school / alternative school	End the reliance on curiosity-stifling schools and introduce various methods of schooling.
Virtual learning	A high-tech alternative to end the reliance on textbooks and supersede the mindless and rote drudgery in many secondary classrooms and a window to opportunity for communities in need.
National curriculum standards	Federal, state, and local oversight for education and schooling required since taxpayer money spent.
Mastery tests	Minimum curriculum standards established by schools of education and teachers. What knowledge, skills, and proficiencies should children and youth attain?

Individualized learning from home offers parents a myriad of schooling choices. Placing education into the hands of families allows for learning based on millions-year-old human development theory (Bernhard, 1988). Parents, instead of public or private school systems, educate their children and raise them safely as they see fit.

Small and other alternative school initiatives will end the reliance on the factory model school concept. This idea provides all families who choose not to give up a career to raise their progeny. Smaller school settings seemingly improve student–teacher relationships and make education personal and significant as individual student curiosities are tapped. Alternative settings can help foster relevant learning situations as students participate in internships and apprenticeship learning settings.

Adding this variety of school settings will give families choices and decrease reliance on the curiosity-stifling factory model school. Smaller egg-crate schools do not inherently improve teaching and learning. At the same time, a marketplace of schools and teachers should exist from which families can choose.

Virtual learning classes and schools can aid in this choice. When communities do not offer good schools and teachers to its families, the virtual world can supplant these inadequacies. Students should not be educationally limited as a result of geography, ethnicity, gender, religion, or economic status. A virtual marketplace of schooling and teachers can assist especially vulnerable families and overcome community deficiencies.

Another important feature of successful school reform is the creation of national curriculum standards. The role of the federal government in education is to provide money and oversight while educators create a set of national standards over which all students progressively attain mastery.

The educational setting can be of any variety—home based, small school, virtual, or other. Students are mentored by an adult, by a person Vygotsky termed the *more competent other*, to help meet the standards. National standards promote choice because a variety of school settings are acceptable as long as standards are met. Mastery tests must be developed and aligned with standards to measure individual student progress.

A criterion-referenced mastery testing program must be developed to assess individual student performance on proficiencies. Mastery must be demonstrated during teenage years. Criterion-referenced tests measure student mastery on information as opposed to norm-referenced tests that measure students against each other on the same test. Students are permitted to take the proficiency tests and prove aptitude at any time, enhancing the functionality of individualized educational settings.

As long as students sit passively disengaged in rows of desks while teachers talk and textbooks guide all instruction for fragmented curricula, radical change is needed. Taxpayer money no longer needs to be spent on textbooks, buildings, facilities and furniture, teacher salaries and benefits, school district staff salaries and benefits, and transportation. As it stands, taxpayers are funding a system of education that dulls natural human curiosity and stifles learning.

New ultrasophisticated technological advances can offer an enriching alternative form of education never before possible in human history. For example, a young student can receive education online from a personal computer at home. She learns Chinese from a teacher in Beijing, math from an educator in another state, geography from a scientist living and working in Antarctica. Her father provides supervision while work with online teachers is undertaken. Progress is monitored regularly by her father.

After lunch, her father takes her to a museum for a lesson in astronomy. Her community soccer team provides her with a late-afternoon opportunity to interact with other kids while promoting physical fitness and team-building skills. Periodic criterion-referenced mastery tests based on national curriculum standards serve as an audit of her educational experience.

Reform plans from this study, spanning over 200 years of school reform history, were least successful with the teaching profession element and the school power and politics element. The five reform ideas described here offer new opportunities for the educational enterprise to address these elements. Table 4.6 lists the 10 variables from these two elements. These 10 variables were used to assess the success potential of the five new initiatives that educational policymakers should support.

Table 4.7 lists the results of plugging in the indicators to the new school reform proposals. Although small school / alternative school initiatives were popular in 2007—the Gates Foundation funded many of these—based on the results of this study, they were deemed least effective of the five initiatives. According to the results, time and money should be spent creating mastery tests and national curriculum standards, and then students should be afforded the opportunity of virtual learning or a process of individualized learning from home. Additional nontraditional arrangements must be made for children from dysfunctional homes.

Mastery tests improve on the teaching profession element because they allow students the freedom to attain schooling and prove competency without inadequate teacher interference. Teacher development, the unlearning process, teacher education programs, pedagogy, and productive teaching defined are all superseded. The macro-educational indicators from the school power and politics element are significantly addressed by mastery tests because they prescribe a governmental role, and the middle-class ethic and school bureaucracy indicators are supplanted.

At this time, alternatives to traditional schooling are mushrooming in popularity. Homeschooling, charter schools, and privatization of school management are examples of the changes occurring. Also, the high-tech explosion allows for more creative working environments. Many professionals are able to work from home, communicating and producing work through computers.

The traditional school model provides child care for students while their parents are at work. Taking children out of the home for childrearing and education may not provide the best result for society. Any change that places education back in the hands of families will require federal, state, and local governments as well as businesses to lead the way. Government

Table 4.6. Indicators From the Teaching Profession and School Power and Politics Indicators

Indicator	Description
Teacher development	The teacher development indicator stresses a change in teacher education based on the fact that once a teacher is hired he or she is not fully trained in teaching and learning and needs additional support and training.
Unlearning process	The unlearning process indicator requires a method to change minds or at least to understand and neutralize differences teachers may have.
Teacher education programs	The teacher education programs indicator calls for collaboration with schools of education for future hires and staff development for experienced teachers.
Pedagogy	The pedagogy indicator identified the need for taking into account the daily life of teachers.
Productive teaching defined	The productive teaching defined indicator involves the development of a definition of good teaching.
Government involvement	The government involvement indicator highlights the fact that government controls education and a reform plan must gain governmental support.
Middle-class ethic	The middle class ethic indicator asks a question: what should education for lower-class students include.
School bureaucracy	The school bureaucracy indicator says that the bureaucratic school structure inhibits collaboration and stifles any student or teacher power.
Research and development	The research and development indicator requires the reform plan to conduct meticulous evaluation and adjustments as necessary.
Silent axioms and educational policymakers	The silent axioms and educational policymakers indicator states that government and business leaders (the educational policymakers) have ingrained notions of education and the reform plan must effectively account for this reality

and businesses control the economy, and persons are dependent on them to a greater or lesser extent to provide the impetus for meaningful reform.

These new reform ideas are not the final answers for reforming schools. Individualized learning from home, small schools / alternative schools, and virtual learning do not overwhelmingly reform teaching, as evidenced

Table 4.7.   New School Reform Concepts and How They Rate With Select Indicators

	Individualized Learning From Home	Small Schools / Alternative Schools	Virtual Learning	National Curriculum Standards	Mastery Tests
Teacher development	N	N	Y	Y	Y
Unlearning process	N	N	N	Y	Y
Teacher education programs	Y	N	Y	Y	Y
Pedagogy	N	N	N	Y	Y
Productive teaching defined	Y	N	N	N	Y
Government involvement	Y	Y	Y	Y	Y
Middle-class ethic	Y	N	Y	Y	Y
School bureaucracy	Y	N	Y	N	Y
R&D	Y	Y	Y	N	Y
Silent axioms / educational policymakers	Y	N	Y	Y	Y

Note: Y = yes, the reform initiative satisfies the criteria for the particular indicator; N = no, the reform initiative does not satisfy the criteria for the particular indicator.

by the results with the teacher development, the unlearning process, teacher education programs, pedagogy, and productive teaching defined indicators. Ultimately, Sarason's plea for fundamental teacher preparation reform cannot be ignored.

It will take decades for Sarason's vision of improved teaching to be realized because, as a society, we have not even defined productive versus unproductive learning. In the meantime, new models of schooling should begin as alternatives to the traditional schooling structure. Only a small percentage of the population will buy in to the new concepts. Most people will favor the system of schooling that they experienced as children. Ideally, after years of research and development, government, businesses, and citizens at large will begin to embrace a form of education that is more natural and consistent with millions-year-old human developmental strategies (Bernhard, 1988).

Childrearing and educational opportunities will be provided more often by primary caregivers who model effective learning and differentiate instruction based on the natural curiosities and individual developmental needs of their progeny. More of these generally described natural learning situations will tug at the traditional schooling ideal for decades. Advocates of the more natural learning environments will have to lobby governments and businesses to reconfigure society to allow people to more directly participate in the education of their children. Ultimately, schooling as it is known will end as children are raised and educated at home or in small apprenticeship settings.

When a new conceptualization of schooling becomes a reality, it will end the following school norms, which are well known and with which schools continue to struggle:

Ability grouping
Adequate yearly progress
After-school detention
Alternative discipline schools
Behavior specialists
Block schedule versus traditional schedule
Booster clubs
Bullying in school
Central office personnel
Class rings
Comprehensive high schools
Dean of students
Desegregation of student populations
Dropouts
Drugs and alcohol in school
Expensive school construction and maintenance
Extracurricular sports
Federal lunch program
Homecoming
Homeroom
Letterman jackets
Middle school
Modal classroom
Nap time
NCLB
Office referrals
Open house

Out-of-school suspension
Principals and assistant principals
Prom
PTA
Recess
Retention versus promotion
School boards
School bureaucracy
School clubs
School dances
School dress codes
School psychologists
School reform plans
School report cards
School security guards
School social workers
School support staff
School uniforms
School violence
Student code of conduct
Superintendents
Tardy students
Textbooks
Worksheets and busywork
Yearbooks
Yellow school buses

A great deal of time, energy, human capital, and taxpayer monies are put into the listed items. Unfortunately, nothing on this list significantly contributes to advancing Sarason's idea of a concept of productive learning. In contrast, I believe that everything on this list impedes progress toward Sarason's conceptualization of a process for effective education.

Critics may rail against the five proposals—individualized learning, small school / alternative school, virtual learning, national curriculum standards, and mastery tests—as elitist initiatives. Partisan politics will undoubtedly alter and possibly warp even the best of these new educational plans. New York University law professor Derrick Bell (1980a,

1980b) cautions against optimism with lessons of the interest-convergence dilemma—that the dominant group in society goes along with ideas intended to help the disadvantaged groups only if the dominant group primarily benefits from the plan.

All reform plans must represent the best interests of the common good. New schooling proposals put forth in this study will serve low socioeconomic status students better than traditional schooling will because the initiatives offer alternatives to the bureaucratically social class–biased system of schooling that currently exists. Adults living in public housing, for instance, will be given choices in deciding who will teach their children, and they will be given greater leverage in deciding where and how their children are educated.

Students from families of low socioeconomic status are typically the abnormalities in the middle-class-based, factory-model schooling process. They do not easily find success in school and are often a source of frustration for teachers and schools. Providing the lower-class citizenry with real choices in teachers, school settings, and modes of educational delivery is real school reform. Government agencies should play a role, but they should no longer serve in loco parentis.

CONCLUSION

The top power brokers in education have historically been state legislators, governors, and, to an increasing degree, the federal government. Solutions advanced by the federal administration in 2007 included school vouchers, charter schools, standardized tests, strict teacher accountability standards, and adequate yearly progress goals. All of these proposed solutions, however, failed to address the fundamental problems in society that affected learning—poverty, unemployment, and lack of community.

The current federal NCLB does not live up to its claim of helping students and families who need it most. Rather, NCLB further exacerbates the problems inherent in the educational enterprise. Instead of helping children who are doubtlessly "left behind," this act has served to stigmatize and alienate the schools and the public from our neediest students.

In 2007, norm-referenced standardized test scores inevitably measure the socioeconomic status of each student's family. NCLB seemingly requires states to provide yearly standardized norm-referenced tests to measure students against their peers born in the same year. Students from families with all the advantages in life score in the upper quartile on these tests, whereas students who experience developmental gaps in childhood generally score in the lower quartile when rated against same-age peers. The NCLB federal law helps perpetuate the socioeconomic caste system in America.

The reality is that schools and teachers who serve greater numbers of poor children produce lower test scores and face sanctions, including job loss. The State of North Carolina serves as a prime example of this; a state judge there has accused teachers of committing "academic genocide" because their high-poverty schools scored below those of their same-age peers on standardized tests. As a result, people who choose teaching as a profession seek out schools and students that will produce high standardized test scores to provide them a sense of accomplishment and job security.

NCLB actually perpetuates low socioeconomic status students being left behind. Since 2001, presumably more teachers have sought out teaching positions in schools with large percentages of high socioeconomic status students, driven away from high-poverty schools. Teachers are more hesitant to take on the noble work of serving in high-need schools for fear of personal career damaging sanctions as a result of predictably low test scores.

Despite the century-old American myth that education is the great equalizer and the road to a better life, the United States continues to struggle to provide quality schooling to poor and minority students. M. B. Katz (1971) writes that "people ask no more of schools today than they did a hundred and twenty-five years ago. . . . Even then the schools were asked to do the impossible" (p. 141). Spring (2000) adds that "it has never been proved that a relationship exists between the amount and quality of education available in a society and a decrease in crime, unemployment, and other social, economic, and political problems" (p. 214).

The originating goal of the American public school system is obsolete. The ideal of schooling is no longer socialization of the masses and the preparation of workers for mindless drudgery. However, the public school system is still set up to accomplish these two principles.

The primary education goal for 21st-century youth should be the development of critically minded, reflective thinkers who can come up with creative solutions to problems novel to their times. The egg-crate, curiosity-stifling, discipline-based 19th-century government-controlled and private organization–controlled schooling configuration cannot produce this result. The search for new ways of schooling is long overdue.

Glossary

adequate yearly progress—According to the No Child Left Behind Act of 2001, "test scores must be disaggregated by major racial and ethnic groups, English language proficiency status, students with disabilities as compared to all other students, economically disadvantaged students as compared to students not economically disadvantaged, migrant status, and gender" (English, 2005, p. 408). The federal government measured schools and school district test results to determine if adequate yearly progress was reached according to each subgroup.

archival data—Factual information collected in a library or other storage area and made available for historical research.

assessment and modification—Created new information and identified new opportunities. The school development plan was data driven, which permitted orderly changes and adjustments (Comer, 1996).

bureaucracy—"In the early part of the twentieth century, the bureaucratic model of organization became firmly rooted in our school systems with the superintendent at the top and the teacher at the bottom. In between came a whole echelon of generalist and specialist personnel" (Oliva & Pawlas, 1999, p. 8).

Carnegie unit—"The curricula of the schools often seemed structured in such a way as to imply that all knowledge is equally valuable." Each high school course counted for one equal unit of credit (Oliva & Pawlas, 1999). Furthermore, in Charlotte-Mecklenburg Schools, North

Carolina, for example, a student in 2006 had to earn 28 units of credit to graduate from high school.

civil rights movement—An African American–led movement that reached its prime in the 1960s. The movement put pressure on the government until it ended legally sanctioned segregation laws and granted full citizenship rights to African Americans (Palmer, 1998b).

climate—According to Comer, "the school's climate . . . defined as the frequency and quality of interactions among parents, teachers, students, the principal, administrators, and adjunct staff" (Comer et al., 1996, p. 43).

collaboration—Required parents, teachers, administrators, and others involved in a process to respect others' points of view. It encouraged inclusion and respect among all members of the school community (Comer, 1996).

Comer school development plan—A data-driven, site-based management school reform plan that operated under its three guiding principles of consensus, collaboration, and no-fault. Dr. Comer originally created the school development plan to help two high-poverty African American elementary schools in New Haven, Connecticut, that struggled to effectively educate its students.

comprehensive school plan—Focused on sharing information between schools and community; setting social and academic climate goals; and defining curriculum, instruction, and assessment (Comer, 1996).

consensus—This concept discouraged the idea of voting on particular issues. It urged all concerned to work toward an agreed solution that was acceptable to everyone (Comer, 1996).

constructivist learning theory—"The work of Piaget and Vygotsky, among others, asserts that learning takes place as the individual internalizes and reshapes information and experiences into new understandings that are enhanced by social interaction. Constructivists believed that learning cannot be mandated or prevented, but it can be invited and enhanced" (English, 2005, p. 495).

Dalton plan—"It was primarily a plan for individual instruction, and permits the pupil to determine for himself how and when he will do the work in the allotted time" (Cubberley, 1934, p. 528).

de jure segregation—Separation of the races by law. These laws were unjust and discriminated against African Americans and other minorities until they were overturned in the 1960s.

developmental pathways—"Although the child is a seamless whole, a high level of development along the physical, cognitive, psychological, language, social, and ethical pathways is critical for academic learning" (Comer, 1996, p. 15).

Elementary and Secondary Education Act, 1965—"Part of President Johnson's Great Society programs at the height of the civil rights movement. . . . Title I is the best-known section of the ESEA. Title I provides compensatory education in the form of remedial services, typically in mathematics and language instruction for specifically identified children from poor families" (English, 2005, p. 182).

failure—School reform ideas made grand promises, but the results were disappointing. As a result, the educational establishment buried the reform idea and moved on to a new idea. Nothing was learned from the past reform; the next reform did not succeed; and an unproductive cycle began.

historiography—"The writing of history based on critical analysis, evaluation, and selection of authentic source materials and composition of these materials into a narrative subject to scholarly methods of criticism" (*American Heritage Dictionary*, 2006, p. 833).

indicator of observable characteristics—The 26 variables that were identified from Sarason's writings (1990, 1993, 2002, 2004) as the critical components that a reform plan had to include to accomplish its goal of school reform.

IQ—Intelligence quotient. "The labels educators used during the period from 1900 to 1950 indicate a significant shift from the nineteenth century in the way they thought about the 'misfits' in the educational system: *pupils of low IQ* . . . were students who simply did not have the smarts. The scientific solution was to teach them different things in a different way, and perhaps in a different place, from the 'normal' students" (Tyack, 2003, p. 118).

No Child Left Behind Act, 2001—A reauthorization of the federal Elementary and Secondary Education Act: "The act's major provisions include language holding local school boards accountable for student performance and for hiring teachers who are 'highly qualified'" (English, 2005, p. 182).

no-fault—Helped people move past blaming and focused on people's emotions to solve conflicts that were hindering efforts to work collaboratively. It operated "on the premise that other people's mistakes result from misunderstandings, misinterpretations, or miscommunications and not a deliberate attempt to offend" (Comer, 1996, p. 57).

parent team—Brought parents into the school with the PTA as teacher assistants and in special events sponsored by the school. It also wanted to involve parents in the school at some other levels of participation, especially, those parents who were traditionally turned off by the schools and did not play an active role in the education of their children (Comer, 1996).

Sarason, Seymour—Professor emeritus of Yale University, Dr. Sarason predicted in 1965 that all school reform ideas would fail until the methodology for reform was changed. Dr. Sarason believes that a research project must be conducted to create a definition of productive learning. When this occurs, our current concept of schooling will have to be scrapped.

school planning and management team—The governing body of a Comer school. It ensured that all stakeholders had a say in the decision-making process (Comer, 1996).

school reform—Dating from antiquity; according to Noblit and Dempsey (1996), it was the age-old debate between the oratorical concept of "excellence" and the philosophical notion of "equity." Because of this, schools were never reformed; instead, reform was recycled.

site-based management—"The effort to establish school- or site-based management (SBM), which has been popular in some circles during the past 20 years, is an example of creating school communities. An underlying basis for SBM is that those closest to the daily work of schools should be engaged in making decisions about the organization and its structure, management, goals, and objectives" (English, 2005, p. 73).

staff development—These activities were based on training needs that stemmed from the comprehensive school plan. Decisions were made by the school planning and management team with support from central office personnel (Comer, 1996).

student and staff support team—Members included special service personnel, counselors, school psychologists, and the principal and other support staff. They met weekly to discuss mental health issues and discussed referrals from teachers. It helped deal with students who exhibited behaviors that were not conducive to an academic climate by working together with parents and teachers to identify the causes of negative behavior and appropriate modifications to deal with them (Comer, 1996).

theory—"A set of statements or principles devised to explain a group of facts or phenomena, especially one that has been repeatedly tested or is widely accepted and can be used to make predictions about natural phenomena" (*American Heritage Dictionary*, 2006, p. 1794).

three guiding principles—Stakeholders including parents, teachers, administrators, and other adults in the community determined what was to be done in the school, guided by consensus, collaboration, and no-fault (Comer, 1996). The three guiding principles created a theoretical framework for the school within which the adults could operate. The goal was to minimize personal conflicts that interfered with the real work of the school so that most energy went into helping all children develop properly.

three mechanisms—The three mechanisms of the Comer school development plan enabled the adults to work together to best benefit the developmental needs of the children. The school planning and management team took the place of the principal as the primary decision maker. The parent team worked hard to improve the involvement of parents at all levels of the school. The student and staff support team were composed of counselors, teachers, school nurse, school psychologist, and others to provide mental health services (Comer et al., 1996).

three operations—The comprehensive school plan, staff development, and monitoring and assessment (Comer et al., 1996).

Appendix A: The Lancastrian Plan

CHANGE THEORY FOR LANCASTRIAN PLAN:
SOMETIMES EFFECTIVE / NOT EFFECTIVE

"I predicted that as it was being conceived and implemented educational reform would go nowhere" (Sarason, 2002, p. 178).

The Encapsulated Classroom and School: Low

Reigart, 1916, p. 11—One boy reading and 29 writing; old method, 29 doing nothing.

p. 15—"Although a popular method, is one of the most inconsistent, absurd requisitions that was ever forced on human beings."

p. 100—"Imparting of information rather than training in observation and eliciting of thought became the aim."

pp. 54–55—Poor teaching methods.

p. 6—Educational inadequacy almost universally recognized.

p. 41—"The children stood in semicircles and named the letters pointed out by the monitor."

Lancaster, 1973, pp. 37–42. p. 188—Description of the classroom: teaching monitors, inspecting monitors, monitor of absentees, monitor-general, monitor of slates. Education motivates and trains students; method for teaching reading. "Bad accommodation common school-rooms

afford to the poor . . . by the confinement at their seats . . . without varia-
tion." Lancaster school aims to improve upon this.

Riddle, 1905, p. 82—Too much dependence on monitors for teaching—educating the most kids at the least expense, Lancastrian rules. "But
where thorough and complete instruction is sought for, they are constrained to think that other and more successful methods may be found."

Cubberley, 1919, p. 131—Seated in rows, monitor for each row, monitors usually taught groups of 10, stations positioned around the room.

Kaestle, 1973b, p. 166—"The Lancastrian system, with its detailed procedures, prescribed content, authoritarian pedagogy, and hierarchical
teaching structure." Andrews, 1830, pp. 72–74—"As a full description of
the methods employed . . . such information may be obtained by consult-
ing a 'Manual of the Lancastrian System' . . . elementary instruction . . .
founded upon a principle of Order and Discipline, by which the pupils,
under the direction of the master, pursue a course of mutual instruction."

"Unquestioned Bedrock Assumptions" Questioned: High/Medium

Kaestle, 1973b, p. 166—"By bringing the pupils into an obedient subordination, the school imposed order on chaos."

Axiomatic Change—Out of the Box: Medium/Low

Reigart, 1916, p. 99—System of order, organized scheme of classification
and promotion: "Beginners in arithmetic not compelled to commit to
memory meaningless definitions, though there was no provision for teaching the idea of number or an understanding of the mathematical process."

pp. 14–16—Lack of quality teachers prior to Lancastrian: "The common type of illiterate and unprincipled teachers in New York during the
first quarter of the century is pictured in the pages of the Academician. . . .
Our youths are made to languish over books of words accompanied only
by the midnight lamp . . . and compelled to recite these words, not understood, verbatim, on entering school the next morning . . . is one of the
most inconsistent, absurd requisitions."

p. 16—"The method of teaching the science of number was utterly un-
scientific. No recitation rooms were attached to general school rooms."

Cubberley, 1919, p. 134—"Under the plans previously . . . slow and an expensive process . . . individual method of instruction . . . small groups."

p. 135—"Individual method of instruction, with its accompanying waste of time and disorder, continued to be the prevailing method, only a small number of pupils could be placed under the control of a single teacher." Expense made education prohibitive.

Riddle, 1905, p. 23—Blind leading the blind, but large number of children reached.

Intractability of Schools: Medium/Low

Kaestle, 1973b—"Prescribed content," "authoritarian pedagogy," "hierarchical teaching structure."

Note: No cadre of teachers—the student monitors were responsible for the day-to-day teaching.

Reigart, 1916, p. 30—"To the student it makes learning less irksome, by simplifying and facilitating his progress, it gives to instruction more interest, by alternation and variety of exercise, in which physical and intellectual action are combined; it keeps attention awake and interested, by permitting no moment of idleness or listlessness. . . . To the master also, it renders teaching less irksome and more interesting."

Lancaster, 1973, p. 196—"But it is very poor encouragement for a man, having a family, to pass laboriously away the prime of his days, with the cheerless expectation of ending them in a workhouse or prison."

Ongoing Research and Development: Medium

Lancaster, 1973, p. 37—"The influence a master has over his scholars . . . influence they have one over another . . . objects of constant study and practice; it has most happily succeeded in proving, that a very large number of children may be superintended by one master."

p. 53—"Boys who learn by this new mode, have six times the usual practice in writing; but, in the old way the expence is, at the first cost, 5 1/2 d. per month, for writing books, pens, and ink, each boy."

p. 52—"A boy who is associated in a class of an hundred others, not only reads as much as if he was a solitary individual under the master's care, but he will also spell sixty or seventy words of four syllables, by writing them on a slate, in less than two hours: when this additional number of words, spelt by each boy daily, is taken into account, the aggregate will amount to repetitions of many thousands of words annually; when not a word would be written or spelt, and nothing done by nineteen twentieths of scholars in the same time."

Andrews, 1830, pp. 46–47—"And but three persons who have been educated here, have been convicted in our criminal courts."

p. 49—African Free School, New York: "If my eyes had not told me otherwise, I should thought myself in one of the best regulated and best taught schools, composed of the fairest hued children in the land."

p. 55—African Free School, upon inspection: "The progress of the pupils is such as to warrant the conclusion, that they are as susceptible of mental cultivation as the children of the white parents."

p. 68—Six hundred students, Lancastrian method: "The improvement of the scholars is such, as to be satisfactory to the Trustees, and all visitors who come to the school."

pp. 36–37—Audit found schools performing well: "The answers of both boys and girls . . . were prompt and satisfactory. . . . The performances in writing were neat, and in many instances, highly ornamental. . . . The behavior of the children was orderly and creditable to them and their teachers; the whole together furnished a clear and striking proof of the value of the monitorial system of education."

Teachers as Reform Leaders: Low

Reigart, 1916, p. 101—"Even the teacher with the zeal of youth and trained by the modern methods of pedagogy is apt to be overpowered by having his attention directed to the practice of the schools as it *has been* rather than as it *may be*."

Kaestle, 1973b, p. 166—"Prescribed content" and "authoritarian pedagogy"; "NY leaders were attracted by the detailed plans of Lancaster, which could be infinitely duplicated."

Note: No significant cadre of teachers.

Lancaster, 1973, p. 10—"Lancaster's publications, themselves, provide complete directions for organizing a monitorial school, from the construction of the building down to the minute details of curriculum, recitations and school management."

Lang's Five Assumptions: Medium

1. Outside agent.
2. Parents and community involved in the change. Lancaster, 1973, p. 181—"How lamentable a thing it is . . . when the virtuous poor man toils . . . that his children may obtain useful learning, and they yet remain ignorant."
3. Motivate students and families. Lancaster, 1973, p. 188—Criticism of poor parents: "What can we expect from the children of the poor, when the gamester, the drunkard, the profane, and the infidel, are entrusted with their education. Painful instances of this kind have come within my knowledge."
4. Power relationships altered.
5. Less discontinuity between school and nonschool.

Past Reforms' Research: Medium/Low

Reigart, 1916, p. 6—Influence of New York public schools. John Griscom "was a marked factor in the foundation of monitorial schools throughout the country."

p. 99—Lancastrian orderly and organized scheme of classification and promotion in contrast to the schools of that time period.

p. 55—"It is not difficult to discover the superiority of Lancaster's method to the method in vogue at that time. Instead of the long preliminaries and the learning of numbers and rules the pupils were at once set to work in the operations of arithmetic. The children were given something to do, though they were left to the direction of the monitors who knew little more than themselves. . . . The inadequacy of the Lancastrian plan was discovered when comparison was made with the more intelligent methods of Pestalozzi and Warren Colburn."

Andrews, 1830, p. 18—Increase in the number of students and "order and general decorum became objects of favorable remark" both after the introduction of Lancastrian.

p. 44—Outsiders visit: "We never beheld a white school. . . . There was more order, and neatness of dress, and cleanliness of person. And the exercises were performed with a degree of promptness and accuracy which was surprising."

TEACHING THEORY FOR LANCASTRIAN PLAN: NOT EFFECTIVE

"But if we did not have to teach the curriculum, *what would we do with them?*" (Sarason, 1993, p. 42).

Productive Learning: Low

Reigart, 1916, p. 12—"All these little inventions keep children in a constant state of activity, prevent the listlessness so observable in all other institutions for education, and evince . . . a very original and observing mind in him who invented them."

p. 11—"So that there is always one boy reading, and twenty-nine writing and spelling at the same time; whereas, in the ancient method, the other twenty-nine did nothing."

p. 100—Chopping up subject matter, grading pupils based on memorization, universal practice.

p. 101—Monitors did the teaching, teacher no opportunity to "inculcate higher moral standards than those of the youthful monitors."

p. 41—"To facilitate learning a beginner was placed next to a child who had made some progress."

p. 50—Dictation: "It awakens the attention, excites intellectual activity and develops the dormant energies of children more effectually. The process is, itself, the best and most perfect drill for order."

Kaestle, 1973a, p. 184—Monitors instead of "developing, transforming, and almost creative power of an accomplished teacher."

Lancaster, 1973, pp. 50–51—If each boy has a book, how to be sure he is reading? "It will be seen in the article Reading, I do not approve of solitary reading, one by one; it has no emulation with it."

pp. 50–51—"The twentieth boy may read to the teacher, while the other nineteen are spelling words on the slate, instead of sitting idle. . . . If seven hundred boys were all in one room . . . they could all write and spell by this method. . . . The repetition of one word by the monitor serves to rivet it firmly on the minds."

p. 57—"They are required to read every word slowly and deliberately, pausing between each. They read long words in the same manner, only by syllables; thus, in reading the word, Composition, they would not read it at once, but by syllables. . . . This deliberate method is adapted to prevent those mistakes, which boys so often make in reading."

p. 46—Sand cheaper than books, other technology.

pp. 54–55—"I hope to see the day, when slates and slate-pencils will be more resorted to than they have heretofore been, and this afford to every poor child a cheap and ready medium of instruction, in spelling, writing, and arithmetic."

"Pouring in Knowledge" Theory: Low

Reigart, 1916, p. 7—Parrot-like dictation; simultaneous and draft instruction.

p. 100—Mechanical and memorize methods of learning.

pp. 49–50—"In the Lancastrian plans, dictation was employed in the teaching of spelling, reading, writing, and arithmetic."

pp. 54–55—Memorizing: nothing gained but an exercise in memory. Memorize and then recite the words: "This although a popular method, is one of the most inconsistent and absurd requisitions that was ever enforced on human beings."

p. 100—"The imparting of information rather than training in observation and eliciting of thought became the aim. There was developed a catechetical method of teaching which could readily be acquired by the monitor or by the unskilled teacher."

Kaestle, 1973b, p. 83—"Rigid and superficial"—there was a large population increase with no additional monies provided.

Lancaster, 1973, p. 73—"In the instance of dictating the figures 27,935, and any other variations after the same example, the scholars, by writing, acquire a thorough knowledge of Numeration, expressed both in words and figures, without paying any attention to it as a separate rule. In fact, Numeration is most effectually learned by the scholars in my institution, not from the study, but by the practice of it; and I may add, almost every other branch of knowledge, taught in the different classes, is acquired in the same easy and expeditious way."

Students as "Raw Materials" / Military Model: Low

Reigart, 1916, p. 101—Submission to authority; military organization in hands of child monitors. "Apart from obedience, order and cleanliness, the moral influence of the school was neutral or negative."

p. 46—"A place for everything, everything in its place" mechanical refinements that surpassed even those of the noted founder of the system.

p. 46—How the student should stand, hold a book, and so on.

p. 8—Governor Clinton compared Lancastrian system to labor-saving machinery.

p. 75—"Sydney Smith was astonished and delighted to find Lancaster's school a 'perfect machine,' made pleasant and interesting by 'an air of military arrangement.' . . . A very different estimate of the value of the monitorial machinery was made by educators who were able to see below the surface. 'In order to avoid expense, the National and Lancastrian Schools are taught by the boys themselves, the master being rather a governor than a teacher."

Riddle, 1905, p. 24—Human intellect could be molded into almost any shape; system of teaching whose only ability was to combine economy of expense with rapidity of instruction.

Kaestle, 1983, p. 43—"Inculcate not only the traditional values of hard work and obedience but would stress precision, standardization and elaborate routine."

Kaestle, 1973b, p. 164—The school a kind of machine—a positive connotation: "They thought of the technological advantages of automation." Factory was appropriate analogy for school organization.

Lancaster, 1973, pp. 107–108—Military style organization: "It is an important object to secure implicit obedience to those commands . . . seeing them instantly obeyed by the whole class. . . . A number of commands, trifling in appearance, but conducive to good order, are given by the monitors."

Personalized Learning: Medium/Low

Reigart, 1916, p. 100—"The faithful adherence to manuals or the syllabi prepared by school authorities rather than adaptations to the interests of the pupils and the community became the prime duty of the teacher."

p. 34—With the decline of the monitorial system this flexible system of grading and promotion was gradually replaced by the present class system."

Kaestle, 1973b, p. 165—"Content was broken down into small steps and promotion in one subject was independent of promotion in another, a procedure for individual progress that was lost with the introduction of graded schools after 1850."

Lancaster, 1973, pp. 31–32—Economy of time: "'Be careful of time,' says the philosopher, 'for time is the stuff life is made of.'"

pp. 42–43—"A boy who knows how to print . . . is placed by one who knows few . . . to assist him."

p. 93—"The drudgery of teachers is always greater or less, in proportion to the quickness or dullness of their scholars; but, in these modes of teaching all must exert themselves according to their abilities, or be idle."

Kaestle, 1973b, p. 83—"Lancaster, a young schoolmaster and converted Quaker, opened his first school in Southwark in 1798. By experimenting with student monitors and homogeneous grouping, he was able to increase the enrollment from about 60 to 1000 by 1805."

Kaestle, 1983, p. 43—"The Lancastrian school . . . 'allowed the pupils to advance according to their industry and application to their studies.' They 'were not held back by duller scholars,' he said, as is 'often the case under our present school system.'"

p. 41—"A child could proceed at his or her own rate in each subject."

Parental Inclusion: Low

Riddle, 1905, p. 31—"But the poorer classes, for whose education the country was compelled to pay, did not at all times agree with Clinton in looking upon this system as a 'blessing sent down from Heaven.'"

Andrews, 1830, p. 69—Order and system: "Much however depends upon the co-operation of the parents and guardians of the pupils, for it is greatly in their power either to aid or impede its salutary regulations."

Lancaster, 1973, p. 177—"The poor parent becomes sensible that something is amiss, but knows not what. 'Parent changes kid from one school to another and things get worse.' The want of system and order is almost uniform in every class of schools within the reach of the poor, whose indifferent attainments at school, often arise as much from equal impatience and unsettled disposition in their parents, as deficiency of care in the masters, or want of order in their schools."

Student Motivation: High/Medium

Reigart, 1916, p. 30—Learning less irksome by simplifying and facilitating progress; instruction more interesting by alternation and variety of exercise; keeps attention awake and interested, no idle time.

pp. 12–13—"All these little inventions keep children in a constant state of activity, prevent the listlessness so observable in all other institutions for education, and evince (trifling as they appear to be) a very original and observing mind in him who invented them." Punishment by shame instead of pain.

pp. 77–83—Forms of punishment: shame over infliction of pain, system of rewards. "To this conclusion the trustees of the schools were no doubt led by the discovery that the rewards fell into the hands of the strong and the cunning than the meritorious."

p. 90—Criticism of public exhibitions: "learning by rote, pieces which are far above their comprehension, and with the meaning of which, little or no pains are taken to make them acquainted."

Lancaster, 1973, pp. 89–90—"Every boy is placed next to one who can do as well or better than himself: his business is to excel him, in which case he takes precedence of him. In reading, every reading division has the numbers, 1, 2, 3, &c. to 12, suspended from their buttons. If the boy who wears number 12, excels the boy who wears number 11, he takes his place and number. . . . Thus, the boy which is number 12 . . . may be number 1, at the conclusion of it."

p. 94—Silver medals awarded for deserving students.

p. 97—Good monitors who improve their students become "commendable monitor."

Kaestle, 1983, p. 41—"Like traditional pedagogy, the monitorial system emphasized recitation, but now, due to the use of student monitors, children could be almost continuously engaged in active, competitive groups. The constant stimulation of monitorial instruction would increase motivation."

Lower-Class Students: High/Medium

Reigart, 1916, p. 1—Extend education to poor kids that religious schools are not reaching.

p. 3—Several attempts to reach the idleness and viciousness.

p. 13—Poor kids without Lancastrian: "The children of a large portion of the poor population were constantly left a prey to all the evils of ignorance and idleness, and were growing up in habits calculated to fit them for the tenatry of pauper and prison establishments."

p. 99—Education of poor was through churches.

p. 65—"The object, as stated, was to implant in the minds of such children the principles of religion and morality."

Cubberley, 1919, p. 133—"In place of their idleness, inattention, and disorder, Lancaster introduced activity, emulation, order, and a kind of military discipline which was of much value to the type of children attending these schools."

Lancaster, 1973, p. 165—Improvement of the education of the poor: "The number of children that attend a school of this class is very fluctuating . . . disorder, noise, &c. seem more the characteristic of these schools, than the improvement of the little ones."

p. 167—Poor children go to work at an early age; make education worthwhile for them; it is their only opportunity.

p. 168—"Their parents are of the lowest class, by conduct as well as poverty. . . . The improvement of children . . . greatly increased . . . under good regulations."

p. 169—"When the attention of children is occupied, quietness unavoidably follows, and that without the aid of rigour to enforce it."

Andrews, 1830, pp. 32–34—"That the Society, among its earliest acts, provided the means of instruction for the destitute children of color in the city of New York." The society was concerned with ending slavery, protecting free men from being kidnapped into slavery and education.

pp. 113–114—"Now, it is presumed, that a large portion of these poor children might, with proper care on the part of their friends, be sent to school, and, in all probability, by this means, be prevented from becoming inmates of the Bridewell, Penitentiary, or State Prison."

Riddle, 1905, p. 31—"But the poorer classes, for whom education the country was compelled to pay, did not at all times agree with Clinton in looking upon this system as a 'blessing sent down from Heaven.'"

Low IQ and Self-Fulfilling Prophecy: High/Medium

Reigart, 1916, p. 34—"With the decline of the monitorial system this flexible system of grading and promotion was gradually replaced by the present class system."

Kaestle, 1973b, p. viii (Cremin, 1961, said in introduction)—"Our schools have not escaped the preoccupation with classification and output that began with the monitorial school movement, for we still live in that age."

Andrews, 1830, p. 45—Audit visit report: "Those who believe, or effect to believe, that the African race are so far inferior to the whites, as to be incapable of any considerable degree of mental improvement, would not require stronger testimony of the unsoundness of their opinions."

THE TEACHING PROFESSION FOR
LANCASTRIAN PLAN: NOT EFFECTIVE

"Teaching is not a science, it is an art fusing ideas, obligations, the personal and interpersonal. The chemistry of that fusion determines whether or how subject matter matters to the student" (Sarason, 2004, p. 199).

Teacher Development: Low

Reigart, 1916, p. 7—Child monitors.

p. 100—A method of teaching developed that could "readily be acquired by the monitor or by the unskilled teacher."

p. 32—"Two sets of teaching monitors are chosen monthly from the advanced classes, who are employed in teaching the lower divisions in reading, spelling, definitions, arithmetic and sometimes geography; the teaching monitors who have performed these duties, are received into the recitation room for their own instruction; the classes also which they have taught one in larger divisions, at stated times, personally instructed by the principal, assistant principal, and paid monitors."

p. 46—"'A place for everything and everything in its place,' promi-
nently displayed in every school room, resulted in mechanical refinements
which surpassed even those of the noted founder."

p. 53—"So completely was the plan elaborated that 'any boy of eight
years old who can barely read writing, and numerate well, is by mean of the
guide containing sums, and the key thereto, qualified to teach the first four
rules of arithmetic, simple and compound, if the key is correct, with as
much accuracy as Mathematicians who have kept school for twenty years.'"

Kaestle, 1983, p. 41—"Furthermore, by training future teachers as
monitors at model Lancastrian schools and by providing elaborate manuals that explained procedures and lesson plans, the Lancastrian system
promised a virtual guarantee of teacher competence in an age when teachers' qualifications and reputations were low."

Riddle, 1905, p. 25—A teacher traveled all the way to Baltimore to see
Lancaster teach, but Lancaster did not allow other teachers to observe him
teaching.

The Unlearning Process—Unlearning Old Theories: Low

Cubberley, 1919, p. 133—Manuals of instruction.

Teacher Education Programs: Low

Reigart, 1916, p. 99—"The training, however, can hardly be compared
with that of the modern normal school. Six weeks practice as monitors
was deemed sufficient in insure proficiency. In the so-called normal
schools of the society none but academic subjects were taught, the professional training being secured solely from the routine of monitorial practice."

pp. 2–3—"Saturday and evening schools for the instruction of monitors
. . . were more successful, as attendance was compulsory. These schools
were known as 'Normal Schools' though no professional instruction was
given."

p. 91—New York, 1818—"With deep solicitude for diffusing the means
of education among the poor, and for the general extension of the Lancastrian system throughout the country, the trustees invite all those persons
who are desirous of obtaining a knowledge of this method of

instruction to repair to the schools under their charge, where in the space of six or eight weeks, a competent knowledge of the Lancastrian Methods of instruction can be obtained."

Riddle, 1905, p. 82—"Too much dependence was placed on the young and inexperienced beginners."

Lancaster, 1973, p. 64—"I have invented an entire new method of teaching arithmetic."

p. 68—Boys stand in groups of 12, and the monitor asks a boy a question—"How much are 9 and 4?"—and goes around until a boy gets the right answer.

Pedagogy: Low

Reigart, 1916, p. 15—Oral instruction and recitation questioned.

p. 94—Teachers could make no departures from the plans laid down in the by-laws and manuals.

p. 53—Addition taught by dictation of numbers; monitor read from key and inspected slates; greatest of Lancaster improvements according to Sydney Smith; anyone could teach the first four rules of arithmetic.

p. 94—"Teachers were forbidden to make any departure from the plans laid down in the by-laws and manuals."

p. 13—"So that, for the whole school of one thousand boys, there is only one master; the rest of the teaching is all done by the boys themselves."

Kaestle, 1973, p. 164—"Lancastrian system not only cheap and efficient 'it was also considered a more effective way to teach.'"

Lancaster, 1973, pp. 43–44—"The monitor first makes a letter on the sand. . . . The boy is then required to *retrace* over the same letter."

p. 45—"Another method of teaching the alphabet . . . large sheet of pasteboard suspended by a nail on the school wall; twelve boys, from the sand class, are formed into a circle round this alphabet."

p. 46—"It is not the monitor's business to teach, but to see the boys in his class or division teach each other."

p. 84—Lancaster developed keys and therefore: "On this plan, any boy who can read, can teach; and the inferior boys may do the work usually done by the teachers, in the common mode: for a boy who can read, can teach, ALTHOUGH HE KNOWS NOTHING ABOUT IT; and, in teaching, will imperceptibly acquire the knowledge he is destitute of, when he begins to teach, by reading."

Andrews, 1830, p. 73—"The value of the Monitorial System consists in facilitating, in an eminent degree, the business of instruction in the elementary branches of knowledge." Those who have advanced the most, teach the others (monitors).

Productive Teaching Defined: Low

Cubberley, 1919, p. 133—Manuals of instruction complete details "so that the final breakdown of the system in New York City, as elsewhere was due to faults inherent in the system itself. . . . These details teachers were forbidden to depart from, so that the final breakdown of the system in New York City, as elsewhere, was due to faults inherent in the system itself. By carefully studying and following these any person could soon learn to become a successful teacher in a monitorial school."

Lancaster, 1973, p. 58—"This method, also, accustoms the eye at once to read the syllables in every word. . . . For those who are apt to make blunders in learning to read, this mode will be found the best remedy. We are daily in the habit of speaking to each other. . . . Syllables are the component parts of words; those who can read syllables distinctly, will soon learn to combine them into words. Every sentence we express, is a combination of syllables and words."

Kaestle, 1973b, p. 164—"The Lancastrian system of instruction was efficient, both pedagogically and economically, and it demanded highly disciplined procedures."

p. 166—"By bringing the pupils into an obedient subordination, the school imposed order on chaos."

Kaestle, 1983, p. 41—"The highly regimented procedures would maintain order in huge schools as well as inculcate discipline."

Reigart, 1916, p. 9—"Lancaster was nearly overwhelmed by his success in attracting pupils. Necessity led him to utilize the boys who knew a little in teaching boys who knew less."

SCHOOL POWER AND POLITICS FOR LANCASTRIAN PLAN: SOMETIMES EFFECTIVE

"The icing on the cake of vexation was provided by my meetings with policymakers and politicians in Washington and elsewhere. I realized that, however sincere their intentions, they knew nothing about schools and why the school culture, honed over many decades, would resist and defeat reforms attempting to alter the status quo. There are no villains. There is a system. You can see and touch villains, you cannot see a system" (Sarason, 1998, p. 141).

Government Involvement: Medium

Reigart, 1916, p. 4—Slow evolution of tax money to schools.

p. 5—Lack of funds equal monitorial system.

p. 8—"Sydney Smith called George III's support of Lancaster the brightest passage in the history of his long reign. Other advocates: James Hill, Jeremy Bentham, the Duke of Bedford, Sydney Smith, DeWitt Clinton, Thomas Jefferson. . . . The system spread from the Thames to Ganges; it has encircled the equator; it has encompassed the poles; In New York City from 1806 to 1853, 600,000 children were instructed in Lancastrian schools."

p. 94—Adopted by Free School Society, primarily because of its cheapness.

p. 99—Cheapness of monitorial that communities gradually assumed expense of public education.

p. 22—Lancaster wrote a letter to President James Madison: "He ventures to urge the Lancastrian system of instruction as the solution of the Indian problem."

p. 65—"The non-sectarian character of the Lancastrian movement which aroused in England the bitter opposition of zealous partisans such as Mrs. Trimnar and the other supporters of Dr. Bell, serve at first to strengthen the Free School movement in NY and later to facilitate the final merging into the Public School System."

Cubberley, 1919, p. 129—Use of monitors, lack of funds: "The plan was so cheap, and so effective in teaching reading and the fundamentals of religion, that it soon provided England with a sort of a substitute for a national system of schools."

p. 132—"Between 1825 and 1836 the New York legislature passed 13 special acts for the incorporation of Monitorial high schools in the cities and counties of the state."

Riddle, 1905, p. 23—Lancaster met with George III; the plan spread throughout kingdom.

p. 24—Governor DeWitt Clinton: "a blessing sent down from heaven to redeem the poor and distressed."

p. 31—Lawmakers knew its weaknesses; would not replace until something better came along.

p. 34—Lancastrian system merged into free school system 1823 to 1838.

p. 38—General LaFayette visited and praised.

p. 49—Thaddeus Stevens supported it.

pp. 6–7 (Cordasco introduction)—Government support for education absent in the 18th century.

Kaestle, 1983, p. 41—"Lancaster's ideas were not profound, but they were timely. His system was cheap, efficient, and easy to implement."

Lancaster, 1973, p. 7—"It is a remarkable fact that during the whole of the eighteenth century the task of educating the English poor, as far as it was undertaken at all, was left to the different religious denominations, and to the benevolence of individuals and voluntary association without the smallest assistance from the Government."

p. 11—"Its cheapness, above all else, made it attractive to a society which was unwilling to support by taxation or other means a system of popular education."

The Middle-Class Ethic: Medium

Reigart, 1916, pp. 12–13—Punishment by shame instead of pain.

p. 94—Lancastrian alright for poor, Pestalozzian for private schools.

p. 71—Moral training for social and moral improvement.

p. 75—Keep boys busy and they will not get into trouble.

p. 77—Punishments and rewards.

Kaestle, 1973, p. vii—"Katz . . . has portrayed the system as the key element in the class-biased educational program of the New York Public School Society, attesting the Society's aim of ensuring 'social order through the socialization of the poor in cheap, mass schooling factories.'"

Kaestle, 1973b, p. 166—"By bringing the pupils into an obedient subordination, the school imposed order on chaos."

Kaestle, 1983, p. 41—"In an age when urban reformers worried about the moral education of the poor, the system promised to inculcate obedience, promptness, and industry."

p. 43—"Lancaster's methods did answer a new concern among educational spokesmen for moral education that would inculcate not only the traditional values of hard work and obedience but would stress precision, standardization, and elaborate routine."

Lancaster, 1973, pp. 183–184—Cannot educate the poor if the public does not want nor support it; public schooling for the poor, not to socialize in the vision of the elites: "It would be almost sure of success, if the active members of a society established for that purpose, were inclined to meet the poor as men, as brethren, as Christians, and the sincere teachers of youth: not with an intention to dictate to them, but to give additional force to their well-meant endeavours, and raise them to public esteem."

p. 185—Purpose of schooling: "The promotion of good morals; and the instruction of youth in useful learning, adapted to their respective situations."

p. 6 (Cordasco introduction)—"It was not the monitorial system of education which was controversial, or Joseph Lancaster. What was disputed was the education of the poor: its desirability, its form and its cost."

Andrews, 1830, p. 54—"Unquestionably, the most efficient means of promoting the moral improvement of this degraded portion of the human family, is the institution of schools."

School Bureaucracy: Low

Reigart, 1916, p. 3—School board set up, destroyed Public School Society (end of monitorial system).

p. 97—Monitorial system, long life owed to support of society.

Research and Development: Medium

Lancaster, 1973, p. 9 (Cordasco introduction)—"Lancaster whose school in Southwark, London, adopted basic monitorial principles when it opened in 1798. Although the techniques were very old (extending back to the efforts of John Brinsley [c. 1570–c. 1630], with evidences of the use of monitors in Elizabethan grammar schools), it was Lancaster who established in the monitorial system a practical and inexpensive method of instruction for poor children on a large scale. The term 'monitorial' derives from the practice of employing the older or more intelligent children to teach small groups of the other children and, indeed, it was an ancient technique."

Silent Axioms and Educational Policymakers: Medium

Reigart, 1916, p. 5—The friends supported Lancaster (over Bell) because nonsectarian.

p. 6—New York public schools John Griscom, marked factor in spreading monitorial schools throughout United States.

p. 98—"While it seems surprising that the monitorial system was so long maintained in New York, there is less occasion for criticism regarding the introduction of the system when there is taken into consideration the lack of educational facilities at the beginning of the nineteenth century, the crude methods employed, and public indifference towards the education of the masses in all the great cities of Europe and America."

p. 3—"Other denominations also opposed the Society's maintenance of a monopoly of public education in the city."

p. 94—Educational policymakers believed the Lancastrian plan suitable for adapting charity schools to it; elite schools, Pestalozzian.

Lancaster, 1973, p. 55—Keeping all students active by buying one book in large print and nailing each page to the wall. Then, 12–30 or more students stood and learned from one page. Only one book is needed, and money is saved. The plan keeps all students busy and is supported because it saves money.

Andrews, 1830, p. 55—"We are convinced that the instruction and right education of the children of the African race, will do more to advance the cause of universal emancipation than all other means put together."

Riddle, 1905, pp. 32–33—"While there seems to be no record of this committee's findings, the grand jury reported very favorably on the condition of the school at a subsequent sitting." None of the committee was familiar with the Lancastrian plan, but "the fact that they were men of standing and character in their respective localities, was no doubt all-sufficient to render their report highly satisfactory to court and jury."

Kaestle, 1973b—"NY leaders were attracted by the detailed plans of Lancaster, which could be infinitely duplicated. NY became the American Mecca for monitorial school enthusiasts."

p. 83—"Eventually the system became widely criticized for its rigidity and superficiality; but the population was increasing rapidly and the poor were increasing faster than the population. Thus, per capita resources for schooling were reduced while the social need for education became more intense. Lancaster offered a panacea for this dilemma."

Lancaster, 1973, p. 6—"It was not the monitorial system of education which was controversial, or Joseph Lancaster. What was disputed was the education of the poor: its desirability, its form, and its cost."

Appendix B: The Age-Graded Plan

CHANGE THEORY FOR AGE-GRADED PLAN: SOMETIMES EFFECTIVE

"**I** predicted that as it was being conceived and implemented educational reform would go nowhere" (Sarason, 2002, p. 178).

The Encapsulated Classroom and School: Low

Martin, 1972, p. 29—One-room schoolhouse; older students helping younger students; the children are all different; "some things than he is in others."

Mann, 1844, p. 84—"The first element of superiority in a Prussian school, and one whose influence extends throughout the whole subsequent course of instruction, consists in the proper classification of the scholars. In all places where the numbers are sufficiently large to allow it, the children are divided according to ages and attainments; and a single teacher has the charge only of a single class."

Messerli, 1972, p. 341—Textbooks helped shape graded instruction: "William Holmes McGuffey devised an incredibly popular series of reading books of graduated difficulty. At last teachers finally had the means for arranging their pupils according to a Procrustean classification of grades. . . . A rationally managed system made possible predictable outcomes and a closer control over input and output. Change, spontaneity, creativity, and individual differences were sacrificed."

"Unquestioned Bedrock Assumptions" Questioned: Low

Bernhard, 1988, p. 144—Age-grading detrimental to adult life.

Mann, 1844, p. 84—Classification of scholars, based on textbooks.

p. 60—"I saw many Lancastrian or Monitorial schools in England. . . . One must see the difference, between the hampering, blinding, misleading instruction given by an inexperienced child, and the developing, transforming, and almost creative power of an accomplished teacher."

Axiomatic Change—Out of the Box: Medium

Messerli, 1972, p. 347—"Mann never envisioned that graded instruction could also mean a mind-numbing regimentation as repressive as anything accomplished by the Boston masters, nor did he expect that children someday would spend one-sixth of their most formative years, in an environment of cells and bells."

Intractability of Schools: Medium

Goodlad and Anderson, 1987, p. xxxv—"The larger the schooling enterprise became, the more accepted and intractable the graded system became."

Ongoing Research and Development: High/Medium

Anderson, 1993, p. 10—No research supporting "segregating students by age and providing them with a standard curriculum."

M. B. Katz, 2001, p. 56—"Graded school systems had still more benefits. . . . High school would raise inadequate educational attainment of the children. . . . Pupils would strive for the prestige of success in the entrance examinations, and teachers would strive for the prestige of having successful pupils." Also, separating older and younger kids eliminates a great deal of discipline problems.

Bernhard, 1988, p. 149 — Piaget's thoughts lend support to age segregation: "Surely if our sole interest in the education of children is to develop their intellectual abilities as efficiently as possible, it makes sense to segregate them on the basis of age."

p. 17 — Humans have been foragers for 99% of their existence.

Anderson and Pavan, 1993, p. 100 — Torrance plan data showed older kids learned just as much or more in multi-age groupings; "re-visiting material already mastered and reorganizing it in their own mind in order to 'teach it.'"

Teachers as Reform Leaders: Medium

Cubberley, 1919, p. 232 — "The waste in maintaining two duplicate schools in the same building, each covering the same two or three years of school work, when by re-sorting the pupils the work of each teacher could be made more specialized and the pupils better taught, was certain to become obvious as soon as school supervision by teachers began to supersede school organization by laymen."

Lang's Five Assumptions: Low

1. Outside agent. Tyack, 1974, p. 44 — "From Horace Mann in Massachusetts to Calvin Stowe in Ohio to John Pierce in Michigan, leading common school crusaders urged communities to replace the heterogeneous grouping of students with a systematic plan of gradation based on the Prussian model."
2. Parents and community involved in the change. M. B. Katz, 1971, p. 35 — Taking local control away from the communities and creating a school bureaucracy, more efficient. Bernhard, 1988, p. 128 — "The modern educational environment — large in size, isolated from family life, specialized and segregated — cannot tolerate anything like the full range of learning styles and activities that constitute the human evolutionary heritage."
3. Motivate students and families.
4. Power relationships altered. M. B. Katz, 1971, pp. 35–36 — Taking power from local communities and creating a school bureaucracy, with a superintendent at the top of the power structure.

5. Less discontinuity between school and nonschool. Bernhard, 1988, p. 120—"Social involvement in the elementary school is pretty weak. But being in an elementary school is like being in a hunting-and-gathering band compared with what comes next." p. 144—Age-graded detrimental to preparation for adult life.

Past Reforms' Research: Medium

Tyack, 2003, p. 124—One-room schools deemed inefficient; "Urban educators . . . built a graded system of instruction in which academic standards were clear and challenging, instruction was uniform."

M. B. Katz, 2001, p. 55—District system, educators thought "unsound": "In most district schools children of all ages were taught in one room by one teacher. Throughout the pre-Civil War period educators argued that this was an inefficient method of instruction and that children would acquire a better education in graded schools. . . . Both younger and older children suffered, and the harried teacher was unable to do anything effectively. . . . Graded schools, in which students of the same age worked together and stimulated each other, were a more effective and efficient pedagogical device."

TEACHING THEORY FOR THE
AGE-GRADED PLAN: NOT EFFECTIVE

"But if we did not have to teach the curriculum, *what would we do with them?*" (Sarason, 1993, p. 42).

Productive Learning: Medium

B. F. Brown, 1963, p. 224—"The textbook publishers will take a back seat to the curriculum researchers in determining what our students will read and learn."

Goodlad and Anderson, 1987, p. xxxiii—ethnology, anthropology, educational history, and research; age segregation is not necessary or natural; "worse, it appears to have far more negative than positive consequences."

p. xxxiii—Pratt found "whereas same-age groups create increased competition and aggression, multiage groups promote increased harmony and nurturance."

p. 3—"The realities of child development defy the rigorous ordering of children's abilities and attainments into conventional graded structure."

Messerli, 1972, p. 346—"In attempting to broaden and systematize the function of schooling, and create a uniformity of what took place in the classrooms of the Commonwealth, he was inadvertently narrowing the concept of education. To create an educational ecology of formalism was to risk sacrificing many of the imaginative, spontaneous, poetic, and aesthetic indigenous lessons to be experienced in the emerging American culture."

Mann, 1844, p. 85—Teach to stimulate all five senses: "much easier to keep the eye and hand and mind at work together, than it is to employ either one of them separately from the others."

p. 84—"The first element of superiority in a Prussian school . . . the proper classification of scholars. . . . The children are divided according to ages and attainments; and a single teacher has the charge only of a single class."

Bernhard, 1988, p. 149—"Piaget's thought lends authority to the separation of children into age-groups during their educational experiences. If children in a particular stage are *incapable* of understanding certain concepts or performing certain kinds of operations, it follows that in school they should be grouped together in terms of the stages of their development."

p. 149—"Develop their intellectual abilities as efficiently as possible, it makes sense to segregate . . . [by] age."

p. 179—"An evolutionary perspective also makes it clear that, in order for children to learn naturally, they need to have consistent yet varied adult models."

Tyack, 1974, p. 202—"'Retardation' was manmade, of course, an educational artifact. The classification of pupils was not divinely inspired or imbedded in the order of nature; much less were the curriculum and standards of promotion unalterable."

"Pouring in Knowledge" Theory: Low

B. F. Brown, 1963, p. 18—Muscle mental theory and gifted education; gestalt psychology.

Anderson, 1993, p. 10—"Graded schools, with its overloaded, text-book-dominated curriculum, and its relatively primitive assumptions about human development and learning."

Martin and Harrison, 1972, p. 12—"The curriculum is still packaged for instruction despite the evidence that decades of graded lessons have failed to reach or teach the great diversity among children even of the same age."

Students as "Raw Materials": Low

Martin, 1972, p. 31—"Putting children of the same age together into a classroom is an artificial social event encountered only in schools."

Goodlad and Anderson, 1987, p. xxi—Age-graded, lockstep, and rigid curriculum based on age.

Tyack, 2003, p. 104—"Gradation of classes became popular in large part because it promised the efficiency of the division of labor common in factories. . . . Educators arranged the curriculum into standardized parts that corresponded with the grades, year by year."

Messerli, 1972, p. 342—Mann believed tighter supervision and centralization needed: "He thought of children not as individuals but as masses of pupils or an entire generation to be trained."

p. 341—"Thus, as in the production of material goods, so in the education of children, the entire nation would experience a shift from *Gemeinschaft* to *Gesellschaft*."

Bernhard, 1988, p. 154—"In both primate and nomadic foraging societies, youngsters grow and learn in a framework of intimate relationships between subsistence and sociality. . . . Children *must* have adult models, and the point is that they *do* have them whether or not the adults like it."

Personalized Learning: Low

Martin, 1972, p. 15—"For more than one hundred years the organization of children into grades has inhibited the behaviors necessary for children to learn as individuals."

p. 29—"The one-room school forced the teacher to cater to the differences within each child."

p. 30—"Why, after forty years' advocacy of individualization of instruction, is it so difficult to find . . . evidence that what there is to learn has been effectively tailored to individual children?"

p. 31—One-room older kids helped manage younger ones.

p. 32—One-room classroom students help each other; graded classroom, this is known as cheating.

Goodlad and Anderson, 1987, p. 1—"The quick are compressed and contracted to fit the grade. In time, they learn to adapt to a pace that is slower than their natural one."

p. 3—A typical first-grade classroom has a span of 4 years.

p. 21—"We believe that abolition of grade barriers frees each child, whatever his ability, to move forward in his learning as rapidly and as smoothly as possible. But we also believe that such structure is in harmony with his social and emotional well-being."

Bernhard, 1988, p. 118—Children's biological needs not met in school; "Must socialization in a modern industrial culture work against children's natural inclinations and needs to be successful? If not, how may we change the environment of the school? If so, what may we learn about our society from the way we treat our children?"

Hunter (from Morgenstern, 1966)—All children grow and learn at different rates. "Materials that are inappropriate or improperly or partially learned are not only wasteful in themselves but they interfere with previous and future learning." "Wasteful to ask a child who has achieved a learning objective to idle his intellectual motor while the rest of the group catches up to him."

Parental Inclusion: Not Applicable

No evidence noted.

Student Motivation: Medium/Low

M. B. Katz, 2001, p. 56—"Most educators . . . competition was necessary as a stimulus. . . . Competition with oneself would produce an equal amount of effort without harmful social implications, without reinforcing the enervating and disastrous competition characteristic of a materialistic society. Intra-personal was the type of competition encouraged in graded schools."

Lower-Class Students: Low

B. F. Brown, 1963, p. 222 — "Students of all socio-economic backgrounds will be the realistic concern of the schools. A breakthrough in keeping all students in school longer will come when more guidance counselors are a part of the school staff. When the schools' ungraded program allows culturally disadvantaged youngsters to be a part of a special program geared to their previous experiences and unique needs, a major hurdle will have been cleared."

Anderson and Pavan, 1993, p. 11 — "It appears a nongraded environment especially benefits boys, blacks, underachievers, and students from lower socioeconomic groups, with the benefits increasing the longer that children remain in that environment".

Tyack, 2003, p. 107 — "The uniform graded school may have been efficient for the majority of students. . . . But for vast numbers — especially impoverished immigrants and blacks — the system was geared to produce failure."

Low IQ and Self-Fulfilling Prophecy: Medium/Low

B. F. Brown, 1963, p. 221 — "The ungraded school is a common-sense approach for differences between and within people. Some youngsters are able at mathematics and poor in social science, or vice versa."

Goodlad and Anderson, 1987, p. 1 — "The slow are pulled and stretched to fit the grade" (Procrustes, Greek mythology, made the visitors fit the size of the bed).

pp. 3–4 — Mental age important.

p. 8 — "The achievement range begins to approximate the range in intellectual readiness to learn soon after first-grade children are exposed to reasonably normal school instruction."

p. 9 — Data suggest two major generalizations: First, spread of intellectual readiness (mental age) grows as children go to second year of school;

second, "spread in achievement in the various subject areas also grows greater, closely approximating the spread of mental age."

Tyack, 2003, p. 106—Normal students were those who advanced at the regular graded school pace: "The student who flunked the promotion exam was held back and considered to be 'retarded,' or 'laggard,' a failure."

Tyack, 1974, p. 199—"In an age that worshipped efficiency, over-aged students and school leavers were signs of malfunction. . . . Besides the waste of money and effort, forcing children to repeat grades was inhuman."

TEACHING PROFESSION FOR
AGE-GRADED PLAN: NOT EFFECTIVE

"Teaching is not a science, it is an art fusing ideas, obligations, the personal and interpersonal. The chemistry of that fusion determines whether or how subject matter matters to the student" (Sarason, 2004, p. 199).

Teacher Development: Low

B. F. Brown, 1963, p. 225—Internships for teachers' psychology of learning; less emphasis on history of American education; "increased salaries will contribute to general interest in teaching as a career"; merit pay.

Goodlad and Anderson, 1987, p. 204—"Unprecedented numbers of pupils pouring into the schools during the second half of the [19th] century." The division of subjects and so forth "simplified the task of preparing needed teachers quickly."

The Unlearning Process: Low

No evidence noted.

Teacher Education Programs: High/Medium

Goodlad and Anderson, 1987, p. 47—Rise of normal schools helped spread the graded structure; 1836, McGuffey Reader.

Pedagogy: High/Medium

B. F. Brown, 1963, p. 222—"Teachers will spend more time listening. . . . The teacher will make appropriate learning prescriptions to get at increased knowledge."

Cubberley, 1919, p. 229—"It began by the employment of assistant teachers, known as 'ushers,' to help the 'master,' and the provision of small recitation rooms, off the main large room, for their use in hearing recitations."

Tyack, 1974, p. 44—"In the one-room school, or its inflated urban counterparts containing 200 or more pupils of varying advancement, the instructor hardly had time to teach, so varied were the tasks he faced."

Messerli, 1972, p. 341—Textbooks helped shape graded school structure, William Holmes McGuffey: "At last teachers finally had the means for arranging their pupils according to a Procrustean classification of grades . . . a rationally managed system made possible predictable outcomes and a closer control over input and output. Change, spontaneity, creativity, and individual differences were sacrificed."

Productive Teaching Defined: Medium/Low

Goodlad and Anderson, 1987, p. 47—"Concept of progressively more difficult instructional material is bad."

p. 59—"But when he does understand what nongrading permits . . . more creative teaching . . . select a range of books without concern for their grade level . . . need not worry about the fact that Tommy's reading is so far in advance of his arithmetic."

p. 59—No fear of failing students not up to grade standard; better analysis of individual students' progress with ability.

Mann, 1844, p. 84—More orderly: "While attending to the recitation of one, his mind is constantly called off, to attend to the studies and the conduct of all the others. . . . All these difficulties are at once avoided by a suitable classification."

p. 60—"One must see the difference, between the hampering, blinding, misleading instruction given by an inexperienced child, and the developing, transforming, and almost creative power of an accomplished teacher."

Tyack, 1974, p. 44—"Methods of discipline, teaching style, school furniture, and intellectual content should be adjusted to the maturity of pupils, and this could be done only where the children were properly classified."

p. 45—"The teacher's time and talents being concentrated upon certain work, it becomes easier by repetition, and, therefore, is likely to be performed more efficiently."

SCHOOL POWER AND POLITICS FOR THE AGE-GRADED PLAN: SOMETIMES EFFECTIVE / NOT EFFECTIVE

"The icing on the cake of vexation was provided by my meetings with policymakers and politicians in Washington and elsewhere. I realized that, however sincere their intentions, they knew nothing about schools and why the school culture, honed over many decades, would resist and defeat reforms attempting to alter the status quo. There are no villains. There is a system. You can see and touch villains, you cannot see a system" (Sarason, 1998, p. 141).

Government Involvement: High/Medium

B. F. Brown, 1963, p. 223—"The schools of the future will be assisted by more state and federal money, requirements and advisory counseling."

Cubberley, 1919, p. 238—Chicago: "In 1853 the city council appointed a city superintendent of schools to unify the work done in the districts. He at once graded and reorganized the instruction, and introduced uniform records and textbooks."

p. 304—"Boston offers a good illustration of the beginnings of school grading, out of many that might be cited. . . . In addition to the division of the schools horizontally into Primary Schools and English Grammar Schools, and the subdivision of the latter vertically into writing and reading schools, a beginning of classification and the grading of pupils had been made, by 1823, by the further subdivision of the reading school into four classes."

pp. 309–310—"The next step in the evolution of the graded system was the division of each school into classes. . . . It began by the employment of assistant teachers, known as 'ushers,' to help the 'master,' and usually the provision of small recitation rooms."

p. 311—"The third and final step in the evolution of the graded system was to build larger schools with smaller classrooms, or to subdivide the larger rooms . . . sort and grade the pupils, and outline the instruction by years; and the class system was at hand."

Tyack, 1974, p. 44—"But it fell to a practical man, John Philbrick, actually to provide a concrete model for his urban colleagues. Philbrick knew that educational function necessarily reflected architectural form. He convinced the Boston school board, therefore, that the proper classification of pupils required a new kind of building . . . 'egg-crate school.' . . . Every teacher had a separate classroom. . . . And thus was stamped on mid-century America not only the graded school, but also the pedagogical harem."

The Middle-Class Ethic: Medium/Low

Anderson, 1993, p. 10—"Educators and business leaders to continue viewing the tax-supported public school system largely as a funnel for producing unskilled workers at a time when there are no longer an abundance of jobs available."

Messerli, 1972, p. 348—"As in other opinions, Emerson [Ralph Waldo] preferred to meditate and write rather than act. Many of his contemporaries, on the other hand, preferred to follow an idea or movement rather than listen to a critique. Hence, they were ready to march behind the new organizational banners which Mann had unfurled."

School Bureaucracy: Medium/Low

Goodlad and Anderson, 1987, p. 46—Mann visited Germany in 1843.
Tyack, 2003, pp. 103–104—Making schools uniform and graded produced "laggards." "They wanted to avoid the haphazard and diverse character of rural schools."

Tyack, 1974, p. 44—"Crucial to educational bureaucracy was the objective and efficient classification, or 'grading,' of pupils. In 1838, Henry Barnard first gave his lecture . . . which he would repeat in more than fifty cities. . . . He maintained that a classroom containing students of widely varying ages and attainment was not only inefficient but also inhumane."

Research and Development: Medium/Low

Anderson, 1993, p. 10—"Most of the studies show neutral or inconclusive outcomes when graded and nongraded groups are compared, but results favoring the nongraded approach are growing in both quantity and quality."

Martin, 1972, p. 30—Graded school and one-room schoolhouse "required contrary learning patterns."

Goodlad and Anderson, 1987, p. 2—There is overwhelming evidence for nongraded schooling.

p. 3—Graded hierarchy, teachers get frustrated and so do students; parents disappointed.

p. 46—"The factory system superseded the craftsman, bringing to industry the mass production of the assembly line. . . . The graded system was to provide an orderly means of classifying the many young people who were to come to school as a result of increased public interest in schooling."

p. 47—The textbook "had its own considerable influence on the movement toward graded structure."

p. 69—Age graded: "Sometimes lost in the discussion of graded organization is the fact that an artificial and unnatural homogeneity of chronological age and academic experience is engendered by the arrangement of one-grade-per-class"; unhealthy attitude created toward other age groups, especially toward younger kids.

p. 226—"A compatibility between the nongraded structure and continuous pupil progress, longitudinal curriculum development, and integrated learning becomes obvious."

Bernhard, 1988, p. 128—"Students in school are segregated by age to such an extent that the mixed-age groupings that occur naturally in foraging societies are impossible. . . . A world in which children are categorized according to age and grade is highly artificial, and children's gradual perception of these segregations and hierarchies as normal makes it all the more difficult for them to learn normally."

Anderson and Pavan, 1993, p. 98—"From an evolutionary perspective, age-homogeneity is not only unnatural but perhaps even destructive."

p. 98—Age-graded neither natural or universal: "It is a relatively recent phenomenon in the human experience, and 'runs counter to the pattern of upbringing of the young which previously existed for millions of years.'"

p. 98—"We gain a strong impression that the much-publicized failure of American schools could well be traced at least in large measure to the unnatural conditions imposed upon children by age segregation."

Silent Axioms and Educational Policymakers: High/Medium

Anderson, 1993, p. 10—"Born of administrative practicality and puritanical traditions"; Horace Mann got it from Prussia.

Cubberley, 1919, pp. 223–224—"The early courses of study adopted for the cities of the time reveal the same studies in the schools, as well as the beginnings of the classification of the pupils on the basis of the difficulty of the subjects. . . . Though ungraded in character, the beginnings of a grading of schools is nevertheless evident."

p. 311—"The greatest impetus to the establishment of this graded-class organization came from Horace Mann's Seventh Annual Report, in 1844, on the graded school system of Prussia. . . . The transition to the graded system, it is seen, came naturally and easily. . . . By the time of the beginnings of state and city school supervision the school systems of the cities only awaited the touch of an educational organizer to transform them from a series of differentiated and largely independent schools into a series of graded schools that could be organized into a unified system, with a graded course of study."

Appendix C: The Gary Plan

CHANGE THEORY FOR THE
GARY PLAN: SOMETIMES EFFECTIVE

Sarason, 2002, p. 178—"I predicted that as it was being conceived and implemented educational reform would go nowhere."

Levine, 2002, p. 52—1920s school systems struggled with burgeoning student enrollment, and platooning promised a way to accommodate the increased number of students.

The Encapsulated Classroom and School: Medium

Hartwell, 1916, p. 54—Special work, play, and classroom; "initial motivation . . . attack the seat-bound academic formalism that . . . bored children."

Elwell, 1976, p. 192—Swimming pools.

Bourne, 1970, p. 222—Gary plan ideologies expressed, but the school leaders "leave the teaching staff largely to realize these aims in their own way."

p. 240—"Unfortunately, many of the teachers have not been at Gary long enough to catch the spirit, some who sympathize with its spirit have not been effectively assisted to abandon or modify their former habits. . . . Many teachers at Gary are not doing so well as they have previously done under other conditions." No guarantees that the encapsulated classrooms for the three *R*s changed.

Bourne, 1970 (Levine, 2002, footnote regarding Flexner and Bachman), p. 237—Brick-and-mortar innovation much easier than program innovation. "The development of Community Mental Health Centers, which do more of the same, offering 'old wine in new bottles,' is a case in point in the field other than education."

"Unquestioned Bedrock Assumptions" Questioned: Medium

Elwell, 1976, p. 17—Eight hours a day, six days a week, learning art, music, crafts, entertainment, and the three *R*s.

Levine, 2002, p. 52—The school a miniature community (Dewey).

Axiomatic Change—Out of the Box: Medium

Elwell, 1976, p. 17—Work, study, play.

Levine, 2002, p. 52—Vocational education, art and literature, and recreation.

Bourne, 1970, p. 158—"'This is the age,' says Superintendent Wirt, 'of the engineer, of machinery, and of big business. The school business enterprises offer a type of industrial and commercial education facilities . . . adapted to modern industry and business. There are big business problems and machinery problems in the school.'"

Intractability of Schools: Medium/Low

Gary—Wirt started from scratch, still did not last; people not convinced in Gary after his death in 1938.

Levine, 2002, p. 55—Detroit teachers go along and afraid to voice disapproval of plan (but really against it). Teacher complaints about discipline in platoon schools.

Bourne, 1970, p. 149—"It must be remembered that the Gary plan postulates an educational philosophy different from that of the ordinary public schools. Teachers trained in schools managed with rigid administrative and disciplinary methods naturally find adjustment difficult in a system which repeatedly calls upon them for initiative, alters their relations to the pupils, and requires a more practical attitude of 'application' toward the subject-matter of instruction."

Ongoing Research and Development: Medium

Elwell, 1976, p. 20—Unflattering Rockefeller funded report.

p. 20—"No systemized means for determining whether or not its innovations were working." Some changes based on research.

Bourne, 1970, p. 156—"Whether it is to be his vocation or not, the Gary school believes that such work is a good thing in the education of all children."

Teachers as Reform Leaders: Low

N/A (Teachers did not serve as reform leaders since the reform started prior to their arrival in Gary.)—Wirt began the school system with the platoon school plan.

Ravitch, 1988, p. 228—In New York City, "by acting imperiously and not building broad support for the plan, they failed to get public approval."

Lang's Five Assumptions: Medium

1. Outside agent—Wirt, positive.
2. Parents and community involved in the change, negative.
3. Motivate students and families, postive/negative; the extras create community involvement, but the teaching and learning aspects still not inclusive.
4. Power relationships altered, negative.
5. Less discontinuity between school and nonschool, positive.

Bourne, 1970, p. xlii—"Many of the children and their parents had but the vaguest ideas of the Gary plan goals."

Past Reforms' Research: Medium/Low

Power relationships altered theoretical framework of reform.
  Dewey.
  Not observed.

TEACHING THEORY FOR THE
GARY PLAN: SOMETIMES EFFECTIVE

"But if we did not have to teach the curriculum, *what would we do with them?*" (Sarason, 1993, p. 42).

Productive Learning: Medium

Hartwell, 1916, p. 26—Physical training.

Cremin, 1961, p. 101—Granville Stanley Hall, John Dewey, William Wirt (Dewey was Hall's student at Johns Hopkins, and Wirt was Dewey's at Chicago).

p. 103—Child-centered school.

Callahan, 1962, p. 162—Child centered.

Elwell, 1976, p. 20—"Designed for education of whole child."

Bourne, 1970, p. 173—"Children learn by watching and asking questions—'picking up'—in the most natural way in the world, in contrast to the formal and stilted ways of the traditional classroom work."

"Pouring in Knowledge" Theory: Medium/Low

Elwell, 1976, p. 20—Rockefeller student found old-fashioned teaching methods still being used.

Bourne, 1970 p. 241 (Flexner and Bachman)—"But departmentalization tends in a measure to interfere with the direct use of literature, science, and games as means of making the three R's less formal and more appealing."

p. 244—"Little attention was devoted to meaning or use. Only once in the classes observed were children required to re-tell the story or to summarize the main points of the narration after the reading."

p. 247—Learning liquid measure: "But there was nothing for the children to measure; they merely looked at the measures, observing their relative sizes."

Students as "Raw Materials": Low

If operating under a business model, then it is hard to stay away from the concept of students as raw materials.

Levine, 2002, p. 53—Good example of scientific management and efficient plant use.

Personalized Learning: Medium

Wirt believed in Dewey's "school is life."

Elwell, 1976, p. 17—Play, gardening, nature study. Lockers: seen by some as the trademark of the Gary plan.

Bourne, 1970, pp. 228–229—Some students extra time in gym and less time in three *R*s.

Parental Inclusion: Medium/Low

Elwell, 1976, p. 20—Adult classes in the evenings (large numbers of non-English-speaking immigrants).

Bourne, 1970, p. 164—The Gary plan makes the school the social center of the community.

Student Motivation: Medium/Low

Constructivist teaching methods.

Hartwell, 1916, p. 26—Physical training.

Cremin, 1961, p. 59—"Democratic principles to school conduct and discipline."

Lower-Class Students: Medium

Hartwell, 1916, p. 11—Ohio compulsory education laws.

p. 14—"[Wirt's] attempt to . . . meet the . . . needs of many differing classes."

Bourne, 1970, pp. xii–xiii—"The Gary system provided for diverse interests and aptitudes and tried to prevent the failure of children who could not perform well in the usual schools' circumscribed and prescribed program."

Low IQ and Self-Fulfilling Prophecy: Medium/Low

Cremin, 1961, p. 186—Binet IQ testing.

Bourne, 1970, p. xii—Provide for and prevent failure of children who are not performing well in the school's circumscribed and prescribed program.

TEACHING PROFESSION FOR THE GARY PLAN: NOT EFFECTIVE

"Teaching is not a science, it is an art fusing ideas, obligations, the personal and interpersonal. The chemistry of that fusion determines whether or how subject matter matters to the student" (Sarason, 2004, p. 199).

Teacher Development: Medium/Low

Levine, 2002, p. 54—Departmentalization benefits teachers.

p. 55—Schools about teachers, too.

Bourne, 1970, p. 151—Departmentalization, grade teachers do not have to worry about teaching subjects such as music and drawing; "enables them to concentrate on the subjects which interest them, rather than diffuse their attention among many."

p. 157—"An undemocratic and invidious distinction between the manual worker and the brain worker."

p. xlii—"There were legitimate grievances, which the Gary supporters had tried to deny. The program was installed with inadequate preparation of facilities, and before teachers and principals had been properly trained."

The Unlearning Process—Unlearning Old Theories: Low

Bourne, 1970, p. 238 (Flexner and Bachman) —"We have said that thoroughgoing reform can proceed only as a new body of teaching material is developed and teachers of a new type are trained."

p. 240—"Unfortunately, many of the teachers have not been at Gary long enough to catch the spirit; some who sympathize with its spirit have not been effectively assisted to abandon or modify their former habits; in consequence, despite some excellent work, which we do not overlook, many teachers at Gary are probably not doing so well as they have previously done under other conditions."

Teacher Education Programs: Low

Bourne, 1970, p. 239 (Flexner and Bachman)—"Even teachers trained in the most cut and dried fashion have in large numbers been aroused to the futility of abstract drill in grammar and arithmetic and to the uselessness of a mechanical grind in geography and history."

Pedagogy: Medium/Low

Hartwell, 1916, p. 52—"Enrichment of courses of study . . . overloaded pedagogically . . . more efficient in concentrating energy."

p. 77—Regrouping of teachers into regular and special teachers.

Elwell, 1976, p. 20—Teacher specialization by subject.

Bourne, 1970, p. 153—"The emphasis on discussion rather than formal recitation, even takes a certain amount of actual teaching out of the hands of the teachers. . . . The teacher, as in the Montessori method, becomes the guide and mentor rather than direct preceptor."

p. 173—"The 'helper and observer' system, applied not only in the relations between children, but between teachers, and between teachers inside the school and visitors, is one of the most valuable features of the Gary plan."

Productive Teaching Defined: Medium/Low

Specific goals for student motivation, skill development, lifelong learning.

Elwell, 1976, p. 21—One-hour-per-day auditorium program can address the chair and organize their thoughts.

Bourne, 1970, p. 222—"Assistant superintendents, supervisors, etc. lay out plans and ideals based on Gary plan ideology and leave it to teachers to realize the aims in their own way."

SCHOOL POWER AND POLITICS FOR THE GARY PLAN: SOMETIMES EFFECTIVE / NOT EFFECTIVE

"The icing on the cake of vexation was provided by my meetings with policymakers and politicians in Washington and elsewhere. I realized that, however sincere their intentions, they knew nothing about schools and why the school culture, honed over many decades, would resist and defeat reforms attempting to alter the status quo. There are no villains. There is a system. You can see and touch villains, you cannot see a system" (Sarason, 1998, p. 141).

Government Involvement: Medium

Hartwell, 1916, p. 21—Money, space better utilized.

    p. 20—20% savings.

    p. 51—Divide all children into two platoons.

Cohen and Mohl, 1979, p. 36—New York City only interested for money, tarnished image of Gary plan.

Bourne, 1970, p. xxiii—"Compulsory school attendance laws, often passed in conjunction with child labor regulations, brought all children into the schools and attempted to keep them there."

    p. xxx—1906, Wirt impressed the mayor and the three school board members—a civil engineer, a surveyor, and a railroad engineer.

    p. xlii—Houghton Mifflin made large financial contributions to the Mitchel campaign for New York City; Mayor Mitchel supported the Gary plan in New York City because of the potential savings. He believed that more students could be educated at less expense.

The Middle-Class Ethic: Medium/Low

Ravitch, 1988, p. 228—Segregated like other schools.

Bourne, 1970, p. xxv—"As the immigrants poured into the cities, the schools' problems increased. The schools were inadequate for the discipline, health, and delinquency problems and evidences of family disorganization that came to their direct attention."

School Bureaucracy: Medium/Low

Elwell, 1976, p. 21—Wirt in complete charge during 31 years. He criticized New Deal, and his reputation suffered as a result.

Cohen and Mohl, 1979, p. 15—Hierarchical bureaucracy kept to a minimum.

Research and Development: Medium/Low

Bourne, 1970, p. xxiv—"The demand for change was expressed in an idiom quite familiar to our present day. Schools were to become more relevant to the conditions of modern industrial life."

p. xxx—"Wirt showed how his plan could produce more classes at a lower cost, while including innovative features in curriculum and methods, in school building, and in the relationships of the schools to other community resources."

Silent Axioms and Educational Policymakers: Low

Like Gary because of money saved (two times the number of pupils accommodated).

Bourne, 1970, p. 236 (Flexner and Bachman)—"An entire school system can only gradually promote radical reform in the substance and manner of classroom instruction. The course of study may indeed be expressed in terms so general that large leeway is left to the grade teachers. . . . The conventional character of available textbooks in most subjects, generally speaking, handicap wide departure by an entire system from established practices."

Appendix D: The Trump Plan

CHANGE THEORY FOR TRUMP PLAN: SOMETIMES EFFECTIVE

"I predicted that as it was being conceived and implemented educational reform would go nowhere" (Sarason, 2002, p. 178).

The Encapsulated Classroom and School: High/Medium

Beggs, 1964, p. 4—"To do the job the staff felt needed to be done students had to be freed from the lock-step rigidity of the self-contained classroom."

pp. 25–26—"The small groups were designed to be student centered, and were to be characterized by a high degree of student involvement through individual participation by discussion and work with teacher or fellow students. Each student was given a large block of time for independent work, during which time he was to prepare for the large and small group activities. It was intended that emphasis be placed on the development of personal responsibility for learning."

Trump, 1959, p. 13—Current lock-step schedule too inhibiting: "Today's school schedules students tightly so that they go from one class or study hall to another, six or more periods a day, with the same periods repeated five days a week."

p. 61—Some secondary students, more time at work than school. "This cooperative school–work program will contribute to closer ties with business and industry."

p. 117—"The purpose of schedule modification is to make it more flexible so that students and teachers can break out of the conventional, standard-size period, five days a week, each period slated for a self-contained classroom."

pp. 112–113—New technological devices.

Trump and Baynham, 1961, p. 47—"The self-contained classroom locks them in and denies their differences. It makes a farce out of the concept of equality of educational opportunities for all students because it refuses them access to the wide range of varied talents possessed by different teachers."

Ridgewood High School, 1965, p. 14—"The computer-built schedule of 20–minute modules has permitted truly flexible scheduling. 'The number of combinations possible with 21 periods per day makes it possible to do almost anything. It lends itself to improvisation outside the formal structure laid down by the computer.' There's flexibility for teachers and students during the fairly large time portions not scheduled into groups."

Doremus, 1982, p. 347—"It soon became apparent that the schedule, though different from traditional schedules, was no more flexible. . . . The scheduling within that system was just as rigid as in any other high school."

"Unquestioned Bedrock Assumptions" Questioned: High

Beggs, 1964, p. 221—"The ungraded school is a common-sense approach to providing for differences between and within people. Some youngsters are able at mathematics and poor in social science, or vice versa."

p. ix—a new organizational pattern for instruction based on large group and small group instruction and independent study.

Ridgewood High School, 1965, p. 13—"Classes of different lengths overlapped almost all day. There were no passing bells. And the teachers were left unscheduled for nearly half of their time."

Pileggi, 1969, p. 568—"School programs should reduce the time required for listening to teachers' talk. Conversely, the school should provide more time and better places for pupils to engage in independent study, covering required content as well as materials of special interest. . . . The school program needs to help pupils to find avenues of social action in the community."

Trump and Baynham, 1961, p. 41—"Tomorrow's schools will put flexibility of school arrangements ahead of the rigidity of the bell. The day will be divided into 15– to 20–minute modules of time."

Trump, 1959, p. 7—Large-group and small-group instruction and individual study time; 40% of study time to work independently.

Beggs, 1964, p. 17—"Yet we go on in much the same way as we have since 1643 [Boston Latin grammar and the lockstep graded organization]. True, we have refined the imperfect fabric of graded instruction for all students by means of various ability-grouping systems."

Axiomatic Change: High

Beggs, 1964, p. 26—"Emphasis was placed on students 'doing.' . . . Learning was meant to be an active process for the learner. The teaching job was to get the students involved in mental and mechanical operations."

p. xii—"Basically a system of instruction employing—team teaching, large and small group instruction with individual study, multimedia teaching aids, flexible scheduling."

Trump, 1959, p. 19—"The secondary school of the future will provide for closer relationships between students and teachers."

Trump and Baynham, 1961, p. 111—"A beginning can be made by setting aside one or two periods a month where the emphasis is completely on creativity. Students will not be told what to do but rather will be given questions and suggestions."

pp. 76–77—"In most large classes, a few students were both willing and anxious to ask questions. Four or five pertinent queries usually covered any special problems in the lesson. Students were encouraged to ask questions; they were expected to respond to those asked by the teacher."

Ridgewood High School, 1965, p. 13—"Students also conducted their own discussion periods ('seminars') while teachers apparently looked on from the sidelines."

p. 16—An intermediate phase in the conversion to the large-group, small-group, independent study plan: "This intermediate phase, with the aim of putting the teacher and student in a closer relationship than independent study allows, employs a 'learning laboratory' for each subject field."

Intractability of Schools: Medium/Low

Beggs, 1964, p. 4—Staff wanted to individualize instruction; central office stayed out of the way of the plan: "Sole responsibility was placed on the Lakeview staff for the Plan's evolvement and implementation. The central office officers seldom visited the school."

Trump, 1959, p. 14—"The school of the future will schedule students in class groups an average of only 18 hours a week, instead of the present 30 hours."

Trump and Baynham, 1961, p. 85—"There is a different spirit in team teaching and team classes. It's more demanding for students and more stimulating for teachers."

Doremus, 1982, p. 347—"Foreign language teachers were the first to opt out. They wanted small classes meeting daily to emphasize conversation. . . . Other departments soon followed. . . . Most still use the large-group technique occasionally. . . . Few teachers are still involved in team teaching and planning."

Ridgewood High School, 1965, p. 16—Superintendent Howard: "All of our people long for the good old days, the easy days, now and then. But we haven't given up and we won't."

Ongoing Research and Development: Medium

Beggs, 1964, p. 7—"Do students learn more by the trial and error method with supporting help than by listening to formal lectures? What place does crisp logical content presentation have in instruction?"

Trump, 1959, p. 10—Experimentation used to determine who, what, how long, and so on.

p. 14—"Experience and judgment will determine how many hours yearly are desirable in such fields."

Trump and Baynham, 1961, p. 68—"Data much broader in scope than those collected today will answer such questions as: Did the students learn more? Were teacher competencies better utilized and morale raised? Were the new procedures financially feasible and economically efficient?"

p. 93—Technology: "A final report indicated that spelling can be taught at the seventh-grade level as effectively by tape as by teachers using the same word list or current spelling book. Also, they found that spelling tapes can be made in such a way that the class can function without any supervision from the teacher."

p. 112—Try out these ideas first with more mature students: "A total program of reorganized instruction is easiest to start with the more able students in the senior year."

pp. 126–127—Teachers to state clearly what they want; data collection-satisfaction of parents, students, teachers, and others.

Doremus, 1982, p. 348—"Those who do vaguely remember standardized tests being administered during the innovation period, but none can remember what the data indicated. The decision to make program changes was not the result of careful evaluation. One teacher told me, 'We didn't look at the program and evaluate it and throw out what wasn't working; we just made decisions on what we liked.'"

Ridgewood High School, 1965, p. 14—There have been some problems with scheduling, seminars, and independent study.

Teachers as Reform Leaders: High

Beggs, 1964, p. 5—Central office seldom visited the school; plan totally fashioned at the school level.

p. 5—"The basis of school improvement begins and must be carried out at the building level."

Beggs, 1964, p. 27—Teachers as reform leaders: "A certain lack of respect for the counsel of the educator may be the reason so little pointed reform has gone on in the schools."

Trump and Baynham, 1961, p. 59—"Proposed changes will be determined also by answers to these questions: Do the teachers consider the changes desirable? Will the changes meet professional standards? Are the changes financially feasible?"

pp. 114–115—"The teachers could further provide their own guidelines to more flexible curriculum organization. . . . Which of the following instructional methods is best? . . . It is intended simply as an aid in making decisions about the most effective methods and best school settings for accomplishing present purposes."

Doremus, 1982, p. 347—Foreign language teachers first to opt out; other departments followed.

Lang's Five Assumptions: Medium/Low

1. Outside agent. J. Lloyd Trump created and published the plan as president of the National Association of Secondary School Principals because of a teacher shortage. "In 1955 . . . 45,000 more teachers than were readily available were needed in high schools" (Trump and Baynham, 1961, p. 1); the plan included support personnel to do a great deal of the nonteaching work. Doremus, 1982, p. 348—First 10 years of operation at Wayland High, four principals, several superintendents and many teacher and department head changes: "None of his successors advocated the Trump Plan as strongly as the original principal."

2. Parents and community involved in the change. Trump, 1959, p. 35—Community relations: school buildings located near center of town. "They will call upon community experts or specialists to serve as instruction assistants or consultants." Trump and Baynham, 1961, pp. 125–126—Community members involved in decision making: "The potential for the public in bringing fresh ideas and lending support to new approaches in education is purposely emphasized."

3. Motivate students and families—Trump and Baynham, 1961, p. 70.

4. Power relationships altered. Trump and Baynham, 1961, p. 125— "The school staff, the administration, the board of education, the students, their parents, and other members of the community need to study, work, and plan together if changes are to be understood, accepted, and put into effect."

5. Less discontinuity between school and nonschool. Trump and Baynham, 1961, p. 70—"In tomorrow's schools, more members of the community at large will be employed to teach and perform other school services, and the education of students will take place in the community as well as within the four walls of the school building."

Past Reforms' Research: Medium/Low

Power relationships altered theoretical framework of reform.

TEACHING THEORY FOR TRUMP PLAN: SOMETIMES EFFECTIVE

"But if we did not have to teach the curriculum, *what would we do with them?*" (Sarason, 1993, p. 42).

Productive Learning: High

Beggs, 1964, p. 6—"Regardless of the motive of the teachers, learning doesn't take place unless the procedures used in teaching are appropriate for student understanding."

pp. 12–13—"Basically the Decatur-Lakeview Plan involved: 1. Large group instruction for content presentation. 2. Independent study for individual work. 3. Small group activity for discussion and idea reinforcement. 4. Team teaching to bring the combined talents of teachers together in common instructional problems. 5. Use of technological aids and programmed instruction wherever possible to stimulate and clarify learning. 6. Varied time allotments for different courses and diverse learning groups."

p. 12—Decatur-Lakeview plan, small-group activity for discussion and reinforcement.

Trump, 1959, p. 8—"These large-group activities will occupy about 40 per cent of the students' time."

Trump and Baynham, 1961, p. 115—"Conventional evaluation methods do not measure such highly important goals as development of independent responsibility for learning, growth in creativity and inquiry, ability to think and discuss effectively in small groups, and development of satisfaction in learning."

p. 6—"We must develop the spirit of inquiry in young people. As they go through school, they should learn to react intrinsically to what they read and hear and to approach problems with the curiosity, the will, and the techniques to solve them."

Ridgewood High School, 1965, p. 16—Learning laboratory and seminars: "The aim, aside from teaching the student, is to make him see that he can undertake a project and finish it." Superintendent Howard, on learning laboratories: "As the step that can move a student from the conventional classroom approach to independent study." On seminars: "Some seminars are extremely effective and some are not . . . give students a chance to put ideas from lectures and their own reading and independent study projects to work."

"Pouring in Knowledge" Theory: High

Beggs, 1964, p. 10—Learning takes place through action, not listening, alone.

pp. 19–22—Different learning theories debunked: Decatur-Lakeview learning theory—students learn when they see purpose to learning; learning is an active process; change in behavior is the central goal of instruction; students learn at different rates and on various levels of comprehension in different content areas; students learn best as a result of the appeal to the senses (seeing, hearing, touching, and smelling); the environments for learning, psychological and physical, are contributing to successful outcomes; learning is affected by the students' concept of themselves and their attitude toward others.

p. 18—"At one time it was assumed the mind was like a muscle, and that hard work alone would develop mental powers. . . . An outgrowth of this theory is the belief that bright youngsters should be in souped-up classes. . . . The recommendations that bright students do more work is a basic premise of those who believe in the 'muscle' theory of learning."

Trump, 1959, p. 14—"An underlying purpose of the school will be to develop ability to study, think, and solve problems, in contrast to today's emphasis on memorization."

p. 26—"The secondary school will place less emphasis on mass classroom recitations which permit relatively little attention to the individual."

B. F. Brown, 1963, p. 224—"The textbook publishers will take a back seat to the curriculum researchers in determining what our students will read and learn."

Students as "Raw Materials": High

Beggs, 1964, p. 12—Decatur-Lakeview plan, independent study for individual work.

pp. 19–20—Learning by filling up the pitcher, and teachers talked and talked; learning as the result of transfer of generalizations; learning as the response of a structured stimulus.

Personalized Learning: High

Beggs, 1964, p. 9—Student centered; English students writing; science students doing.

pp. 25–26—"The large groups were expected to be teacher-centered, but students were expected to be actively involved."

p. 30—Students learn by doing.

p. 12—Decatur-Lakeview plan, varied time allotments for different courses and diverse learning groups.

p. 222—"Teachers will spend more time listening. . . . The teacher will make appropriate learning prescriptions to get at increased knowledge."

Trump, 1959, p. 10—"Conferences between students and instructors will be held whenever necessary to clarify goals, content, and personal problems."

p. 36—Evaluation: "Evaluating the total growth of students, rather than merely finding out what facts they possess, will take more time, imagination, and skill on the part of teachers and students."

p. 66—"They will understand that individual students learn more readily through the use of different types of instructional aids."

p. 66—Learning resource center: "students' individual or group reading, viewing, listening, and writing."

p. 78—Small-group discussion: "They provided a setting where teachers came to know and understand individual students better and where students further explored the ideas suggested by large-group presentations."

Trump and Baynham, 1961, p. 118—"The first step in serving individual differences among teachers and students is to plan specific, individual programs only with and for those teachers and students who are particularly interested."

p. 80—Small-group discussions: "They provided a setting where teachers came to know and understand individual students better and where students further explored the ideas suggested by large-group presentations."

"A 'Trump Plan' 4 Years Later," 1965, p. 15—"Students are not born with the ability for independent study. Some students don't even have it when they enter graduate school. . . . We ask students to participate in planning their own learning and then to put the plan in effect."

Trump and Baynham, 1961, p. 7—In today's classroom, too little done to deal with individual differences.

Parental Inclusion: Low

Not included.

Student Motivation: Medium

Trump, 1959, p. 10—"*Study* activities will require students progressively to take more responsibility for self-direction. The amount of time will vary according to subject and student maturity."

Trump and Baynham, 1961, p. 76—Fewer discipline problems in the large classes.

p. 97—Seniors excused from study hall and allowed independent study time: "Students in these projects developed better independent study habits and concern for individual work."

Lower-Class Students: Low

Beggs, 1964, p. 9—Reduction of dropouts a big goal; high-level academic experiences.

p. 222—"Students of all socio-economic backgrounds will be the realistic concern of the schools. A breakthrough in keeping all students in school longer will come when more guidance counselors are a part of the school staff. When the school's ungraded program allows culturally disadvantaged youngsters to be a part of a special program geared to their previous experiences and unique needs, a major hurdle will have been cleared."

Low IQ and Self-Fulfilling Prophecy: Medium

Beggs, 1964, p. 29—More low-ability students staying in school longer.

Ridgewood High School, 1965, p. 16—Superintendent Howard: "We have found, too, that seminars can be effective with low-ability students.

They like to express their ideas, the same as anyone else. Discussions are as meaningful to them as to gifted children."

THE TEACHING PROFESSION FOR
TRUMP PLAN: SOMETIMES EFFECTIVE

"Teaching is not a science, it is an art fusing ideas, obligations, the personal and interpersonal. The chemistry of that fusion determines whether or how subject matter matters to the student" (Sarason, 2004, p. 199).

Teacher Development: High/Medium

Trump, 1959, p. 23—"Many basic assumptions underlying present standards of teaching loads will be changed. The professional teacher working with large groups will need more time for preparing and planning his instruction. He will spend fewer hours a week before classes than today's teacher."

p. 25—"The career teachers will have more time to devote to studying new developments and research findings in their own fields, building teaching aids, improving evaluation, and doing other professional tasks."

p. 42—Provide time for professional development.

Trump and Baynham, 1961, p. 52—"Here are some concepts about tomorrow's teachers as professionals: They will differentiate between what they must do and what sub professional assistants and machines can do."

p. 66—Highly diversified staff; significant degree of selection, coordination, in-service training, team-teaching setting.

p. 86—"Teachers' schedules were arranged as nearly as possible so that team members had a common free period during the day for conferences or lesson planning, assigning responsibilities for various tasks, project coordination, and evaluation. Where daily meetings were impossible, regularly scheduled weekly meetings were held."

p. 103—Improved teachers' morale.

p. 120—"Provisions for salary, advancement, and supervision are interrelated . . . raise professional standards . . . advancement by remaining primarily as classroom teachers."

p. 8—"Lack of time for professional work damages professional pride."

Beggs, 1964, p. 225—Internships for teachers. "Increased salaries will contribute to general interest in teaching as a career."

Doremus, 1982, p. 348—"New department heads and teachers weren't trained for team teaching."

The Unlearning Process: Medium/Low

Beggs, 1964, p. 6—Teachers work in isolation; no educational psychology invested in; teachers institutes are holdover from one-room schoolhouse days, talked about calendar, textbooks.

p. 24—"The chapter on in-service education will describe the techniques used for this. The point is this: While we accepted some beliefs about learning, we didn't always employ them in day-to-day instructional practice . . . as a staff we had to do some changing in our operational behavior in the classroom."

p. 225—Psychology of learning; emphasis on history of education.

Trump and Baynham, 1961, pp. 104–105—40% independent study; 40% large group; 20% small group.

Doremus, 1982, p. 348—"Many new staff member indicated a preference for being left alone to teach in their own rooms."

Teacher Education Programs: Low

Trump, 1959, p. 27—Better teacher training. "The fetish of uniformity that seems to be dooming the teaching profession to mediocrity will be discarded."

p. 31—Closer relationships with colleges and universities.

p. 32—University/secondary collaboration.

Trump and Baynham, 1961, p. 123—College students who want to be teachers should work as clerks and instructional assistants while in college. Plan with college of education for training teachers.

p. 83—Collaboration with Harvard University an effective method for more students writing "contract correcting."

Pedagogy: High

Beggs, 1964, pp. 8–9—"How could we expect real quality in education if every teacher was expected to be equally expert at all phases of the teaching process?"

p. 30—"Instead of five lectures a day, they can give one. The rest of the day can be spent in working with students or doing a better job of preparation for the next lecture."

p. 12—Decatur-Lakeview plan, large-group instruction for content presentation and team teaching to bring the combined talents of teachers together in common instructional problems.

p. 226—Some teachers will work with large groups; some, small groups; some, independent study students.

Trump, 1959, p. 13—"Teachers will have more time to plan and conduct evaluations that will be helpful to students in showing progress toward achieving all the purposes of instruction rather than merely the possession of facts, the principal area of evaluation at present."

Trump and Baynham, 1961, p. 106—Team teaching; "As more teachers and students are involved in team-teaching activities, however, greater flexibility in scheduling and more effective use of the special talents of different teachers will result."

p. 107—Team teaching.

p. 8—Teachers provided more time for lesson plan development and grading student papers and projects and less time on clerical and other nonprofessional duties.

p. 92—Closed-circuit television, overhead projector, and tape recorders used: "More than 500 transparencies were created and prepared in one year, and teachers discovered the added advantage of being able to review an entire unit of work."

p. 103—Team teaching: "Teachers found increased satisfaction in teaching and their morale was raised as their special abilities were tapped to a greater degree."

p. 109—"Today's teachers are scheduled for too many class hours per week, and the classes are *uniformly* too large."

p. 108—Employ teacher assistants and other clerical staff to make the day-to-day work of teachers more about lesson planning and teaching.

Keefe, 1971, p. 3—"The team-teaching approach allows greater specialization . . . as each teacher, for example, can take the lead on a unit in the curriculum they like or has special expertise in and the others can complement this effort." Help from instructional assistants to supervise independent study times; clerical assistants for typing, copying, and record keeping; and general aides for general supervision and other duties.

Ridgewood High School, 1965, p. 14—"To give teaching teams a half-day to plan together and to meet with students, it was attempted at first to schedule all humanities classes in the morning and all science-math classes in the afternoon."

Productive Teaching Defined: High

Beggs, 1964, p. 10—Learning takes place through action, not listening, alone.

p. 28—Work changing; "We don't know the issues youngsters will face, but we do know we must teach them to think, to reason, to judge and to create."

p. 12—Decatur-Lakeview plan, use of technological aids and programmed instruction wherever possible to stimulate and clarify learning.

Trump, 1959, p. 7—Large group instruction: "Instruction and discussions will be conducted by teachers who are particularly competent, who have more adequate time to prepare, and who will utilize the best possible instructional aids."

Trump and Baynham, 1961, p. 114—"In effect, these are the questions that teachers will answer for each unit in their present courses," content, and purposes; students of differing ability levels learn via independent study, which requires motivation, explanation, demonstration, large-group instruction—what requires teacher–student interaction? Small group.

p. 85—Teacher statement regarding team teaching at Evanston High: "If there is any flat statement that can be made, it is that there is a different spirit in team teaching and team classes. It's more demanding for students and more stimulating for teachers."

p. 103—"Students had improved learning opportunities because they came in contact with more teachers, and with the best competencies of those teachers, either as they met them in person or were aided by technological instructional devices."

Keefe, 1971, p. 3—"The Trump plan sees the teacher in the role of facilitator of learning and teacher advisor."

SCHOOL POWER AND POLITICS FOR TRUMP PLAN: SOMETIMES EFFECTIVE / NOT EFFECTIVE

"The icing on the cake of vexation was provided by my meetings with policymakers and politicians in Washington and elsewhere. I realized that, however sincere their intentions, they knew nothing about schools and why the school culture, honed over many decades, would resist and defeat reforms attempting to alter the status quo. There are no villains. There is a system. You can see and touch villains, you cannot see a system" (Sarason, 1998, p. 141).

Government Involvement: Medium

Beggs, 1964, p. 223—"The schools of the future will be assisted by more state and federal money, requirements and advisory counsel."

Doremus, 1982, p. 347—"To accommodate the program, the town of Wayland built a facility that consisted of six (now eight) separate buildings, each with an overhang to shelter pupils during class changes."

p. 348—When the grant money ended, budget problems occurred, and class loads for teachers increased.

p. 348—"When the district had to expand the high school to keep pace with enrollment increases, it chose to build one wing with regular classrooms and labs and a second with a library/media center. . . . This decision closed all decentralized resource centers except science."

The Middle-Class Ethic: Medium

School Bureaucracy: Low

Keefe, 1971, p. 2—It attempts to break down hierarchical levels that exist in schools and make the principal, for example, the "instructional leader," instead of the boss.

p. 3—"This plan suggests a team teaching approach . . . does not imply a hierarchy of teachers; it proposes a team of peers working together, utilizing their different talents for the common good of the students."

Doremus, 1982, p. 348—New principals were less enthusiastic about the Trump plan than the original principal had been.

Research and Development: Medium

Trump and Baynham, 1961, p. 127—"Have the students learned more under the changed program than under conventional procedures? Has the job satisfaction of the teachers been raised significantly? Are the changed procedures logistically and financially feasible?"

Doremus, 1982, p. 347—"The use of teacher aides, provided by a Ford Foundation grant, to help staff the resource centers."

Silent Axioms and Educational Policymakers: Low

Appendix E: The Coalition of Essential Schools Plan

CHANGE THEORY FOR CES PLAN: SOMETIMES EFFECTIVE

"I predicted that as it was being conceived and implemented educational reform would go nowhere" (Sarason, 2002, p. 178).

The Encapsulated Classroom and School: High/Medium

Sizer, 1996, p. 154—"Curricular decisions should be guided by the aim of thorough student mastery and achievement rather than by an effort merely to cover content."

p. 155— Principle 7: "The tone of the school should explicitly and self-consciously stress values of unanxious expectation."

p. 152—"The more I came to believe that while what we were doing in our schools was generous and well intentioned, the design of the work often defied common sense when scrutinized carefully. Teach mathematics and physics or literature and visual art as utterly separate entities? Break the day into little fifty-minute globules of time and expect thoughtful work?"

Sizer, 1992, pp. 207–208—Principle 1: "The schools should focus on helping adolescents learn to use their minds well. Schools should not attempt to be 'comprehensive' if such a claim is made at the expense of the school's central intellectual purpose." Principle 5: "The governing metaphor of the school should be student as worker, rather than the more familiar metaphor of teacher as deliverer of instructional services. Accordingly, a prominent pedagogy will be coaching, to provoke students to learn how to learn and thus to teach themselves."

Sizer, 2004, p. 104—"Few serious business enterprises, save those expecting only mindless labor, break up their intellectual work into snippets of time, arranged in no intellectually coherent order."

"Unquestioned Bedrock Assumptions" Questioned: High

Muncey and McQuillan, 1996, p. 14—"The Coalition proposed changing many aspects of traditional school life—including student–teacher relations, classroom pedagogy, departmental structures, and budget priorities."

Sizer, 1984, p. 223—"The weaknesses of the high school lie deeper, in how it is organized and in the attitudes of those who work there."

Sizer, 1996, p. 153—Essential; "focus on the intellectual core of schooling, at the expense of 'extras,' which appeared to them and us to be weakening the ultimate work of the students."

Sizer, 1992, pp. 207–208—Principle 1: "The schools should focus on helping adolescents learn to use their minds well. Schools should not attempt to be 'comprehensive' if such a claim is made at the expense of the school's central intellectual purpose." Principle 5: "The governing metaphor of the school should be student as worker, rather than the more familiar metaphor of teacher as deliverer of instructional services. Accordingly, a prominent pedagogy will be coaching, to provoke students to learn how to learn and thus to teach themselves."

Cushman, 1989, p. 2—"The way one construes knowledge today is in some ways profoundly different from the way it was construed in the late 19th century."

Axiomatic Change—Out of the Box: High

Exhibitions to demonstrate student mastery.

Sizer, 1992, p. 211—Switching from traditional course coverage to "a course of study . . . rich, genuine, and compelling . . . " is not an overnight process.

Sizer, 1996, p. 153—"Why 'essential'? We had a double meaning in mind: essential in that the work we envisioned was tellingly needed, and essential in that the schools choosing to be involved would focus on the intellectual core of schooling, at the expense of 'extras,' which appeared to them and us to be weakening the ultimate work of the students."

Sizer, 1992, pp. 207–208—Principle 2: "The school's goals should be simple: each student should master a number of essential skills and be competent in certain areas of knowledge . . . 'less is more' . . . curricular decisions are to be directed toward the students' attempt to gain mastery rather than by the teachers' effort to cover content." Principle 6: "Students embarking on secondary school studies are those who show competence in language and elementary mathematics. . . . The diploma should be awarded on a successful final demonstration of mastery for graduation— an Exhibition. . . . The emphasis is on the students' demonstration that they can do important things."

Cushman, 1989, p. 2—"Can anyone believe that students should be passive recipients of teacher's talk for up to 90 percent of the time?"

Intractability of Schools: High

Muncey and McQuillan, 1996, p. 8—"The Coalition central staff does not offer member schools a model or even a suggested starting point for change but rather emphasizes local control and autonomy."

McDonald et al., 1999, p. 17—"Change-minded schools often bump up against constraints created at the district and state level. School change is never entirely the business of the school alone."

Sizer, 1992, p. ix—"The early 1990s are witnessing the confrontation of two forces: the protection of the culturally important and remarkably stable form of secondary education that Americans have shared for almost a hundred years and the press for new and more efficient forms of schooling."

p. 3—"Like most high schools, it just rolls on, fettered by routine of long standing. The result is a cacophony of jumbled practices, orchestrated only by a complex computer-driven schedule whose instrument is a bell system whose ushers are assistant principals."

Sizer, 1996, p. 153—"Accordingly, we prescribed no 'model' to 'implement'. We came with no panacea. We believed that each community had to find its own way. However, what we accepted in common was a set of ideas, ones that appeared to us to invest every good school we knew."

Ongoing Research and Development: High

McDonald et al., 1999, p. 15—Coalition roots in study of high schools from 1979–1984; Ted Sizer and group "investigated the evolution and condition of the American high school."

Sizer, 1992, pp. 211–212—Smaller schools have success with lower truancy and dropout rates.

Muncey and McQuillan, 1996, p. 290—"Over time, however, the enthusiasm of Coalition proponents often waned; and those who were initially skeptical about the need for reform were unlikely to change their minds when the benefits of doing so seemed uncertain and the drawbacks readily apparent."

Sizer, 2004, p. 96—Dennis Littky and Deborah Meier.

Sizer, 1996, p. 153—Key elements not meant to be exhaustive, to provide guidance.

p. 160–161—"Most studies have focused on implementation issues and the effects of Coalition-like restructuring on school life. This research has helped to clarify the goals of restructuring, reveal the complex and often puzzling nature of implementation, and identify promising strategies."

p. 162—"The Center on Organization and Restructuring of Schools . . . has sponsored several sets of studies . . . large scale and asks whether school restructuring increases student achievement. The second set narrows the focus to twenty-four restructuring schools to examine whether they promote intellectual rigor and if so, how."

Teachers as Reform Leaders: High

Muncey and McQuillan, 1996, p. 7—"Teachers had to be at the heart of school reform."

McDonald et al., 1999, p. 6—"The focus of the CES work is less on issues than the life of schools and classrooms, and the work is predicated on the idea that the issues and the stimulus for change should come from the practitioners themselves."

p. 46—"Underlying these ideas is a school-centered theory of action, one that views school reform from the school up."

Sizer, 2004, p. 94—"A uniform Plan might suit his place well in theory, but if the people who were going to live that plan were not part of its conception and if it did not reflect the best of their setting, then it would fail, if not at first then in the long run."

p. 97—Voluntary faculty and students.

Lang's Five Assumptions: Medium

1. Outside agent. Sizer, 2004, p. 94—"At the same time, to expect that all professional wisdom will arise locally is equally wrong-headed."
2. Parents and community involved in the change. Sizer, 1992—Include community and draw on strengths of faculty. Sizer, 1996, p. 153—"Our view was that excellence and vitality in schools arises from the particular people within them and the community in which that school resides." Principle 10: The school should demonstrate nondiscriminatory and inclusive policies, practices, and pedagogies. It should model democratic practices that involve all who are directly affected by the school. The school should honor diversity and build on the strength of its communities, deliberately and explicitly challenging all forms of inequity.
3. Motivate students and families, no significant involvement in curricular decision making, but the concept of "all children can" means schools must do a great deal to connect to all families and communities (Sizer, 1996, p. 36).
4. Power relationships altered.
5. Less discontinuity between school and nonschool.

Past Reforms' Research: Medium/Low

Power relationships altered theoretical framework of reform.

Sizer, 2004, pp. 93–94—High School Study, a consuming issue: "I was encouraged by the founders of the Study and others to move next to remedies. The result was the Coalition of Essential Schools."

McDonald et al., 1999, p. 15—"The Coalition of Essential Schools has its roots in a study of high schools (1979–84) . . . They found that for historically predictable reasons, the high school was failing in three interrelated respects. Its curriculum was disjointed and shallow—lots of coverage or poorly connected subjects, in little depth. Second, it lacked the capacity to know its students well, and it treated them as passive rather than active learners. Third, its teachers worked in isolation from each other and at an unproductively frenetic pace."

TEACHING THEORY FOR CES PLAN: VERY EFFECTIVE

"But if we did not have to teach the curriculum, *what would we do with them?*" (Sarason, 1993, p. 42).

Productive Learning: High

McDonald et al., 1999, p. 16—"The principles build on the central idea that a school's mission should be to help students to learn to use their minds well, and that learning should be a personalized, active, and meaningful experience for both teachers and students."

Sizer, 1992, p. 25—"Why an *Exhibition*? The word clearly states its purpose: the student must Exhibit the products of his learning."

Sizer, 2004, p. 95—Principle 2: Less is more (curriculum).

Sizer, 1992, pp. 207–208—Principle 1: "The schools should focus on helping adolescents learn to use their minds well. Schools should not attempt to be 'comprehensive' if such a claim is made at the expense of the school's central intellectual purpose." Principle 5: "The governing metaphor of the school should be student as worker, rather than the more familiar metaphor of teacher as deliverer of instructional services. Accordingly, a prominent pedagogy will be coaching, to provoke students to learn how to learn and thus to teach themselves."

"Pouring in Knowledge" Theory: High

Muncey and McQuillan, 1996, p. 14—"The Coalition of Essential Schools initiated its reform effort with the intention of 'creating schools where the rigorous use of the mind for all kids, without exception, is the highest priority.'"

McDonald et al., 1999, p. 15—"Its curriculum was disjointed and shallow—lots of coverage of poorly connected subjects, in little depth."

Sizer, 1992, p. 25—"To shoot baskets well one needs to practice. To think well one needs to practice."

p. 26—School about studying "complex ideas, those of fundamental consequence for oneself and for the culture. It is not merely about 'coverage.'"

Sizer, 2004, p. 95—Student-as-worker principle.

Sizer, 1996, p. 131—Passive disengagement: "Will and his pals and his teachers spent the day going through the motions, covering the ground, getting the job done, playing out the routines of school."

p. 146—"Serious secondary education requires the commitment of its students. They have to work hard; they are not merely genial empty vessels waiting to be filled with knowledge."

pp. 154–155— Principle 6: "The diploma should be awarded upon a successful final demonstration of mastery for graduation—an 'Exhibition.'"

Sizer, 1992, pp. 207–208—Principle 2: "The school's goals should be simple: each student should master a number of essential skills and be competent in certain areas of knowledge. . . . 'Less is more.' . . . Curricular decisions are to be directed toward the students' attempt to gain mastery rather than by the teachers' effort to cover content." Principle 5: "The governing metaphor of the school should be student as worker, rather than the more familiar metaphor of teacher as deliverer of instructional services. Accordingly, a prominent pedagogy will be coaching, to provoke students to learn how to learn and thus to teach themselves."

Students as "Raw Materials": High

McDonald et al., 1999, p. 15—"Second, it lacked the capacity to know its students well, and it treated them as passive rather than active learners."

Sizer, 1992, p. 210—"The student-as-worker principle has been another likely point of entry, because it can be addressed even within a traditional structure. Teachers can readily talk less and stimulate more, become coaches and questioners more often than lecturers."

pp. 207–208—Principle 3: "The school's goals should apply to all students, but the means to these goals will vary as these students themselves vary. School practice should be tailor-made to meet the needs of every group of adolescents."

Sizer, 1996, p. 154— Principle 5: "The governing practical metaphor of the school should be student-as-worker rather than the more familiar metaphor of teacher-as-deliverer-of instructional-services."

Personalized Learning: High

Sizer, 2004, p. 95—Mastery through exhibition.

p. 106—"Silence masks our fear of the young. If we refuse to hear their legitimate complaints, we can live with limited obligations to them."

Sizer, 1984, p. 231—"I'm opposed to schooling that focuses narrowly on particular job training."

Sizer, 1996, p. 152—"Defied common sense . . . treat every child of the same age in essentially the same way?"

p. 153—"School practice should be tailor-made to meet the needs of every group or class of adolescents."

Sizer, 1992, p. 210—Many schools begin with the three principles of student as worker, personalization, and exhibitions.

p. 207–208—Principle 3: "The school's goals should apply to all students, but the means to these goals will vary as these students themselves vary. School practice should be tailor-made to meet the needs of every group of adolescents." Principle 2: "The school's goals should be simple: each student should master a number of essential skills and be competent in certain areas of knowledge. . . . 'Less is more.' . . . Curricular decisions are to be directed toward the students' attempt to gain mastery rather than by the teachers' effort to cover content." Principle 5: "The governing metaphor of the school should be student as worker, rather than the more familiar metaphor of teacher as deliverer of instructional services. Accordingly, a prominent pedagogy will be coaching, to provoke students to learn how to learn and thus to teach themselves." Principle 4: "Teaching and learning should be personalized to the maximum feasible extent. No teacher should have direct responsibility for more than eighty students; decisions about the course of study, the use of students' and teachers' time, and the choice of teaching materials and specific pedagogies must be placed in the hands of the principal and staff."

Parental Inclusion: High

Sizer, 1992, p. 175—"Families must feel welcome to address their concerns *directly* to the people who have the power to make or change decisions affecting their children." Principle 10: "The school should demonstrate nondiscriminatory and inclusive policies, practices, and pedagogies. It should model democratic practices that involve all who are directly affected by the school. The school should honor diversity and build on the strength of its communities, deliberately and explicitly challenging all forms of inequity."

Student Motivation: High

Sizer, 1992, p. 25—"If he does that well, he can convince himself that he can use knowledge and he can so convince others. It is the academic equivalent of being able to sink free throws in basketball."

pp. 207–208—Principle 2: "The school's goals should be simple: each student should master a number of essential skills and be competent in certain areas of knowledge . . . 'Less is more.' . . . Curricular decisions are to be directed toward the students' attempt to gain mastery rather than by the teachers' effort to cover content."

Lower-Class Students: High

p. 36—"We decide about children by how they appear and what we have been expected to believe about their appearances."

Sizer, 2004, p. 95—Helping young people use minds well and all students.

p. 106—"We know that the rich get the better scores and the poor get the compromises."

Sizer, 1992, pp. 207–208—Principle 3: "The school's goals should apply to all students, but the means to these goals will vary as these students themselves vary. School practice should be tailor-made to meet the needs of every group of adolescents." Principle 7: "The tone of the school should explicitly and self-consciously stress the values of unanxious expectation ("I won't threaten you, but I expect much of you"), of trust (unless it is abused), and of decency (the values of fairness, generosity, and tolerance). Incentives appropriate to the school's students and teachers should be emphasized, and parents should be treated as essential collaborators."

Low IQ and Self-Fulfilling Prophecy: High

Sizer, 1992, p. 32—"But people do not learn alike, and to run a school on the basis of One Best Curriculum . . . is itself profoundly discriminatory."

p. 37—"A student who is not challenged for a period of years, or even months, finds it difficult to catch up with students who have been stretched during the same period. . . . Indeed, the very struggle of trying to catch up often tells the student that she *is* inferior, just as the school said she was. . . . The late bloomer flourishes all too rarely. The waste to that student—and to society at large—is prodigious."

pp. 207–208—Principle 3: "The school's goals should apply to all students, but the means to these goals will vary as these students themselves vary. School practice should be tailor-made to meet the needs of every group of adolescents."

TEACHING PROFESSION FOR CES PLAN: SOMETIMES EFFECTIVE

"Teaching is not a science, it is an art fusing ideas, obligations, the personal and interpersonal. The chemistry of that fusion determines whether or how subject matter matters to the student" (Sarason, 2004, p. 199).

Teacher Development: High/Medium

Sizer, 2004, p. 107—Philosophy and secondary education "places where fundamental thinking of the enterprise might happen, these generally are peripheral electives disconnected from the bread-and-butter certification programs."

Sizer, 1996, p. 155—Principle 9: Competitive salaries for staff; time for "collective planning."

The Unlearning Process: Medium

Muncey and McQuillan, 1996, p. 289—Making intellectual focus "a top priority in schools has proven difficult."

p. 290—"Over time, however, the enthusiasm of Coalition proponents often waned; and those who were initially skeptical about the need for reform were unlikely to change their minds when the benefits of doing so seemed uncertain and the drawbacks readily apparent."

Sizer, 1996, p. 135—Some teachers passed through schooling unchallenged: "As a result, coming up with demanding intellectual work for the adolescents they teach is difficult, often poignant labor. It starts with the teachers themselves."

Teacher Education Programs: Medium

Sizer, 1992, p. 177—"Learning to teach is much like learning to write: one does it and, if lucky, is assisted by a perceptive editor."

p. 179—"The necessary changes in teacher training and certification are obvious: the general education of teachers must be strengthened and their specialties treated not as separate entities but as part of a larger and more important whole."

Cushman, 1989, p. 5—Teachers as generalists instead of specialists.

Pedagogy: High

McDonald et al., 1999, p. 15—"Third, its teachers worked in isolation from each other and at an unproductively frenetic pace."

Sizer, 2004, p. 95—1:80 teacher to student ratio.

Sizer, 1996, p. 156—"Our research persuaded us that if a teacher could not get to know his or her students well, a great deal of consequence was lost."

p. 100—Teachers cannot teach 120 students well.

Sizer, 1996, p. 133—"In my head I therefore rail about the system (whatever it may be) that grandly tolerates routines that force good and decent people into disrespectful and ineffective practice."

p. 152—Not providing teachers time to grade writing assignments.

p. 153—Teachers should have no more than 80 students so that they can effectively personalize the lessons.

p. 155—Principle 9: Common planning time for teachers.

Sizer, 1992, pp. 207–208—Principle 7: "The tone of the school should be explicitly and self-consciously stress the values of unanxious expectation ('I won't threaten you, but I expect much of you'), of trust (unless it is abused), and of decency (the values of fairness, generosity, and tolerance). Incentives appropriate to the school's students and teachers should be emphasized, and parents should be treated as essential collaborators." Principle 8: "The principals and teacher should perceive of themselves first as generalists (teachers and scholars in general education) and next as specialists (experts in a particular discipline). Staff should expect multiple obligations (teacher–counselor–manager) and a sense of commitment to the entire school."

Cushman, 1989, p. 3—"Our work is in changing *pedagogy*. . . . It starts with kids learning, and how teachers teach them."

Productive Teaching Defined: Medium

Sizer, 2004, p. 95—"Teaching would arise more from a curriculum of questions than a curriculum of answers; the point was to develop the habit of learning well and deeply on one's own. Teaching would therefore emphasize *coaching*."

Sizer, 1984, p. 223—"Less is more." "Thoroughness counts more than coverage."

Sizer, 1996, p. 155—Principle 8: "The principal and teachers should perceive themselves as generalists first . . . and specialists second."

Sizer, 1992, pp. 207–208—Principle 8: "The principals and teacher should perceive of themselves first as generalists (teachers and scholars in general education) and next as specialists (experts in a particular discipline). Staff should expect multiple obligations (teacher–counselor–manager) and a sense of commitment to the entire school." Principle 9: "Administrative and budget targets should include substantial time for collective planning by teachers, competitive salaries for staff, and an ultimate per-pupil cost not more than 10 percent higher than that at traditional schools."

School Power and Politics for CES Plan: Sometimes Effective

"The icing on the cake of vexation was provided by my meetings with policymakers and politicians in Washington and elsewhere. I realized that, however sincere their intentions, they knew nothing about schools and why the school culture, honed over many decades, would resist and defeat reforms attempting to alter the status quo. There are no villains. There is a system. You can see and touch villains, you cannot see a system" (Sarason, 1998, p. 141).

Government Involvement: Medium/Low

Sizer, 1996, p. 141—"Centralized government is an inept and inappropriate tool to set and shape the substance and standards of school policy and practice. They reflect the view that disproportional authority for these purposes should be given to the families affected and the professionals to whom those families entrust their children."

p. 141—"Central government is needed as a financier . . . as a documenter, persuader, supporter, advocate, for neglected children, truth-teller, but not, except at the extremes, a director."

p. 156—"Schools had to work their reform within existing budgets—the assumption being not that more money might not be nice or even needed, but that it was unlikely to be forthcoming. . . . While more moneys are legitimately needed in most places, to hold off reform while waiting for gargantuan budget increases is to wait forever in the current political and economic climate."

p. 48—"For people such as Horace Smith, the process largely missed the point. Few of the compromises that crippled his work were at all addressed by the various state plans."

Sizer, 1992, p. 173—Forward funding: "the current waste and erosion of a cooperative school culture from frequent last-minute major budget decisions is stunning."

pp. 174–175—National standards: "If schools are to be measured by that national standard, what does this say about the state's respect for community standard? Do not families have some rights of control of a public service? To put it most bluntly, are there not proper limits to state power over the minds of adolescents?"

p. 176—"A third duty of the state is to *attract, train, and accredit professionals* to work in the schools. The attitude of the state is crucial here."

The Middle-Class Ethic: High/Medium

Sizer, 1996, p. 49—"The struggle for a new 'one best America'—the best, perhaps, of the word 'multiculturalism'—is with us, and it will affect the schools . . . and reform plans that overlook it or impose simplistic, culturally insensitive remedies will certainly fail."

p. 146—"Public education is an idea, not a structure. The idea is that every citizen must have access to the culture and to the means of enriching that culture."

School Bureaucracy: Medium

Sizer, 1992, p. 173—"The major elements of schooling are controlled outside the teachers' world." State, district, unions, and so on.

Sizer, 2004, p. 96—"Five 'imperatives for better schools': 1. Give room to teachers and students . . . 2. Insist that students clearly exhibit mastery . . . 3. Get the incentives right . . . 4. Focus the students' work . . . 5. Keep the structure simple . . . "'Nice ideas,' I was told. 'But we can't take them seriously.'"

p. 98—"Our agreed-upon task was to reverse at least some of the current of policy influence, traditionally from 'the top' down, now to include imperatives that seemed essential to Horace Smith."

Sizer issued what is more of a manifesto than a plan with teeth.

Sizer, 1996, p. 154—Principle 4: "The choice of teaching materials and specific pedagogies must be unreservedly placed in the hands of the principal and staff."

p. 38—"A new, better system has to be created. In that creation, the issues of *accountable to whom* and *accountable for what* will be nicely and appropriately embedded. A wise resolution will require a new balance of authority between families and government."

Research and Development: Medium

Muncey and McQuillan, 1996, p. 288—"Much of what the Coalition of Essential Schools proposes—in terms of philosophy and practice—as well as the factors that appear to enhance the likelihood of change taking root, run counter to many institutional values and accepted practices in American education and society."

p. 294–295—"Educational change of the scope and nature presently being undertaken nationwide and by such organizations as the Coalition of Essential Schools has little historical precedent."

Sizer, 2004, p. 98—Anonymous donor Education Commission of the States (1988); $500 million from the Annenberg Corporation. The CES reform gained financial support from the Bill and Melinda Gates Foundation.

Silent Axioms and Educational Policymakers: High

Sizer, 2004, p. 98—"Governors go aboard, some (I later realized) merely for the money and the publicity."

p. 99—Lots of national attention and then $500 million from the Annenberg Corporation. "Horace, alas, got lost in all of this. The abrupt arrival of school reform on the national stage energized powers up and down the education system. Horace's school was now the object of attention, and advantages, monetary and political, accrued from it. But authority flowed increasingly upward, away from his beloved Franklin High School and its community's sense of what was wrong and what should be done about it, to the districts then to the states, and eventually to the Federal government"; this is called policy.

Sizer, 1992, p. 173—Give power to local schools.

Cushman, 1989, p. 5—"As I listen to school folk, I sense too little belief that those in policy positions will support powerful new ideas."

Sizer, 1996, p. 41—Sizer example: can ride the train from Lake Forest to the South Side, but the public schools are not open to all. "Not surprisingly, there are profound differences between the schools serving poor communities and those serving rich communities."

Appendix F: The School Development Plan

CHANGE THEORY FOR THE SDP PLAN, EFFECTIVE

"I predicted that as it was being conceived and implemented educational reform would go nowhere" (Sarason, 2002, p. 178).

The Encapsulated Classroom and School: High/Medium

Comer, Haynes, Joyner, and Ben-Avie, 1996, p. 2—"The most appalling thing was that the school staff were trying, but because they were working in isolation, without support, and at odds with one another, they could make no progress."

Comer, Ben-Avie, Haynes, and Joyner, 1999, pp. 278–279—"Teachers who are way makers help students think through five questions: What are the challenges in my life? How can I be who I want to be without hurting myself and others? How can becoming who I want to be help me and others? What resources do I already have to meet these challenges? How can I develop additional resources? The traditional school relies on the individual teacher to organize those experiences and maybe even to deal with questions one and two; the Comer Process involves the entire community."

Bigge and Hunt, 1980, p. 481—SDP theoretical frame: "Much of the inefficiency in education that research has exposed stems from the way most school subjects are organized and presented."

Reiff, 1966—SDP theoretical frame: social action model; school is a social system; to change behavior, one has to modify the environment or social system.

p. 39—Cannot change the social system without having the professional service providers work collaboratively with the clients to solve problems and influence policy.

"Unquestioned Bedrock Assumptions" Questioned: High

Comer et al., 1996, p. 37—"From the four principles of human ecology (the community is client: reduce the use of those community services that maintain the status quo; strengthen community resources; plan for change) emerge part of the theoretical basis for the SDP. Although the focus of school reform is the individual child, the SDP views the child as a part of the family unit and neighborhood as well as a part of the school community."

Axiomatic Change: Medium

Comer, 1996, pp. 39–40—Social action model: "But one cannot successfully change the social system without having the professional service providers work collaboratively with the clients (including the poor, whose needs and concerns must be addressed) to solve problems and influence policy. . . . One must confront issues of power and control." The three guiding principles of consensus, collaboration, and no-fault.

p. 46—"When we focus on social processes, relationships between students and teachers become the vehicle for instruction and are more important than subject area content."

Comer et al., 1999, p. xxiv—Relationships to child development are like location to real estate: relationships, relationships, relationships.

Kelly, 1966, p. 538—From Comer's theoretical frame: "Behavior is not viewed as sick or well but is defined as transactional—an outcome of reciprocal interactions between specific social situations and the individual. Adaptive behavior then can be expressed by any individual in a restricted number of social settings or in a variety of environments. . . . Research task is to clarify the precise relationships between individual behavior and social structure that differentially affect various forms of adaptive behavior."

Reiff, 1966, p. 544—SDP theoretical frame: Maybe forget about treating mental illness so much and concentrate on primary prevention: "The compelling need to direct our energies toward changing social systems for the benefit of whole communities and societies."

p. 543—SDP theoretical frame: "A really innovative community mental health program requires greater clinical skill, knowledge about social process and social organization, and an ability to be versatile in shifting one's focus from individual, to group, to social system."

Becker, Wylan, and McCourt, 1971, p. 414—SDP theoretical frame: "We postulated that if we, in collaboration with the schools, could identify the children who were having trouble and provide remedial experiences for them, we might prevent both the school failure and the later emotional disorder. A goal of equal priority was to increase both the teacher's sensitivity to his pupils and his ability to cope with their needs."

Intractability of Schools: High

Comer et al., 1996, p. 8—"In order to promote such change, mechanisms must be created that allow parents and staff to engage in a process in which they gain knowledge of systems, of child development, and of individual behavior and apply it to every aspect of school programs."

Comer, 1993b, p. 235—Theoretical framework of SDP: "The process model is consistent with the principles of intervention research and an ecological perspective. Human ecology is the study of how people and environment interact. In intervention research it is important to understand the principles of human interaction in a particular environment . . . and develop processes to improve the quality of these interactions."

p. 273—"Our knowledge of organizational behavior suggested it would be wise to structure the intervention so that it would take form from within rather than be imposed from the outside."

Reiff, 1966, p. 546—SDP theoretical frame: "There is a tendency among professionals to ignore power issues and to act as though intelligence and rationality will conquer all. But the power issues are there, and more often than not, determine the outcome of efforts at change and innovation."

Ongoing Research and Development: High

Comer, 1996—SDP data-driven school improvement process seeks to measure impact of its implementation and how to improve school.

p. 123—"Measuring program outcomes, such as improved student performance on standardized tests is meaningless unless there is a commensurate assessment of the level and quality of program implementation." The SDP measures its schools: "to provide formative process data to improve and strengthen program implementation; to provide measures of program impact on salient outcome variables, including those identified in Comprehensive School Plan goal statements; to contribute to the theory on how schools change and how students succeed."

p. 132—SDP students: "greater positive changes in attendance, and teacher ratings of classroom behavior, attitude toward authority, and group participation, when compared to non-SDP students."

p. 145—"It is clear from our research that where the program is implemented well, strong positive school-level and student-level outcomes result."

Comer, 1993b, p. 275—"So we paid attention to test scores. Yet the very nature of our intervention—improved home-school relationships and collaboration to support student development—addressed work and citizenship as well."

p. 285–292—Prince George's County, MD, data.

p. 287—"Efforts to document the effects of the School Development Program have been consistent with our philosophy that educational improvement embodies not only academic growth but social and personal growth as well"; New Haven achievement data increase.

p. 289—"Measures of attendance, suspensions, classroom behavior, group participation, and attitude toward authority were used to assess students' school adjustment"; self-concept study.

p. 290—Classroom environment study: "In a 1989 quasi-experimental study conducted in New Haven and involving 288 students, students in SDP schools reported significantly more positive assessments of their classroom climate than students in non-SDP schools"; 1989, Rockefeller Foundation funding.

Haynes, 1998, p. 309—National survey conducted by SDP staff at Yale; student, parent, and staff perceptions of school climate. "Consideration of school climate becomes especially important in an increasingly complex, competitive, and technologically sophisticated society such as the United States because violence in schools is largely systemic and symptomatic of societal changes . . . addressing the problem of school violence and its impact on children must also be systemic."

Teachers as Reform Leaders: High

Comer, 1993b, p. 149—"I concluded that teacher powerlessness was more the problem than ineffective teaching methods or negative attitudes. . . . There should be an initial period during which teachers learn and share impressions about student needs, try various kinds of programs devised by teachers and educational specialists, and then adopt a flexible but relatively uniform consensus approach to curriculum and teaching."

Comer et al., 1999, p. 281—Chicago Public Schools: "They have created the Collegial Instructors Group (CIG), in which teachers work with other teachers to improve instruction."

Lang's Five Assumptions: High

1. Outside agent, positive. Comer created SDP from the Yale Child Development Center and began it in two New Haven, Connecticut, elementary schools in 1968. Comer et al., 1996, p. 27—"Comer researched the literature of psychiatry, psychotherapy, and psychology for ideas that would form an organizing base or theory. . . . Comer created 'a theoretical formulation that combined elements from several models.'" p. 40—"The change agent must plan with the local people, school staff, parents and community members, and where appropriate, students." p. 155—"An outside change agent can provide the feedback and coaching necessary for enacting new behavior."

2. Parents and community involved in the change, positive. Comer et al., 1996, p. 12—"The PT bridges the gap between home and school. It reduces the dissonance that disadvantaged students experience as they attempt to adjust from one environment to the other. . . . The SDP views parental involvement as the cornerstone for success in

developing a school environment that stimulates the total development of its students." p. 29—"Humans are social beings who need community support and involvement to develop adequately." p. 43—"It takes a whole village to raise a child" is the premise the SDP functions under. Becker et al., 1971, p. 413—SDP theoretical frame: "To be successful the center must obviously relate to the needs of its community."

3. Motivate students and families, positive. Comer et al., 1996, p. 16— "They [parents] lose hope and become less supportive of the school. Some parents, ashamed of their speech, dress, or failure to hold jobs, may become hostile, and avoid contact with the school staff. The result is a high degree of distrust." p. 37—"The SDP views the child as a part of the family unit and neighborhood as well as a part of the school community." p. 49—"The School Development Program gives the parents a framework to work in. These are structures and parent training sessions."

4. Power relationships altered, positive; people most directly affected by decisions should determine what should be done: parents, teachers, administrators, and community members (Comer et al., 1996, p. 59). p. 37—Decrease the use of community services that maintain the status quo.

5. Less discontinuity between school and nonschool. Comer et al., 1996, p. 9—"The SDP's approach, with parents and families at the center of change, is a critical missing link in education reform." p. 33—"School reformers should learn about the child's family and community, and anything that influences the child's life space. They must try to understand the child's behavior before proposing any intervention." p. 29—"Humans are social beings who need community support and involvement to develop adequately."

Past Reforms' Research: High/Medium

Comer et al., 1996, p. 27—"Comer created 'a theoretical formulation that combined elements from several models.' . . . These models included elements of: Lewin's (1936) social psychology theory (field theory) and human ecological systems theory, particularly as explained by Kelly (1966), the population adjustment model by Becker et al. (1971), and Hartman (1979) and the social action model by Reiff (1966)."

TEACHING THEORY FOR SDP PLAN:
VERY EFFECTIVE / EFFECTIVE

"But if we did not have to teach the curriculum, *what would we do with them?*" (Sarason, 1993, p. 42).

Productive Learning: High

Comer et al., 1996, p. 1—"But what happens when children aren't developing well. . . . Some educators blame these children and their families. . . . But we have demonstrated . . . the same children who fail to thrive in a specific setting can become eminently successful *in the same school* when the adults in their lives take the time to create a healthful climate."

pp. 17–18—"In a school environment that overemphasizes the cognitive pathway to the detriment of others, a child may acquire basic academic skills . . . [y]et without support and guidance along the psychological and ethical pathways, the same child will not learn to respect the rights and integrity of others."

p. 33—"School reformers must stress the importance of understanding child and adolescent development along all critical pathways, so that they can arrange the school environment to enhance the life space of all students."

pp. 44–45—"We approach child development with the understanding that the child learns from direct exposure to stimulating and challenging experiences and that the most meaningful learning stems from adult mediation. . . . Children learn by observing how their peers are disciplined, by overhearing how the adults in the building interact with one another, through contact with written and other cultural products, and especially, through significant adults who take an interest. With this, we understand, as Vygotsky discerned, that the higher psychological processes are internalized social relationships."

p. 45—"Comer (1994) notes that the acquisition of a reasonably high level of cognitive skills in knowledge is most often made possible through whole child development. . . . Content in the SDP school is, therefore, seen through the lens of child development. This is a paradigm shift in thinking about the purpose, function, and structure of schooling."

Comer, 1971, p. 274—Teachers need to be firm but fair; deprived children especially need adult authority figures.

p. 275—"The competent caretaker promotes objective, reasoned, and rational thinking, and not loyalty to authority figures, institutions, groups or national values—right or wrong."

"Pouring in Knowledge" Theory: Medium

Comer et al., 1996, p. 45—"In the past, educators considered subject area content knowledge to be most worthwhile. Through mastering disciplines such as science and social studies, we would unlock new knowledge, apply existing knowledge to a wider range of students, and help ensure a better future for our children."

Bigge and Hunt, 1980, p. 485—SDP theoretical frame: "In problem-centered or reflective classes, instruction begins with introduction of an 'I don't know' or problematic situation—one in which students are faced with a question they cannot answer. The problem should be so compelling that students really want to study it."

Students as "Raw Materials": High

Comer et al., 1996, p. 19—Whole-child development; six pathways to development: physical, psychological, social, ethical, cognitive, lingual.

p. 29—Combines social psychology, community health, psychiatry because "humans are social beings who need community support and involvement to develop adequately."

p. 33—"School reform programs should provide experiences that expand options for behavior—the freedom of movement—both for children and for the significant adults in their lives. Enhancing their physical, social, and psychological development is a prerequisite to increasing behavior options."

p. 61—SSST (student and staff support team) works "preventively and prescriptively" to address needs of individual students and the school community as a whole. The SSST works to prevent a crisis from occurring rather than simply reacting to a crisis already developing.

Comer, 1971, p. 267—"The humane being is created (developed), not born. Thus all care and educational methods should be based on what we know about child development and what we know is needed to promote the development of humane beings."

Bigge and Hunt, 1980, p. 30—SDP theoretical frame: B. F. Skinner did not include the concept of motivation in his description of behavior.

Gold, 1999, p. 329—Lewin's field theory found that maladjusted people have problems with daily living because of "unclearness"; they did not get the job maybe because they are a minority, woman, or Jew and "self-hatred" for belonging to an underprivileged group.

Personalized Learning: High

Comer et al., 1996, p. 29—"To change any individual's behavior one must be able to understand that individual's perceptions. To change a child's behavior one must be able to understand that child."

p. 32—"The first prerequisite for understanding a child is to determine the psychological place in which this child is currently situated and his or her freedom of movement region."

Comer, 1993b, p. 224—"Many children appear to have serious psychological problems in difficult social settings but function adequately in good social settings."

Reiff, 1966, p. 546—SDP theoretical frame: "The ability of the non-professionals to do the things that the professionals cannot do, such as, establish a peer relationship, take an active part in the patient's life situation, empathize with his style of life . . . is bound to affect the nature of the mental health services, the role of the professional, and may even have an impact on the ideology of the mental health professional."

Comer, 1971, p. 270—If self-control is not developed in children, then they will be more impulsive, disorganized, and incapable of completing a task.

Parental Inclusion: High

Comer et al., 1996, p. 29—SDP seeks to increase amount of parent and teacher communication and interaction to positively influence and motivate children.

p. 9—Parent team involves parents in the school; especially seeks those traditionally turned off by the schools.

Comer, 1972, p. 223—"Human beings react to a sense of rejections and valuelessness in ways that are harmful to themselves, their children and their society."

p. 38—"Parent participation at every level of school building activity is illustrative of the assumption that the clients for whom a service is being provided should be involved in the design and implementation of that service. This involvement becomes a vehicle for empowering parents and school staff."

p. 51—"Parents in SDP schools participate fully, including planning and making decisions about the academic and social agenda."

Comer, 1993b, p. 225—"It was important for us to have relationships in which parents share with the staff knowledge about their children and community."

p. 226—"Student behavior problems often put parents, teachers, and administrators on the defensive and are a major source of parent-community and school conflict and alienation."

p. 243—"Because the blocks to positive attitude and acceptance have become so pervasive in most communities, and so many people are cynical. . . . Improving schools in communities experiencing severe social stress is almost impossible without influential parent involvement."

Student Motivation: High

Comer et al., 1996, p. 32—"According to Lewin (1936), the first prerequisite for understanding a child is to determine the psychological place in which this child is currently situated and his or her freedom of movement region or 'space of free movement.'"

Bigge and Hunt, 1980, p. 86—SDP theoretical frame, SDP based on Kurt Lewin's motivational theories: "Lewin is generally regarded as being primarily a motivational theorist. . . . He asserted that all behavior was a function of the field prevailing at the time. . . . The conceptual framework within which the characteristics of both individuals and their perceived environments could be studied."

p. 89—"The best reward is psychological—any reward that makes students feel better about themselves—for example, by having satisfied felt needs for competence and self-determination."

p. 113—"Any action that reduces students' feelings of competence and self-determination reduces the amount of internal-intrinsic-motivation. . . . Girls tend to take personally the feedback they get, linking it to their own like-ability, whereas boys treat feedback as information."

p. 31—Blame game, to motivation theory a key component.

Lower-Class Students: High

Comer, 1997, p. 29—At-risk not given the proper preparation needed to succeed and teachers misconstrue as lack of intelligence or effort.

Comer, 1972, p. 221—"Black/white conflict—the failure of this society to develop a social system that enables people to meet their basic human needs at a reasonable level. Until this is done, we will not be able to move beyond black and white."

Comer et al., 1996, p. 37—"[The SSST] allows for the identification of maladaptive behavior in the natural school setting, where both curative and preventive measures are taken."

p. 40—"One cannot successfully change the social system without having the professional service providers work collaboratively with the clients (including the poor, whose needs and concerns must be addressed) to solve problems and influence policy. . . . One must confront issues of power and control that are sure to surface."

p. 7—"Without adequate preparation, school people respond by punishing what they understand as bad behavior and they hold low expectations for underdeveloped or differently developed children. . . . Most schools are unable to address the educational needs of underdeveloped or differently developed children from families marginal to the mainstream of the society."

p. 16—"It is because such circumstances are at variance with mainstream expectations that these children are often considered aggressive or 'bad' and often judged to be of low academic potential."

p. 38—"One such population is the poor, who, according to Becker et al. (1971), are particularly vulnerable to feelings of inadequacy and powerlessness—feelings that adversely affect their mental well-being."

p. 68—"There is a distressing lack of information about the realities poor children face in the United States."

Comer, 1993b, p. 193—"We hypothesized that too many low-income children are not brought into the mainstream social processes through incidental experiences at an early age."

p. 243—"Poor people are hard to work with because they are often angry and alienated. . . . The first task for the development unite team is to demonstrate the commitment and resources to carry out promises."

Comer et al., 1999, p. 278—"Some children are born in very hard places, and that temporarily disrupts their development."

Reiff, 1966, p. 542—SDP theoretical frame: "Low-income people are task oriented, concrete, concerned primarily with the here and now and focused on solving immediate problems. If they have troubles they are interested in finding a way to cope with them. If they are to be helped the response must be to their need, as they see it, for more successful coping techniques." SDP theoretical frame: Self-actualization good for middle- and upper-class patients; lower class "more concerned with the here and now and struggle with 'self-determination' and worry more about survival, about keeping my job, about paying the rent then about becoming an executive, etc." Differences in lifestyle, goals, and so forth, between therapist and low-income patient, effect communication.

Becker et al., 1971, p. 413—SDP theoretical frame: "The pressures and deprivations of living in poverty have a major impact on the self-esteem, self-image, and mental health of the poor. Feelings of helplessness, powerlessness, frustration, and alienation—all too frequent among slum residents—have a deadly effect on their self-image and mental well-being."

Low IQ and Self-Fulfilling Prophecy: High

Comer, 1993b, p. 228—"Students can learn at a reasonable level regardless of their social circumstances."

Comer et al., 1999, p. xx—"Most people assess and understand issues from the dominant cultural perspective that learning is primarily a function of intelligence and will, rather than development."

p. 278—The deficit perspective: "Many teachers labeled many children as being incapable. The deficit perspective assumes that a person's potential is fixed at birth, whereas the developmental perspective assumes that, with enough support, each person can get better in almost any area."

Comer, 1993b, p. 278—"I emphasized that children who are underdeveloped or who developed differently from the way expected in school are viewed as 'bad' and 'dumb.'"

TEACHING PROFESSION FOR
SDP PLAN: SOMETIMES EFFECTIVE

"Teaching is not a science, it is an art fusing ideas, obligations, the personal and interpersonal. The chemistry of that fusion determines whether or how subject matter matters to the student" (Sarason, 2004, p. 199).

Teacher Development: Medium

Comer, 1993b, p. 224—Behavior problems: "But remember that even in the most difficult schools certain teachers and principals are successful. Success usually comes for people who are intuitively expert in human relations. Many more could be expert, given training."

Bigge and Hunt, 1980, p. 223—SDP theoretical frame: "Everything teachers do is colored by the psychological theory they hold. . . . Teachers who do not make use of a systematic body of theory in their day-to-day decisions are behaving blindly. . . . Teachers without a strong theoretical orientation inescapably make little more than busy work assignments."

p. 232—"There are at least five distinctly different ways in which teachers may view their students: 1. innately bad and needing discipline, 2. neutral-active rational animals, 3. active, personalities unfold via native instincts, needs, abilities, talents, 4. passive minds that depend on outside forces for development, 5. purposive persons who develop through interaction with their respective psychological environments."

The Unlearning Process: High/Medium

Comer et al., 1999, p. xxiii—"Staffs can't grow unless they receive the instruction, time, and support to understand the need to change and how to manage the risk involved in thinking and working differently."

Comer, 1993b, p. 277—"In asking professional people to change the way they were working, we were asking them to give up some of the attitudes and methods they had been taught during their own personal and professional development. . . . Among these was the suggestion that children from low income families, marginal to the mainstream, most often minority, could not learn."

Teacher Education Programs: Medium

Comer, 1996, p. 79—"The isolation of the teacher preparation process, the disparity between theory and actual practice, and the lack of what some reformers referred to as the 'depth and breadth' of the liberal arts, science, and mathematics courses became major aspects of the call for reform."

p. 82—Southern University and New Orleans Public School partnership.

p. 96—"A crucial component in teacher preparation is the involvement of either a local mental health agency or a school of social work." Collaboration among universities and K–12 schools needed to improve teacher education programs; often, teacher preparation programs only emphasize cognitive, physical, and language; "preservice teachers encounter children who need daily adult support and guidance along the social, ethical, and psychological pathways because they have to cope with drugs, violence, and issues related to changing values and family structures."

Comer, 1993b, p. 255—"Courses in child development and introduction to teaching would be most helpful if taken during the first year of training" (see also, pp. 256–257).

Pedagogy: Medium/Low

Comer, 1993b, p. 149—"I concluded that teacher powerlessness was more the problem than ineffective teaching methods or negative attitudes."

Comer, 1971, p. 271—"The classroom with no rules, regulations, plans, evaluation, or strategy does not provide the kind of structure or order out of which creative activity can readily flow."

p. 272—"Until they are parents or they spend some time in a classroom. . . . The guiding, directing, value-setting or encouraging, limiting and promoting role of the caretaker is often viewed as unnecessary and even repressive."

p. 273—"The 'tight ship,' harsh or overly strict school situation, does not meet the educational or developmental needs of children. But neither does an approach which permits unstructured social interaction before a child has learned to interact cooperatively and fairly with others."

Productive Teaching Defined: High/Medium

Comer, 1996, p. 46—"When we focus on social processes, relationships between students and teachers become the vehicle for instruction and are more important than subject area content."

p. 46—"Comer's response has been to urge curriculum designers . . . rejects the commonplace practice of designing school curricula solely in cognitive and academic terms."

Comer, 1993b, p. 251—"Teachers must be able to facilitate the academic, social and psychological, and moral development of their students. To do so they must understand child development and how to develop curriculum and utilize materials and activities to facilitate it."

Bigge and Hunt, 1980, p. 224—SDP theoretical frame: "Teachers who are well grounded in scientific psychology—in contrast to 'folklore psychology'—have a basis for making decisions that are much more likely to lead to effectual results in classrooms."

SCHOOL POWER AND POLITICS FOR
SDP PLAN: SOMETIMES EFFECTIVE

"The icing on the cake of vexation was provided by my meetings with policymakers and politicians in Washington and elsewhere. I realized that, however sincere their intentions, they knew nothing about schools and why the school culture, honed over many decades, would resist and defeat reforms attempting to alter the status quo. There are no villains. There is a system. You can see and touch villains, you cannot see a system" (Sarason, 1998, p. 141).

Government Involvement: Medium/Low

For example, Prince George's County, Maryland, was court-ordered to implement the SDP districtwide to ensure equity for all schools and students as mandatory busing for desegregation was ended.

The Middle-Class Ethic: High

Comer, 1972, p. 55—"Too many educators blame the children and their parents. . . . Too many parents and youngsters blame the teachers. Too many critics, who are not in the midst of the problem, cry for the children and assassinate the characters of the educators. What is wrong with the schools is what is wrong with the family is what is wrong with the society. We are a society that has failed to gear itself to enable people to meet their basic needs. The failing public school system is only a by-product of this larger failure."

Comer et al., 1996, p. 5—"Children who underachieved in school and left school without adequate cognitive skills and knowledge were not in significant trouble in our society until about three decades ago."

Reiff, 1966, p. 542—SDP theoretical frame: "There is little hope of getting workers or low-income groups to accept failure to meet the problems of living as an illness, and as long as problems of living continue to be diagnosed as diseases. . . . The alienation will persist."

p. 548—"The greatest social need for mental health services today comes from the low-income groups and the poor. Meeting this need is not primarily a problem of manpower but a problem of ideology."

Comer et al., 1999, p. xx—"Most people assess and understand issues from the dominant cultural perspective that learning is primarily a function of intelligence and will, rather than development."

School Bureaucracy: High/Medium

Comer et al., 1996, p. 37—"Because the emphasis is on changing the social structures and building local capacity and expertise, the governance of the school is placed under the auspices of the . . . (SPMT) that is composed of all the stakeholders, including parents."

p. 8—"The organization and management of the vast majority of American schools are deeply entrenched in the attitudes, values, and ways of the larger society, and are maintained by traditional training and practice."

p. 149—"Consensus is more than a type of decision-making method. . . . It gives voice to the least powerful as well as to the most powerful. It provides a way for the inevitable subgroups in a school's community to connect with one another. . . . Coalition building replaces community building. The genius of consensus is that it forces a transformation from fighting for one's subgroup (teachers, parents, or particular children) to being an advocate for the whole learning community."

Reiff, 1966, p. 39—SDP theoretical frame: "Cannot change the social system without having the professional service providers work collaboratively with the clients to solve problems and influence policy. In doing so, one must confront issues of power and control that are sure to surface."

Research and Development: High

Comer, 1972, p. 55—"With the traditional American flair for ignoring behavioral complexities, the failure of our schools has been reduced to racism, classism and lack of concern. . . . Teachers who do not care are the end products of a long process that is as destructive of them as of the children."

Silent Axioms and Educational Policymakers: Medium

Comer et al., 1999, p. xxiii—"And too many policymakers and practitioners do not understand the need to create a supportive social context because they took their own social context for granted."

Reiff, 1966, p. 546—SDP theoretical frame: "One cannot enter the field of institutional change without forthrightly facing power issues. . . . There is a tendency among professionals to ignore power issues and to act as though intelligence and rationality will conquer all."

Bibliography

Alexander, K., & Alexander, M. D. (1998). *American public school law.* Belmont, CA: Wadsworth.

American heritage dictionary of the English language (4th ed.). (2006). New York: Houghton Mifflin.

Anderson, J. D. (1988). *The education of Blacks in the South, 1860–1935.* Chapel Hill: University of North Carolina Press.

Anderson, R. H. (1993, January). The return of the nongraded classroom. *Principal, 72*(3), 9–12.

Anderson, R. H., & Pavan, B. N. (1993). *Nongradedness: Helping it to happen.* Lancaster, PA: Technomic.

Andrews, C. C. (1830). *The history of the New York African free-schools: From their establishment in 1787 to the present time: Embracing a period of more than forty years.* New York: Negro University Press.

Anson, A. R., Cook, T. D., Habib, F., Grady, M. K., Haynes, N., & Comer, J. P. (1991). The Comer School Development Program: A theoretical analysis. *Urban Education, 26,* 56–82.

Ashmore, H. S. (1954). *The Negro and the schools.* Chapel Hill: University of North Carolina Press.

Ayers, L. P. (1909). *Laggards in our schools: A study of retardation and elimination in city school systems.* New York: Russell Sage Foundation.

Beck, L. G., & Murphy, J. (1996). *The four imperatives of a successful school.* Thousand Oaks, CA: Corwin Press.

Becker, A., Wylan, L., & McCourt, W. (1971). Primary prevention—Whose responsibility? *American Journal of Psychiatry, 128*(4), 412–417.

251

Beggs, D. W., III. (1964). *A practical application of the Trump Plan.* Englewood Cliffs, NJ: Prentice Hall.

Bell, D. A., Jr. (1980a). *Race, racism, and American law.* Boston: Little, Brown.

Bell, D. A., Jr. (1980b). *Shades of Brown: New perspectives in school desegregation.* New York: Columbia University Press.

Bell, D. A., Jr. (1987). *And we are not saved: The elusive quest for racial justice.* New York: Basic Books.

Bell, D. A., Jr. (1992). *Faces at the bottom of the well: The Permanence of racism.* New York: Basic Books.

Bennis, W. G., Spreitzer, G. M., & Cummings, T. (Eds.). (2001). *The future of leadership: Today's top leadership thinkers speak to tomorrow's leaders.* San Francisco: Jossey-Bass.

Bernhard, J. G. (1988). *Primates in the classroom: An evolutionary perspective on children's education.* Amherst: University of Massachusetts Press.

Bigge, M. L., & Hunt, M. P. (1980). *Psychological foundations of education: An introduction to human motivation, development, and learning.* New York: Harper & Row.

Bourne, R. S. (1970). *The Gary schools.* Cambridge, MA: MIT Press.

Boyer, P. S., Clark, C. E., Kett, J. F., Purvis, T. L., Sitkoff, H., & Woloch, N. (1990). *The enduring vision: A history of the American people.* Lexington, MA: D. C. Heath.

Brown, B. F. (1963). *The nongraded high school.* Englewood Cliffs, NJ: Prentice Hall.

Brown, F. (1998, April). Legal perspective: Leandro v. State of North Carolina. *School Business Affairs, 64*(4), 45–47.

Brukacher, J. S. (Ed.). (1965). *Henry Barnard on education.* New York: Russell and Russell.

Bruner, J. (1996). *The culture of education.* Cambridge, MA: Harvard University Press.

Buckingham, B. R. (1921, March). Child accounting. *Journal of Educational Research, 3*(1), 218–222.

Callahan, R. E. (1962). *Education and the cult of efficiency: A study of the social forces that have shaped the administration of the public schools.* Chicago: University of Chicago Press.

Carlson, R. V. (1996). *Reframing and reform: On organization, leadership, and school change.* White Plains, NY: Longman Group.

Cash, W. J. (1941). *The mind of the South.* New York: Alfred A. Knopf.

Cecelski, D. S. (1994). *Along freedom road: Hyde County, North Carolina, and the fate of Black schools in the South.* Chapel Hill: University of North Carolina Press.

Chiles, N., & Hill, C. (1993, December). Making schools work. *Essence*, 86–90.

Clark, R. F. (2002). *The war on poverty: History, selected programs, and ongoing impact*. Lanham, MD: University Press of America.

Cohen, R. D. (1974). Urban schooling in twentieth-century America: A frame of reference. *Urban Education, 8*(4), 423–439.

Cohen, R. D., & Mohl, R. A. (1979). *The paradox of progressive education: The Gary Plan and urban schooling*. Port Washington, NY: Kennikat Press.

Comer, J. P. (1971, Summer). Child development and social change: Some points of controversy. *Journal of Negro Education, 40*(3), 266–276.

Comer, J. P. (1972). *Beyond Black and White*. New York: Quadrangle Books.

Comer, J. P. (1980). *School power: Implications of an intervention project*. New York: Free Press.

Comer, J. P. (1989, Spring). Child development and education. *Journal of Negro Education, 58*(2), 125–139.

Comer, J. P. (1993a). *Making a difference for children*. New York: Teachers College, Columbia Universtiy.

Comer, J. P. (1993b). *School power: Implications of an intervention project*. New York: Free Press.

Comer, J. P. (1996). *Rallying the whole village: The Comer process for reforming education*. New York: Teachers College Press.

Comer, J. P. (1997). *Waiting for a miracle: Why schools can't solve our problems—And how we can*. New York: Penguin Books.

Comer, J. P., Ben-Avie, M., Haynes, N. M., & Joyner, E. T. (1999). *Child by child: The Comer process for change in education*. New York: Teachers College Press.

Comer, J. P., Harrow, M., & Johnson, S. H. (1969, Winter). Summer study-skills program: A case for structure. *Journal of Negro Education, 38*(1), 38–45.

Comer, J. P., Haynes, N. M., & Hamilton-Lee, M. (1988, Winter). The School Development Program: A model for school improvement. *Journal of Negro Education, 57*(1), 11–21.

Comer, J. P., Haynes, N. M., Joyner, E. T., & Ben-Avie, M. (1996). *Rallying the whole village: The Comer process for reforming education*. New York: Teachers College Press.

Cremin, L. A. (1961). *The transformation of the school: Progessivism in American education, 1876–1957*. New York: Alfred A. Knopf.

Crenshaw, K., Gotanda, N., Peller, G., Thomas, K. (Eds.). (1995). *Critical race theory: The key writings that formed the movement*. New York: New Press.

Cuban, L. (1988). *The managerial imperative and the practice of leadership in schools*. Albany: State University of New York Press.

Cuban, L. (1989, June). The "at-risk" label and the problem of urban school reform. *Phi Delta Kappan, 70*(10), 799–801.

Cuban, L. (1993). *How teachers taught: Constancy and change in American classrooms, 1890–1990.* New York: Teachers College Press.

Cuban, L. (2001). *"How can I fix it?" Finding solutions and managing dilemmas.* New York: Teachers College Press.

Cuban, L. (2003). *Why is it so hard to get good schools?* New York: Teachers College Press.

Cubberley, E. P. (1919). *Public education in the United States: A study and interpretation of American educational history.* New York: Houghton Mifflin.

Cubberley, E. P. (1934). *Public education in the United States: A study and interpretation of American educational history.* New York: Houghton Mifflin. (Original work published 1919.)

Cushman, K. (1989, November). At the five-year mark: The challenge of being "essential." *Horace, 6*(1). Retrieved August 15, 2007, from www.essential schools.org/cs/resources/view/ces_res/76

Cushman, K. (1998a). *The collected Horace: Theory and practice in essential schools: Vol. 2. Curriculum, assessment, and whole-school accountability.* Providence, RI: Coalition of Essential Schools.

Cushman, K. (1998b). *The collected Horace: Theory and practice in essential schools: Vol. 4. Leadership in essential schools.* Providence, RI: Coalition of Essential Schools.

Cushman, K. (1998c). *The collected Horace: Theory and practice in essential schools: Vol. 5. Policy and essential schools.* Providence, RI: Coalition of Essential Schools.

Dewey, J., & Dewey, E. (1915). *Schools of to-morrow.* New York: E. P. Dutton.

Doremus, R. R. (1982). What ever happened to . . . Wayland (Mass.) High School? *Phi Delta Kappan, 63*(5), 347–348.

Ducat, C. (1996). *Constitutional interpretation.* Minneapolis, MN: West.

Eggleston, E. (1901). *The transit of civilization: From England to America in the seventeenth century.* New York: D. Appleton.

Elwell, R. (1976, July). The Gary Plan revisited. *American Education, 12*(6), 16–22.

Encyclopaedia Britannica almanac 2003. (2002). Chicago: Author.

English, F. W. (1992). *Educational administration: The human science.* New York: HarperCollins.

English, F. W. (2000). *Deciding what to teach and test: Developing, aligning, and auditing the curriculum.* Thousand Oaks, CA: Corwin Press.

English, F. W. (Ed.). (2005). *The Sage handbook of educational leadership: Advances in theory, research, and practice.* Thousand Oaks, CA: Sage.

English, F. W., & Steffy, B. E. (2001). *Deep curriculum alignment: Creating a level playing field for all children on high-stakes tests of educational accountability*. Lanham, MD: Scarecrow Press.

Fine, M. (1991). *Framing dropouts: Notes on the politics of an urban public high school*. Albany: State University of New York Press.

Fowler, F. C. (2000). *Policy studies for educational leaders*. Upper Saddle River, NJ: Merrill.

Franklin, J. H. (1988). *From slavery to freedom: A history of African Americans*. New York: Alfred A. Knopf.

Franklin, J. H. (1993). *The color line: Legacy for the twenty-first century*. Columbia: University of Missouri Press.

Fried, R. L. (Ed.). (2003). *The skeptical visionary: A Seymour Sarason education reader*. Philadelphia: Temple University Press.

Fullan, M. G. (1991). *The new meaning of educational change*. New York: Teachers College Press.

Gardner, H. (2004). *Changing minds: The art and science of changing our own and other peoples minds*. Boston: Harvard Business School Press.

Gewirtz, S., Ball, S. J., & Bowe, R. (1995). *Markets, choice, and equity in education*. Philadelphia: Open University Press.

Givel, M. (1991). *The war on poverty revisited: The community services block grant program in the Reagan years*. Lanham, MD: University Press of America.

Glazek, S. D., & Sarason, S. B. (2007). *Productive learning: Science, art, and Einstein's relativity in education reform*. Thousand Oaks, CA: Sage.

Gold, M. (Ed.). (1999). *The complete social scientist: A Kurt Lewin reader*. Washington, DC: American Psychological Association.

Goldfield, D. (1990). *Black, White, and Southern: Race relations and Southern culture, 1940 to the present*. Baton Rouge: Louisiana State University Press.

Goodlad, J. I., & Anderson, R. H. (1959). *The nongraded elementary school*. New York: Harcourt, Brace.

Goodlad, J. I., & Anderson, R. H. (1987). *The nongraded elementary school*. New York: Harcourt, Brace. (Original work published 1959)

Graglia, L. A. (1976). *Disaster by decree: The Supreme Court decisions on race and the schools*. Ithaca, NY: Cornell University Press.

Gumbert, E. B., & Spring, J. H. (1974). *The superschool and the superstate: American education in the twentieth century, 1918–1970*. New York: John Wiley.

Hacker, A. (1990). *Two nations: Black, White, separate and unequal*. New York: Columbia University Press.

Hartman, L. (1979). The preventive reduction of psychological risk in asymptomatic adolescents. *American Journal of Orthopsychiatry, 49,* 121–135.

Hartwell, S. O. (1916). *Overcrowded schools and the platoon plan.* Philadelphia: Wm. F. Fell.

Haynes, N. M. (1998). Creating safe and caring school communities: Comer School Development Program schools. *Journal of Negro Education, 65*(3), 308–314.

Hoke County v. North Carolina. (2001). 95 CVS 1158.

hooks, b. (2000). *Where we stand: Class matters.* New York: Routledge.

Johnson, H. M. (1973, December). Are compulsory attendance laws outdated? *Phi Delta Kappan, 55*(4), 226–232.

Kaestle, C. F. (1973a). *The evolution of an urban school system: New York City, 1750–1850.* Cambridge, MA: Harvard University Press.

Kaestle, C. F. (Ed.). (1973b). *Joseph Lancaster and the Monitorial school movement: A documentary history.* New York: Teachers College Press.

Kaestle, C. F. (1983). *Pillars of the republic: Common schools and American society, 1780–1860.* New York: Hill and Wang.

Kahne, J. (1995). *Reframing educational policy: Democracy, community, and the individual.* New York: St. Martin's Press.

Karier, C. J., Violas, P. C., & Spring, J. H. (1973). *Roots of crisis: American education in the twentieth century.* Chicago: Rand McNally.

Katz, M. B. (1971). *Class, bureaucracy, and schools: The illusion of educational change in America.* New York: Praeger.

Katz, M. B. (1987). *Reconstructing American education.* Cambridge, MA: Harvard University Press.

Katz, M. B. (2001). *The irony of early school reform: Educational innovation in mid-nineteenth-century Massachusetts.* New York: Teachers College Press.

Katz, M. S. (1976). *A history of compulsory education laws.* Bloomington, IN: Phi Delta Kappa Educational Foundation.

Keefe, J. W. (1971, January). *Differentiated staffing—Its rewards and pitfalls.* Presentation at the 55th annual convention of the National Association of Secondary School Principals, Houston, TX.

Kelly, J. G. (1966). Ecological constraints on mental health services. *American Psychologist, 21*(1), 535–539.

Kluger, R. (1997). *Simple justice: The history of "Brown v. Board of Education," the epochal Supreme Court decision that outlawed segregation.* New York: Vintage Books.

Kohn, A. (1999). *The schools our children deserve: Moving beyond traditional classrooms and "tougher standards."* Boston: Houghton Mifflin.

Kozol, J. (1991). *Savage inequalities: Children in America's schools.* New York: Harper Perennial.

Lancaster, J. (1973). *Improvements in education as it respects the industrious classes of the community.* Clifton, NJ: Augustus M. Kelley.

Levin, B. (1997). The lessons of international education reform. *Journal of Education Policy, 12*(4), 253–266.

Levine, D. (2002, March). The Milwaukee platoon school battle: Lessons for activist teachers. *Urban Review, 34*(1), 47–69.

Lewin, K. (1936). *Principles of topological psychology.* New York: McGraw-Hill.

Lewin, K. (1938). *The conceptual representation and the measurement of psychological forces.* Durham, NC: Duke University Press.

Lewis, M. S., Bryman, A., & Liao, T. F. (Eds.). (2004). *The Sage encyclopedia of social science research methods: Vol. I.* Thousand Oaks, CA: Sage.

Lightfoot, S. L. (1978). *Worlds apart: Relationships between families and schools.* New York: Basic Books.

Malloy, W. W. (1997). Refocusing drop-out prevention initiatives. *Educational Foundations, 12*(5), 1–17.

Mann, H. (1844). *Seventh annual report of the Board of Education, together with the seventh annual report of the Secretary of the Board.* Boston: Dutton and Wentworth, State Printers.

Mann, M. (1986). *The sources of social power: Vol. 1. A history of power from the beginning to A.D. 1760.* New York: Cambridge University Press.

Martin, J. H. (1972). The grade school came from Prussia. *Educational Horizons, 51*(1), 28–33.

Martin, J. H., & Harrison, C. H. (1972). *Free to learn: Unlocking and ungrading American education.* Englewood Cliffs, NJ: Prentice Hall.

McCullough, D. G. (2001). *John Adams.* New York: Simon & Schuster.

McDonald, J. P., Hatch, T., Kirby, E., Ames, N., Haynes, N. M., & Joyner, E. T. (1999). *School reform behind the scenes: How atlas is shaping the future of education.* New York: Teachers College Press.

McGhan, B. (1997, Winter). Compulsory school attendance: An idea past its prime? *Educational Forum, 61*(2), 134–139.

McLoughlin, W. P. (1972). The effectiveness of the non-graded school. *International Review of Education, 18*(2), 194–211.

Messerli, J. (1972). *Horace Mann: A biography.* New York: Alfred A. Knopf.

Mill, J. S. (1956). *On liberty.* New York: Macmillan. (Original work published 1859.)

Mohl, R. A. (1975). Schools, politics, and riots: The Gary Plan in New York City, 1914–1917. *Paedagogica Historica, 15*(1), 39–72.

Morgenstern, A. (Ed.). (1966). *Grouping in the elementary school.* New York: Pitman.

Muncey, D. E., & McQuillan, P. J. (1996). *Reform and resistance in schools and classrooms.* New Haven, CT: Yale University Press.

Murphy, J. H. (1996). *The privatization of schooling: Problems and possibilities.* Thousand Oaks, CA: Corwin Press.

Murphy, J. H., & Beck, L. G. (1995). *School-based management as school reform: Taking stock.* Thousand Oaks, CA: Corwin Press.

National Commission on Excellence in Education. (1983). *A nation at risk: The imperative for educational reform.* Washington, DC: U.S. Department of Education.

Noblit, G. W., & Dempsey, V. O. (1996). *The social construction of virtue: The moral life of schools.* Albany: State University of New York Press.

Noblit, G. W., Malloy, W. W., & Malloy, C. E. (Eds.). (2001). *The kids got smarter: Case studies of successful Comer schools.* Cresskill, NJ: Hampton Press.

Noddings, N. (1998). *Philosophy of education.* Boulder, CO: Westview Press.

Ogbu, J. U. (1978). *Minority education and caste: The American system in cross-cultural perspective.* New York: Academic Press.

Oliva, P. F., & Pawlas, G. E. (1999). *Supervision for today's schools.* New York: John Wiley.

O'Neil, J. (1997). Building schools as communities: A conversation with James Comer. *Educational Leadership, 54*(8), 6–11.

Orfield, G., & Eaton, S. (1996). *Dismantling desegregation: The quiet reversal of "Brown v. Board of Education."* New York: New Press.

Ott, J. S. (1996). *Classic readings in organizational behavior.* Fort Worth, TX: Harcourt Brace.

Palmer, C. A. (1998a). *Passageways: An interpretive history of Black America: Vol. 1. 1619–1863.* New York: Harcourt Brace.

Palmer, C. A. (1998b). *Passageways: An interpretive history of Black America: Vol. 2. 1863–1965.* New York: Harcourt Brace.

Phillips, D. C., & Burbules, N. C. (2000). *Postpositivism and educational research.* Lanham, MD: Rowman & Littlefield.

Pileggi, N. (1969). Revolutionaries who have to be home by 7:30. *Phi Delta Kappan, 50*(10), 560–569.

Postman, N. (1995). *The end of education: Redefining the value of school.* New York: Alfred A. Knopf.

Pratt, D. (1986). On the merits of multiage classrooms: Their life and work. *Research in Rural Education, 3*(3), 111–116.

Rakove, J. N. (1990). *James Madison and the creation of the American republic.* New York: HarperCollins.

Ravitch, D. (1988). *The great school wars: A history of the New York City public schools.* New York: Basic Books.

Reiff, R. (1966). Mental health manpower and institutional change. *American Psychologist, 21*(1), 540–548.

Reigart, J. F. (1916). *The Lancastrian system of instruction in the schools of New York City.* New York: Columbia University, Teacher College.

Riddle, W. (1905). *One hundred and fifty years of school history in Lancaster, Pennsylvania.* Lancaster, PA: New Era Printing.

Ridgewood High School. (1965, January). A "Trump Plan" school—Four years later. *Education Digest, 30*(5), 13–16.

Sarason, S. B. (1971). *The culture of the school and the problem of change.* Boston: Allyn & Bacon.

Sarason, S. B. (1990). *The predictable failure of educational reform: Can we change course before it's too late?* San Francisco: Jossey-Bass.

Sarason, S. B. (1993). *Letters to a serious education president.* Newbury Park, CA: Corwin Press.

Sarason, S. B. (1996). *Revisiting "The culture of the school and the problem of change."* New York: Teachers College Press.

Sarason, S. B. (1997). *How schools might be governed and why.* New York: Teachers College Press.

Sarason, S. B. (1998). *Political leadership and educational failure.* San Francisco: Jossey-Bass.

Sarason, S. B. (2002). *Educational reform: A self-scrutinizing memoir.* New York: Teachers College Press.

Sarason, S. B. (2004). *And what do you mean by learning?* Portsmouth, NH: Heinemann.

Schaller, M. (1992). *Reckoning with Reagan: America and its president in the 1980's.* New York: Oxford University Press.

Scheurich, J. J., & Imber, M. (1991). Educational reforms can reproduce societal inequities: A case study. *Educational Administration Quarterly, 27*(3), 297–320.

Sergiovanni, T. J. (1992). *Moral leadership: Getting to the heart of school improvement.* San Francisco: Jossey-Bass.

Sergiovanni, T. J. (1994). *Building community in schools.* San Francisco: Jossey-Bass.

Sergiovanni, T. J. (2000). *The lifeworld of leadership: Creating culture, community and personal meaning in our schools.* San Francisco: Jossey-Bass.

Sergiovanni, T. J. (2001). *Leadership: What's in it for schools?* New York: Routledge.

Sizer, T. R. (1984). *Horace's compromise: The dilemma of the American high school.* Boston: Houghton Mifflin.

Sizer, T. R. (1992). *Horace's school: Redesigning the American high school.* Boston: Houghton Mifflin.

Sizer, T. R. (1996). *Horace's hope: What works for the American high school.* Boston: Houghton Mifflin.

Sizer, T. R. (2004). *The red pencil: Convictions from experience in education.* New Haven, CT: Yale University Press.

Sizer, T. R., & Sizer, N. F. (1999). *The students are watching: Schools and the moral contract.* Boston: Beacon Press.

Skowronek, S. (2001). *The politics presidents make: Leadership from John Adams to Bill Clinton.* Cambridge, MA: Belknap Press of Harvard University Press.

Sobol, T. (2006, September 20). Beyond No Child Left Behind: Bigger issues in the room we can't ignore while debating the federal law. *Education Week*, 44.

Spain, C. L. (1925). *The platoon school: A study of the adaptation of the elementary school organization to the curriculum.* New York: Macmillan.

Spring, J. H. (1976). *The sorting machine: National educational policy since 1945.* New York: David McKay.

Spring, J. H. (2000). *American education.* Boston: McGraw-Hill.

Spring, J. H. (2001). *The American school: 1642–2000.* Boston: McGraw-Hill.

Squires, D., & Kranyik, R. (1996). The Comer Program: Changing school culture. *Educational Leadership, 53*(4), 29–32.

Starr, H. E. (Ed.). (1958). *Dictionary of American biography: Vol. 11, Part I, Supplement 1.* New York: Charles Scribner's Sons.

Toulmin, S. (1990). *Cosmopolis: The hidden agenda of modernity.* Chicago: University of Chicago Press.

Trump, J. L. (1959). *Images of the future: A new approach to the secondary school.* Urbana, IL: National Association of Secondary School Principals.

Trump, J. L., & Baynham, D. (1961). *Focus on change: Guide to better schools.* Chicago: Rand McNally.

Tyack, D. B. (1974). *The one best system: A history of American urban education.* Cambridge, MA: Harvard University Press.

Tyack, D. B. (2003). *Seeking common ground: Public schools in a diverse society.* Cambridge, MA: Harvard University Press.

Tyack, D. B., & Cuban, L. (1995). *Tinkering toward utopia: A century of public school reform.* Cambridge, MA: Harvard University Press.

Tyack, D. B., James, T., & Benavot, A. (1987). *Law and the shaping of public education, 1785–1954.* Madison: University of Wisconsin Press.

Walker, V. S. (1996). *Their highest potential: An African American school community in the segregated South.* Chapel Hill: University of North Carolina Press.

Williams, J. (1987). *Eyes on the prize: America's civil rights years, 1954–1965.* New York: Viking Press.

Wills, G. (1994). *Certain trumpets: The nature of leadership.* New York: Simon & Schuster.

Wolcott, H. F. (2001). *Writing up qualitative research.* Thousand Oaks, CA: Sage.

Zinn, H. (1995). *A people's history of the United States: 1492–present.* New York: Harper Perennial.

About the Author

John M. Tharp is a high school principal in the Southeastern United States. He has worked as a public school teacher and administrator in the Southeast and the Midwest. He graduated from the University of North Carolina at Chapel Hill with a doctorate in educational leadership. He earned a master's degree in curriculum and instruction from the University of North Carolina (as a recipient of the James Madison Memorial Foundation Fellowship award) and a history degree from Illinois Wesleyan University.